WELCOME
TO *Fabulous*
LOST VEGAS

MCCANN - LEE

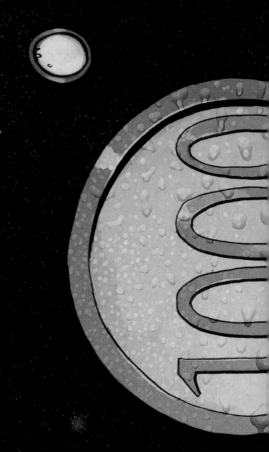

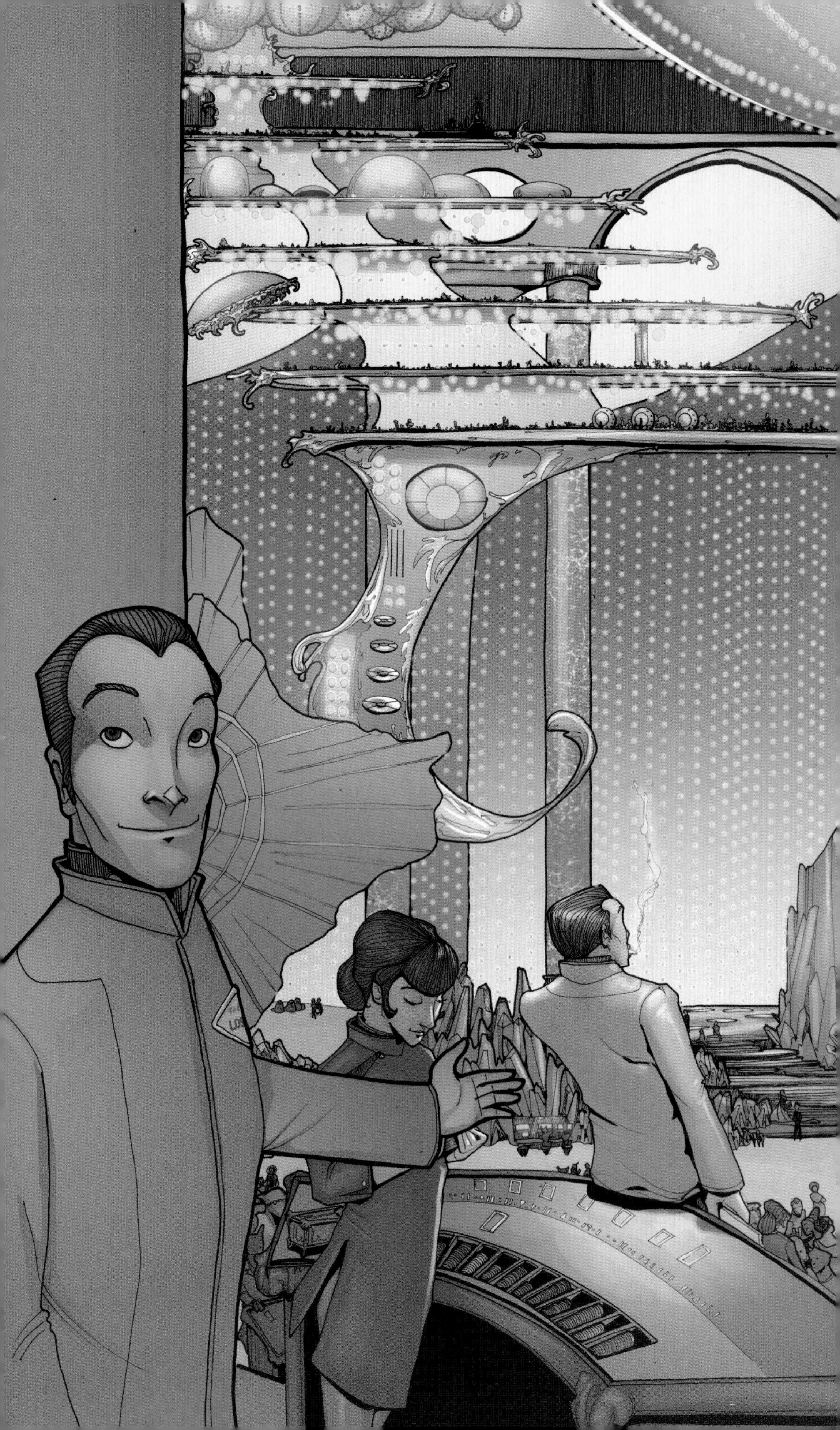

CREATED BY

WRITER
JIM McCANN
&
ARTIST
JANET K. LEE

COLORS
CHRIS SOTOMAYOR

LETTERS
DAVE LANPHEAR

EDITOR
ROB LEVIN

PRODUCTION
DAMIEN LUCCHESE

LOGO
SHANNON FORREY

IMAGE COMICS, INC.
Robert Kirkman – chief operating officer
Erik Larsen – chief financial officer
Todd McFarlane – president
Marc Silvestri – chief executive officer
Jim Valentino – vice-president
www.imagecomics.com

Eric Stephenson – publisher
Ron Richards – director of business development
Jennifer de Guzman – pr & marketing director
Branwyn Bigglestone – accounts manager
Emily Miller – accounting assistant
Jamie Parreno – marketing assistant
Emilio Bautista – sales assistant

Kevin Yuen – digital rights coordinator
Tyler Shainline – events coordinator
David Brothers – content manager
Jonathan Chan – production manager
Drew Gill – art director
Jana Cook – print manager
Monica Garcia – senior production artist

Vincent Kukua – production artist
Jenna Savage – production artist
Addison Duke – production artist

LOST VEGAS TP
ISBN: 978-1-60706-785-6
FIRST PRINTING

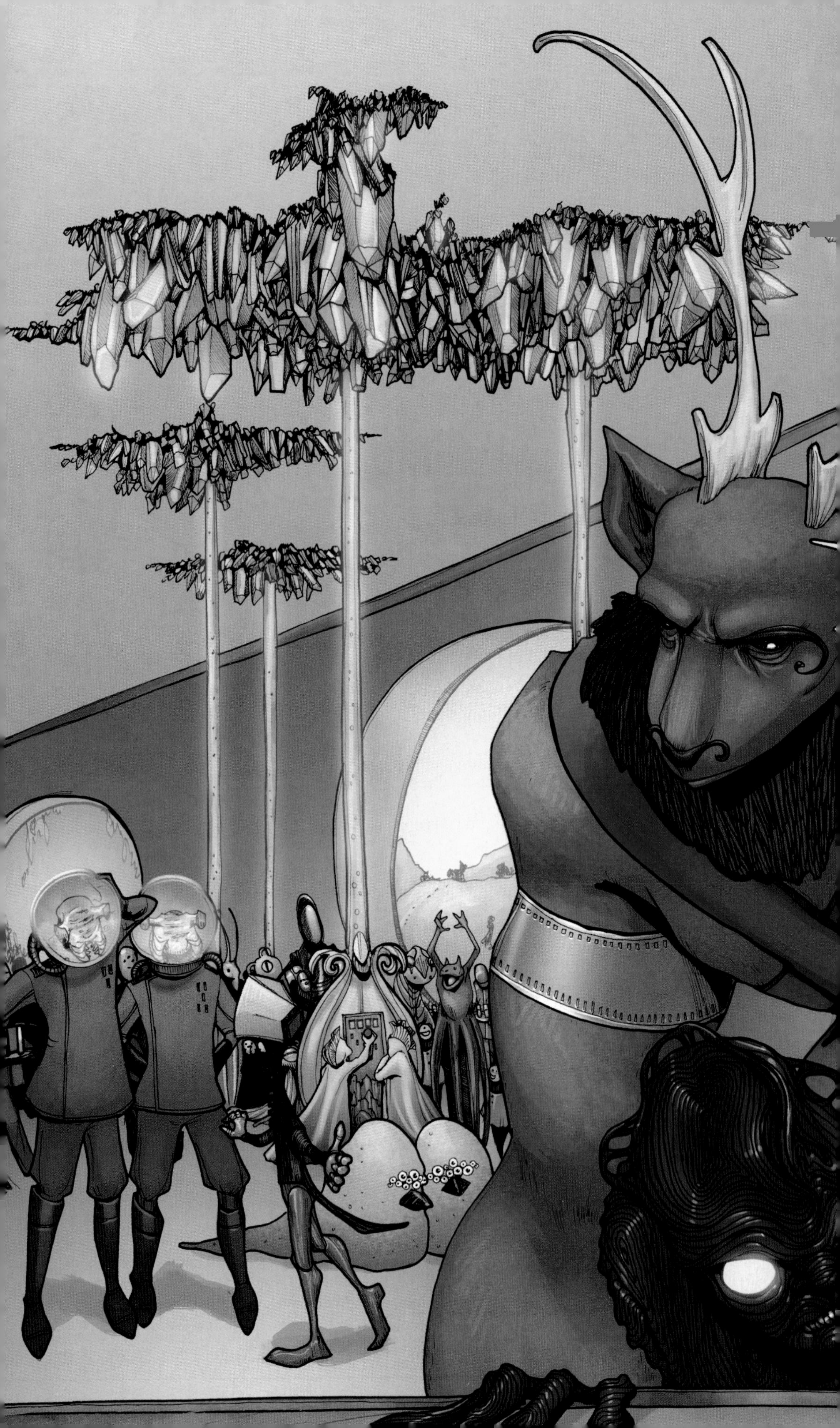

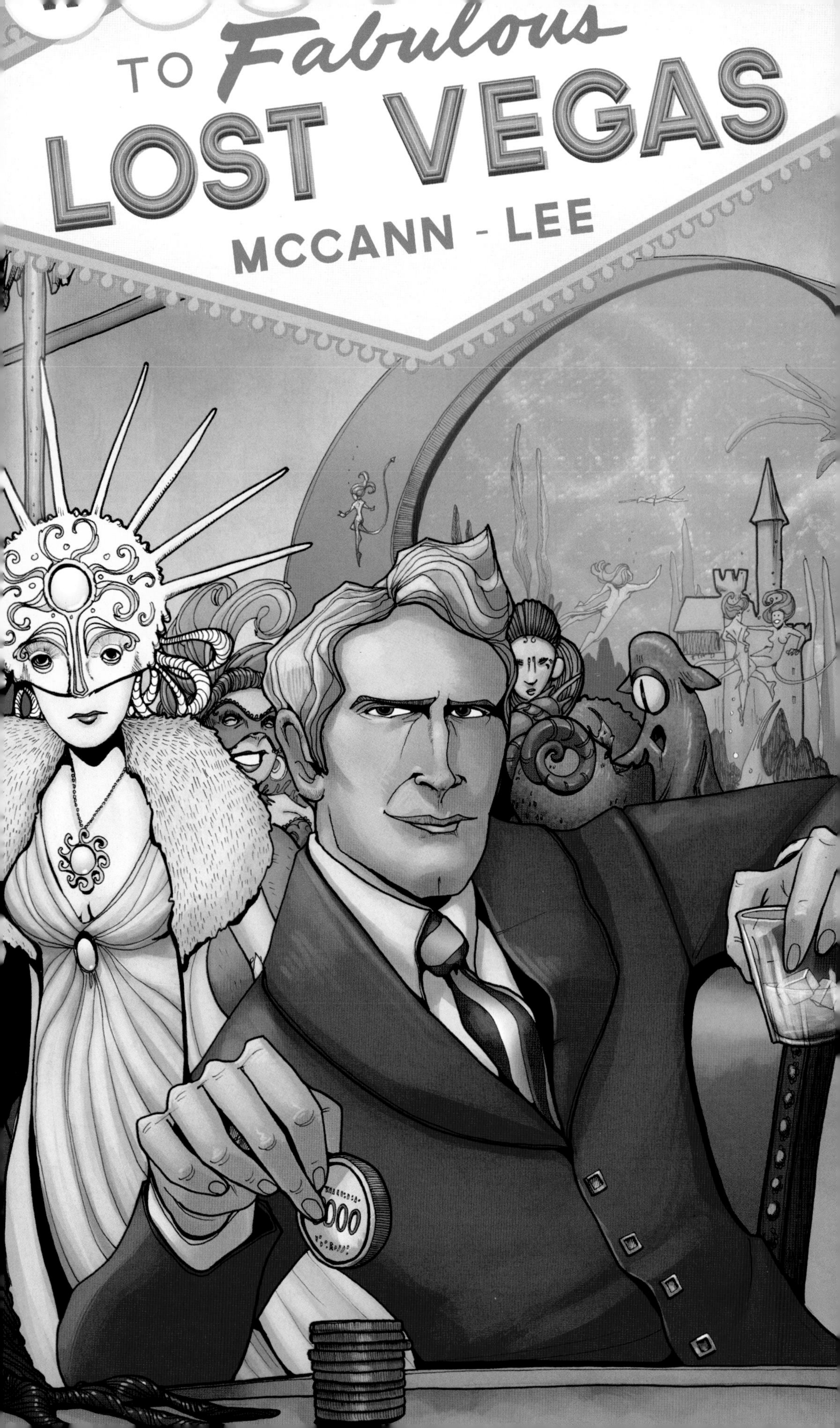
TO Fabulous
LOST VEGAS
MCCANN - LEE

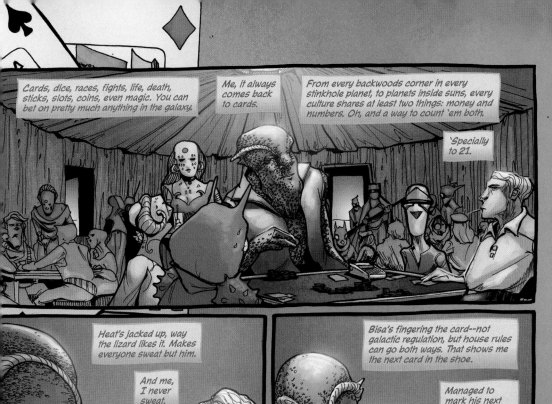

Cards, dice, races, fights, life, death, sticks, slots, coins, even magic. You can bet on pretty much anything in the galaxy.

Me, it always comes back to cards.

From every backwoods corner in every stinkhole planet, to planets inside suns, every culture shares at least two things: money and numbers. Oh, and a way to count 'em both.

'Specially to 21.

Heat's jacked up, way the lizard likes it. Makes everyone sweat but him.

And me, I never sweat.

Bisa's fingering the card--not galactic regulation, but house rules can go both ways. That shows me the next card in the shoe.

Managed to mark his next card--a nine. No way he can win.

Last hand before I can walk outta here with enough to start payin' down every two-bit hustler and high-roller around.

There's a moment at a table when you know, your gut says it for you, the brain doesn't make it happen, the gut does, and your hands are suddenly doubling down, all in.

Figure Bisa's the best chump to try out the fakers I just played while the real chips loaned from Newmey, the last shark in the system, are sittin' safe in my pockets.

When the time comes, you gotta figure how to make your own way.

TOUGH BREAK, BISA. NOW, IF YOUR MAN HERE CAN CREDIT ME OUT--

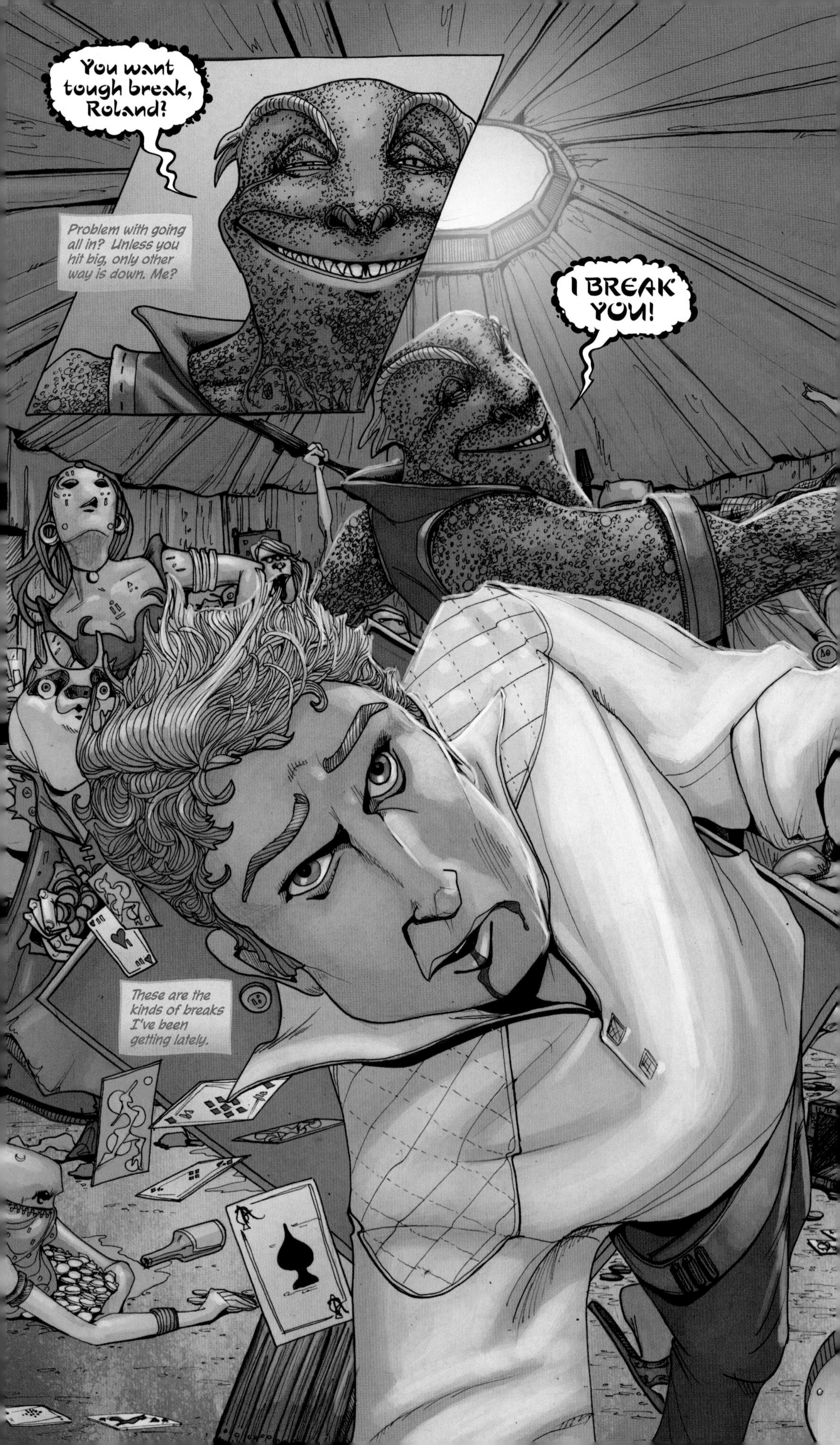
You want tough break, Roland?
Problem with going all in? Unless you hit big, only other way is down. Me?
I BREAK YOU!
These are the kinds of breaks I've been getting lately.

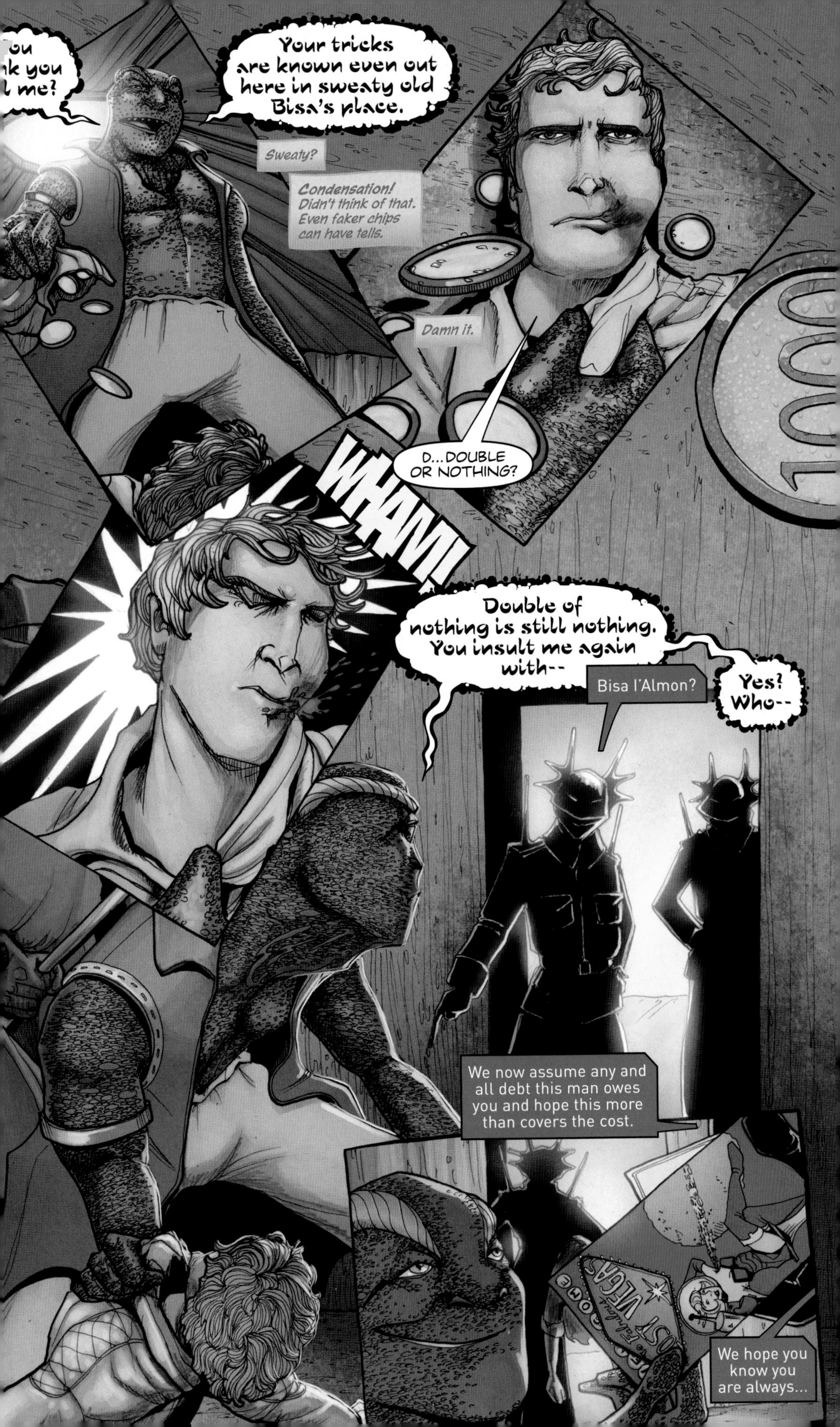

Your tricks are known even out here in sweaty old Bisa's place.
Sweaty?
Condensation! Didn't think of that. Even faker chips can have tells.
Damn it.
D...DOUBLE OR NOTHING?
WHAM!
Double of nothing is still nothing. You insult me again with--
Bisa l'Almon?
Yes? Who--
We now assume any and all debt this man owes you and hope this more than covers the cost.
We hope you know you are always...

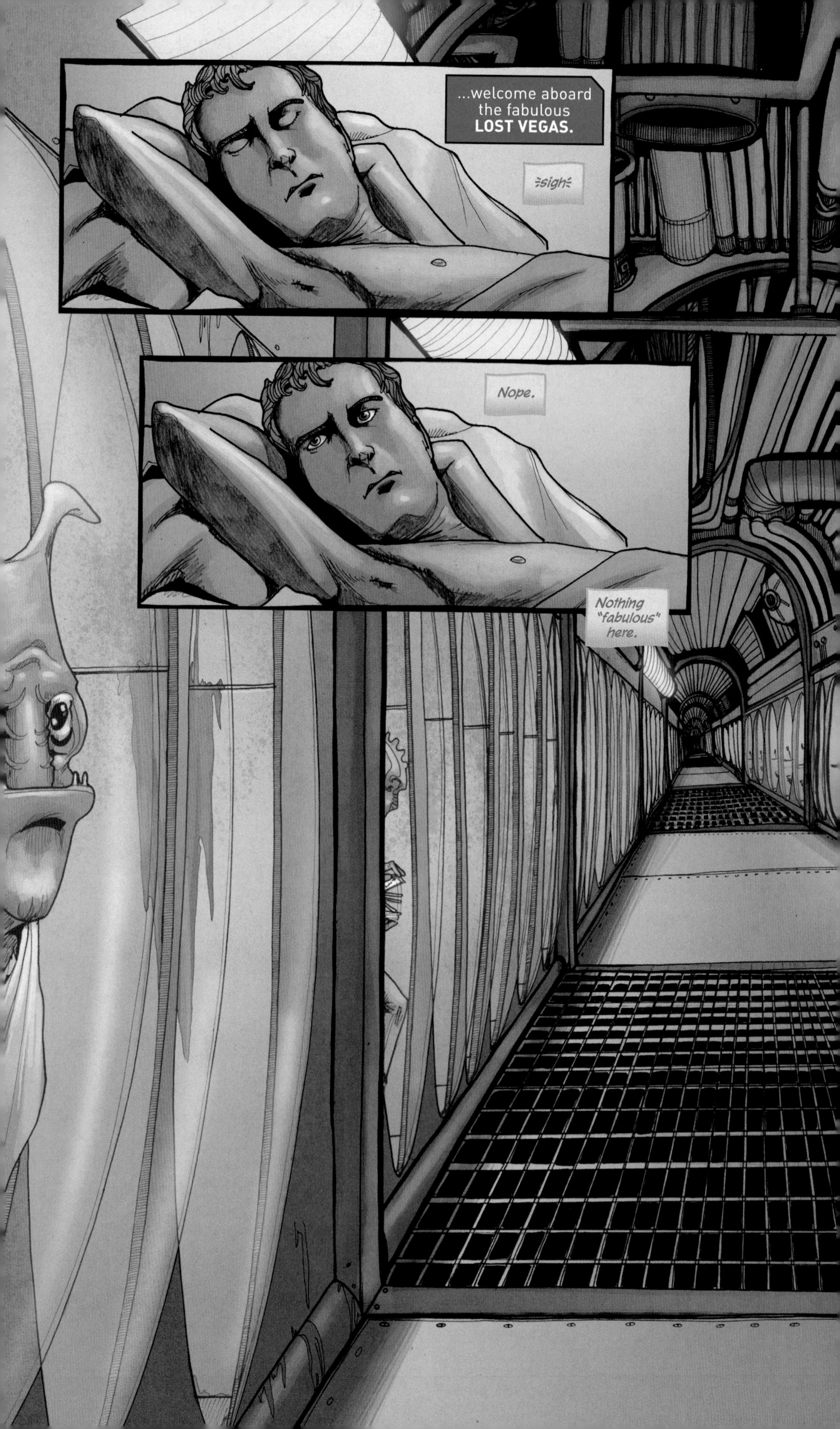
...welcome aboard the fabulous LOST VEGAS.
sigh
Nope.
Nothing "fabulous" here.

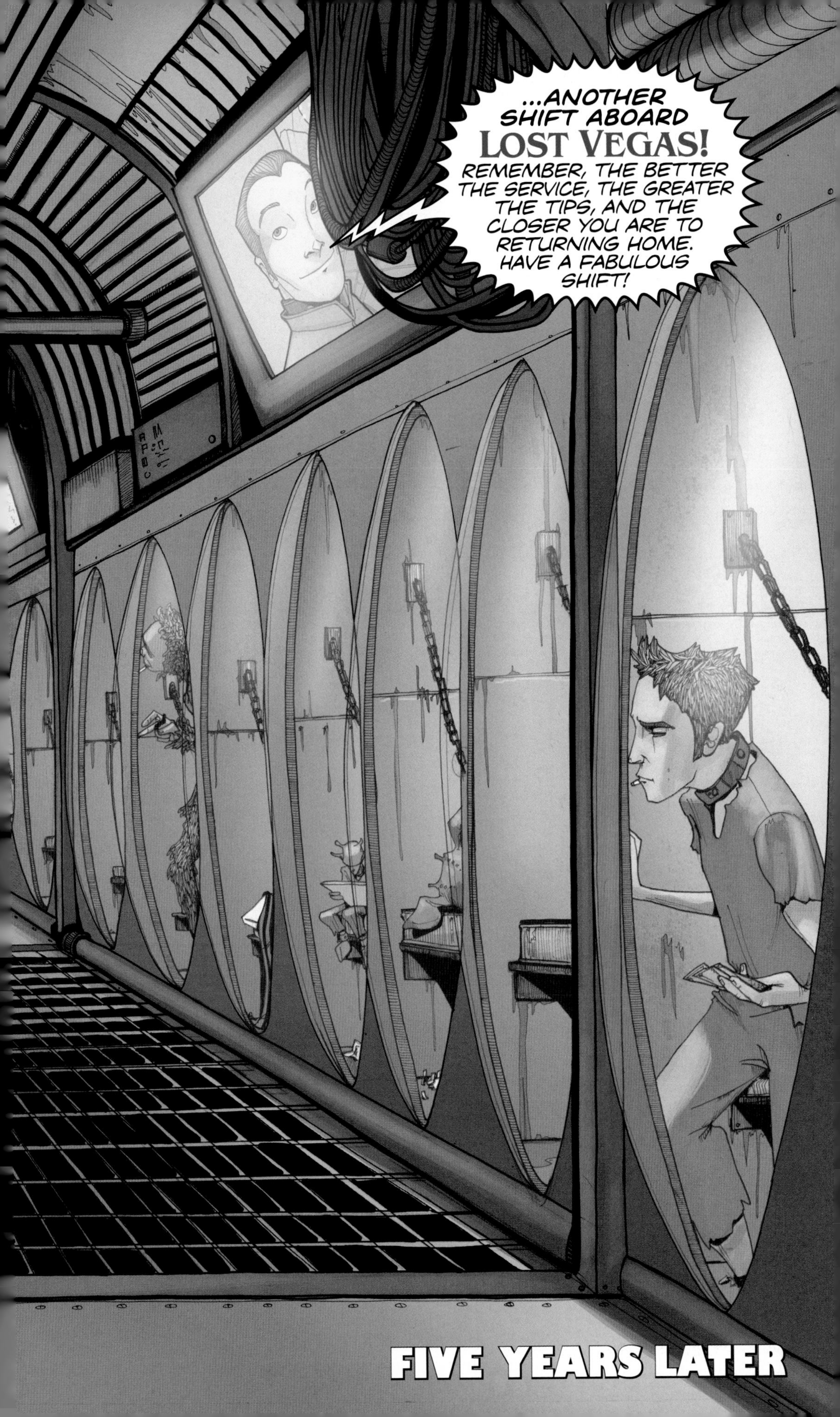
...ANOTHER SHIFT ABOARD LOST VEGAS! REMEMBER, THE BETTER THE SERVICE, THE GREATER THE TIPS, AND THE CLOSER YOU ARE TO RETURNING HOME. HAVE A FABULOUS SHIFT!
FIVE YEARS LATER

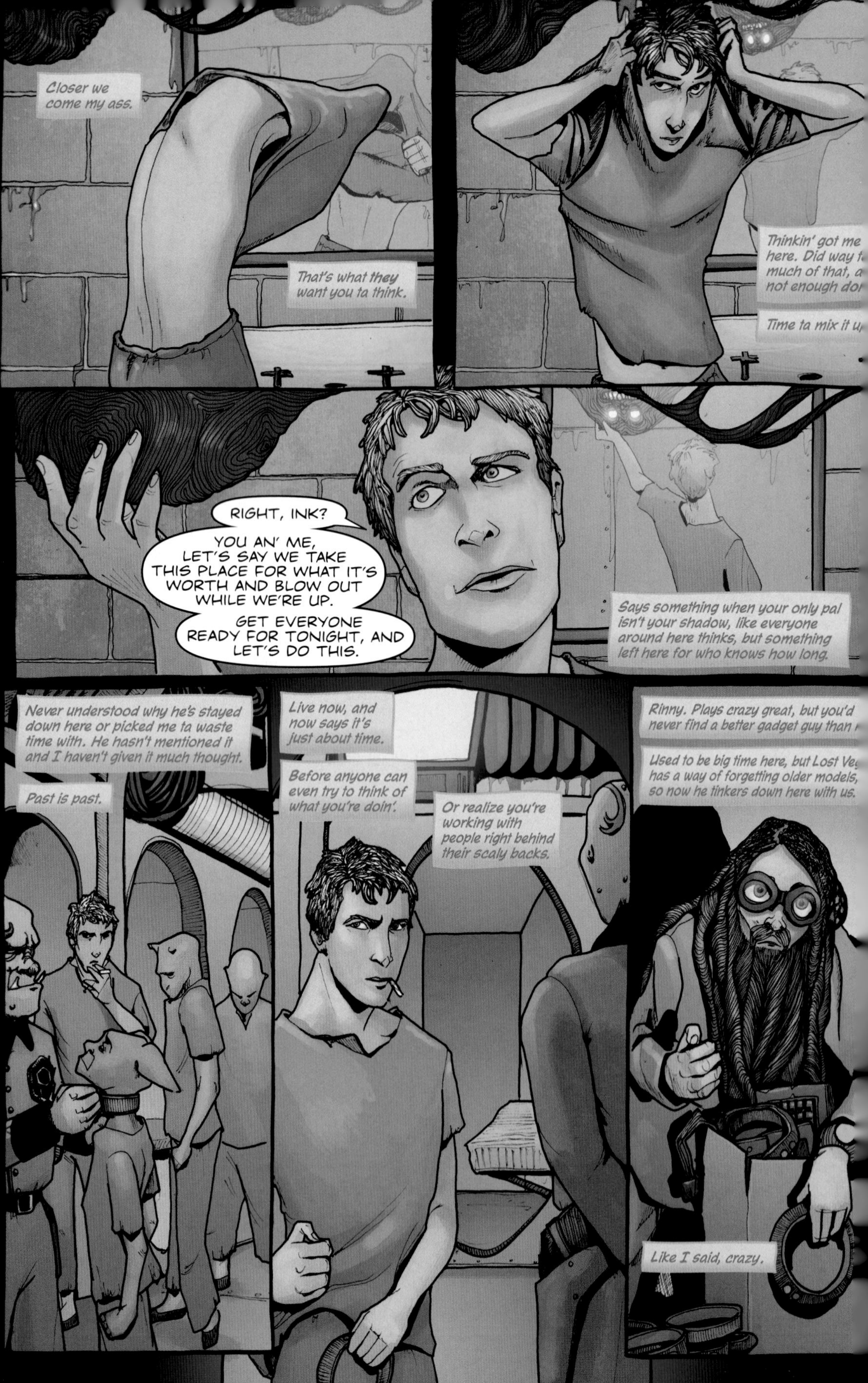
Closer we come my ass.
That's what they want you ta think.
Thinkin' got me here. Did way to much of that, a not enough doi
Time ta mix it u
RIGHT, INK?
YOU AN' ME, LET'S SAY WE TAKE THIS PLACE FOR WHAT IT'S WORTH AND BLOW OUT WHILE WE'RE UP.
GET EVERYONE READY FOR TONIGHT, AND LET'S DO THIS.
Says something when your only pal isn't your shadow, like everyone around here thinks, but something left here for who knows how long.
Never understood why he's stayed down here or picked me ta waste time with. He hasn't mentioned it and I haven't given it much thought.
Past is past.
Live now, and now says it's just about time.
Before anyone can even try to think of what you're doin'.
Or realize you're working with people right behind their scaly backs.
Rinny. Plays crazy great, but you'd never find a better gadget guy than
Used to be big time here, but Lost Ve has a way of forgetting older models, so now he tinkers down here with us.
Like I said, crazy.

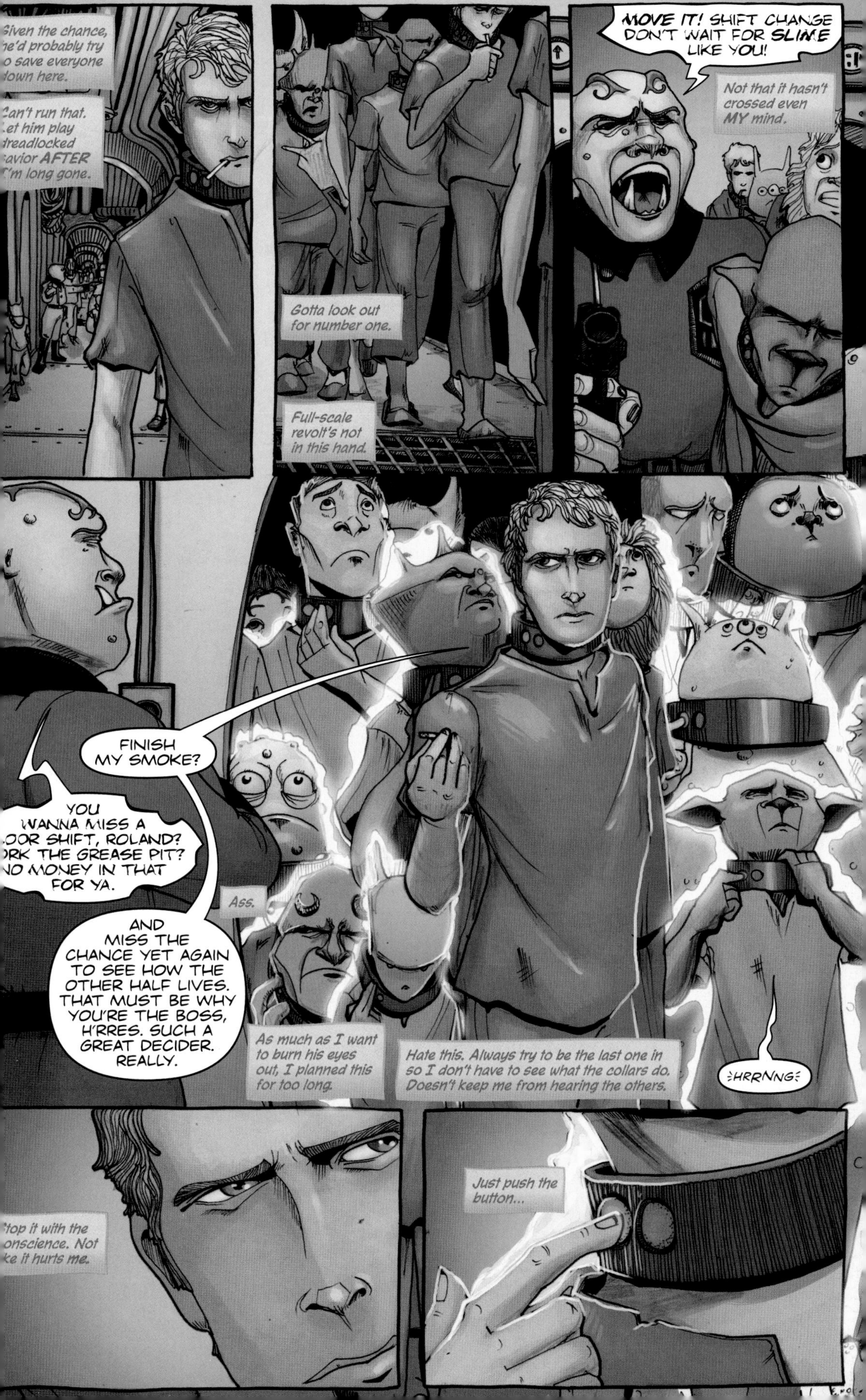

Given the chance, he'd probably try to save everyone down here.
Can't run that. Let him play dreadlocked savior AFTER I'm long gone.
Gotta look out for number one.
Full-scale revolt's not in this hand.
MOVE IT! SHIFT CHANGE DON'T WAIT FOR SLIME LIKE YOU!
Not that it hasn't crossed even MY mind.
FINISH MY SMOKE?
YOU WANNA MISS A OOR SHIFT, ROLAND? ORK THE GREASE PIT? NO MONEY IN THAT FOR YA.
Ass.
AND MISS THE CHANCE YET AGAIN TO SEE HOW THE OTHER HALF LIVES. THAT MUST BE WHY YOU'RE THE BOSS, H'RRES. SUCH A GREAT DECIDER. REALLY.
As much as I want to burn his eyes out, I planned this for too long.
Hate this. Always try to be the last one in so I don't have to see what the collars do. Doesn't keep me from hearing the others.
HRRNNG
Stop it with the onscience. Not ke it hurts me.
Just push the button...

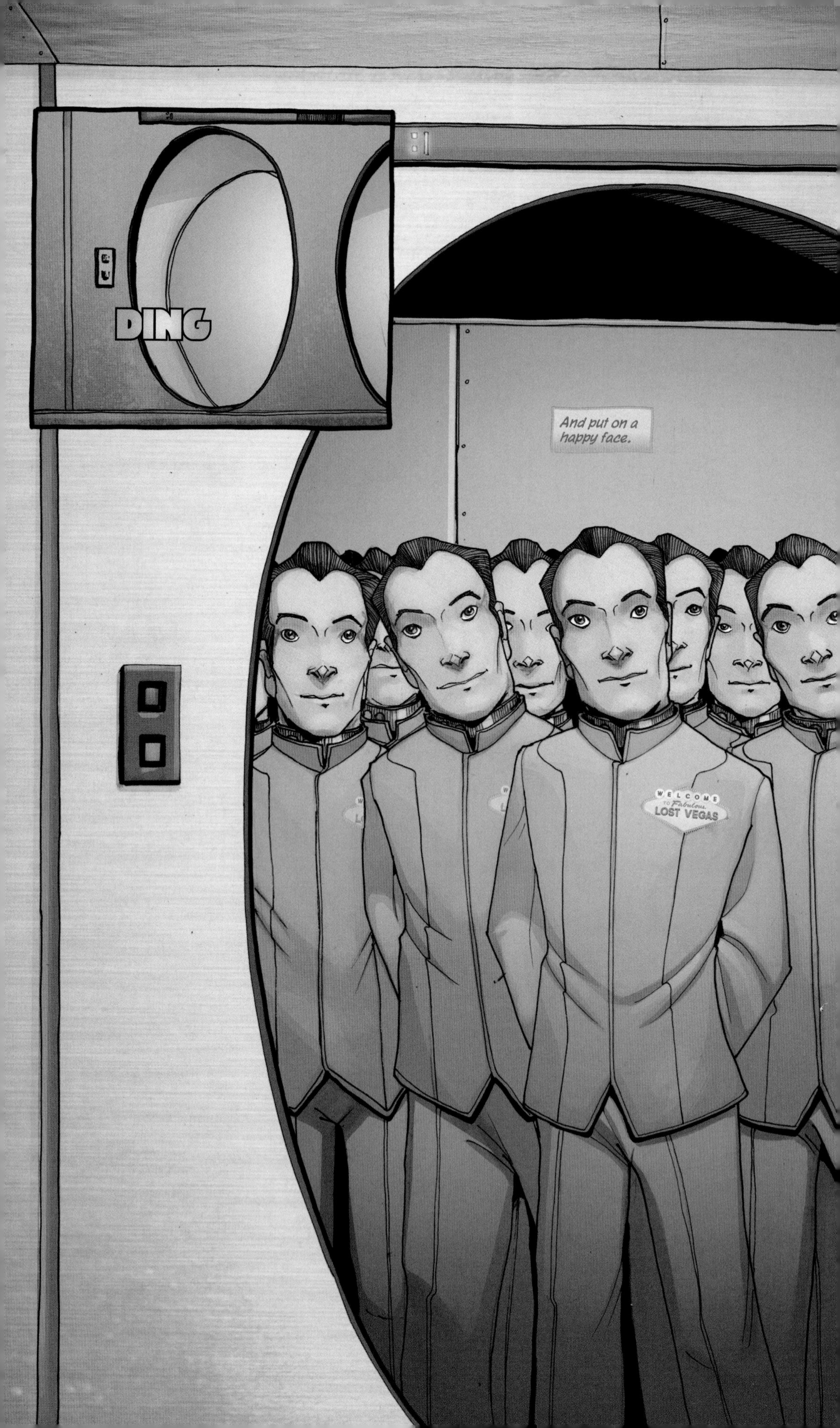
DING
And put on a happy face.
WELCOME TO Fabulous LOST VEGAS

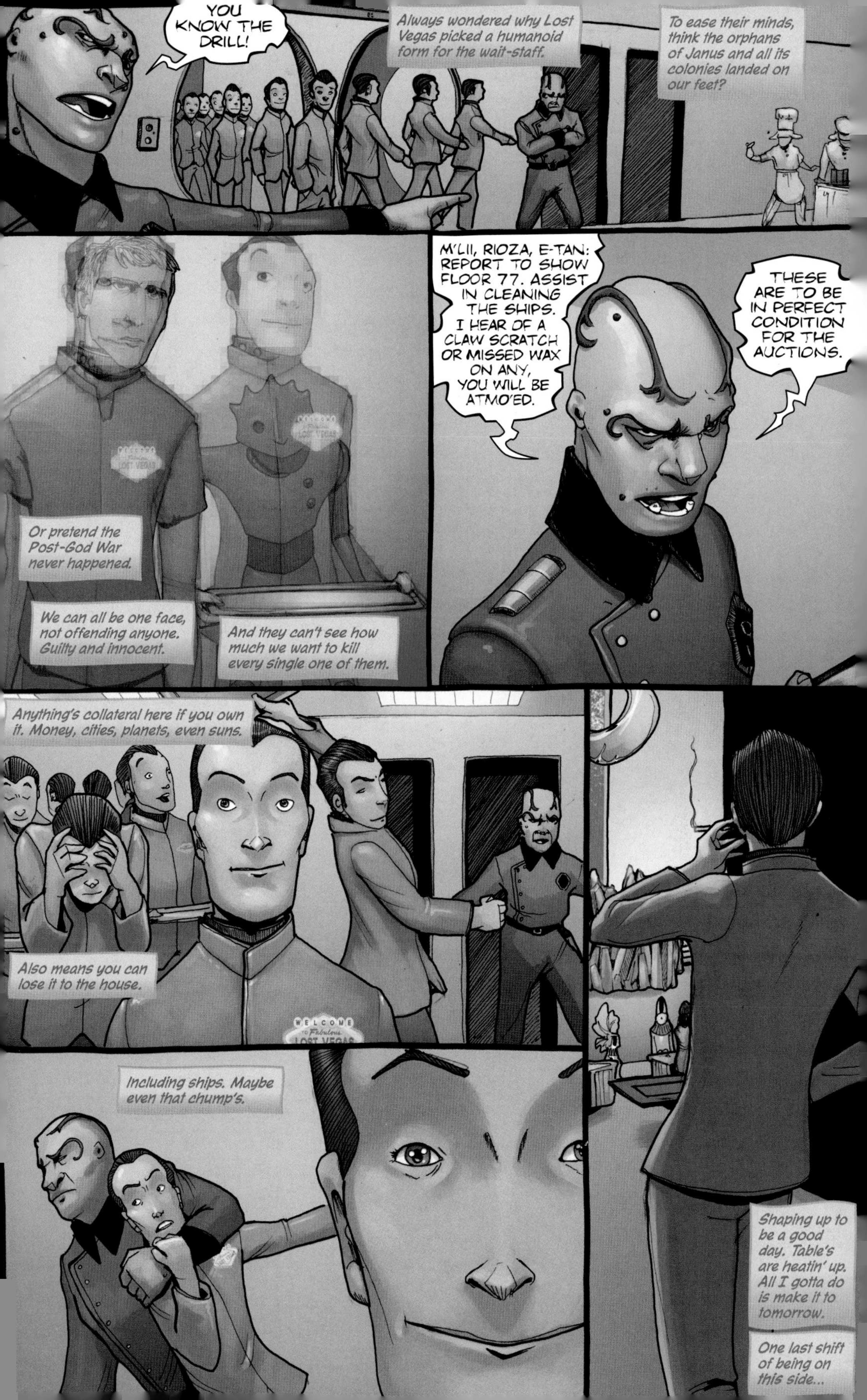
YOU KNOW THE DRILL!
Always wondered why Lost Vegas picked a humanoid form for the wait-staff.
To ease their minds, think the orphans of Janus and all its colonies landed on our feet?
Or pretend the Post-God War never happened.
We can all be one face, not offending anyone. Guilty and innocent.
And they can't see how much we want to kill every single one of them.
M'LII, RIOZA, E-TAN: REPORT TO SHOW FLOOR 77. ASSIST IN CLEANING THE SHIPS. I HEAR OF A CLAW SCRATCH OR MISSED WAX ON ANY, YOU WILL BE ATMO'ED.
THESE ARE TO BE IN PERFECT CONDITION FOR THE AUCTIONS.
Anything's collateral here if you own it. Money, cities, planets, even suns.
Also means you can lose it to the house.
WELCOME TO Fabulous LOST VEGAS
Including ships. Maybe even that chump's.
Shaping up to be a good day. Table's are heatin' up. All I gotta do is make it to tomorrow.
One last shift of being on this side...

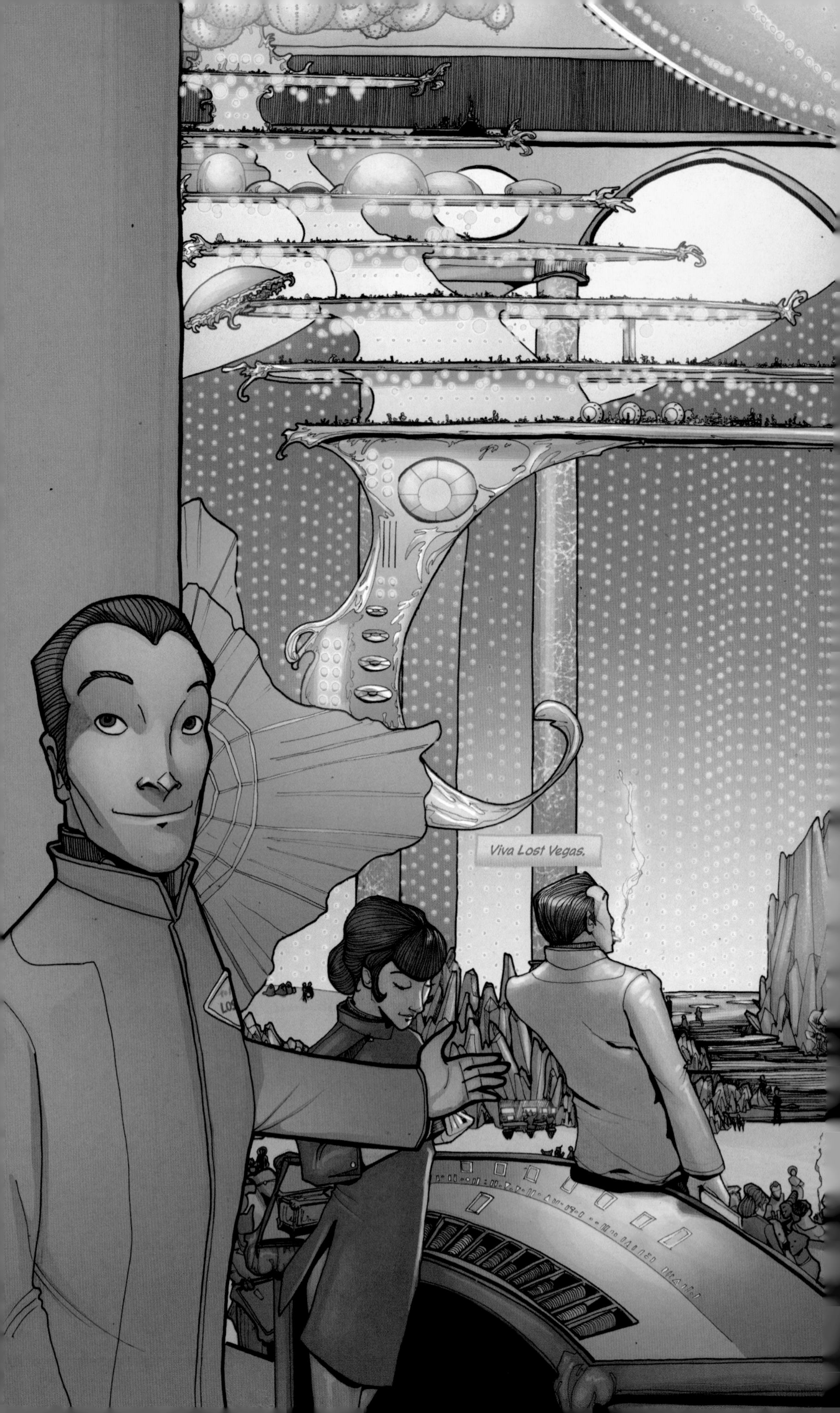
Viva Lost Vegas.

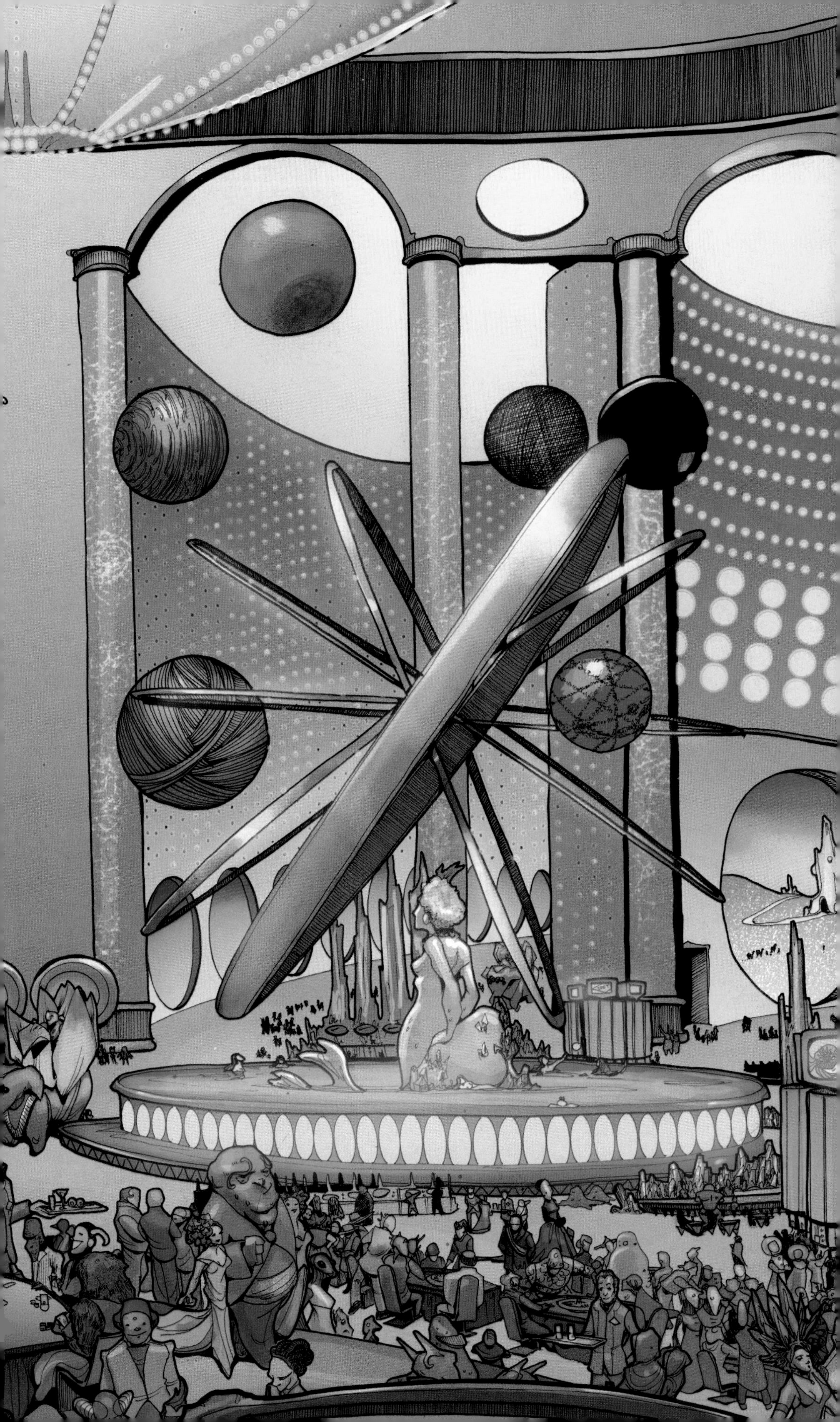

LOST

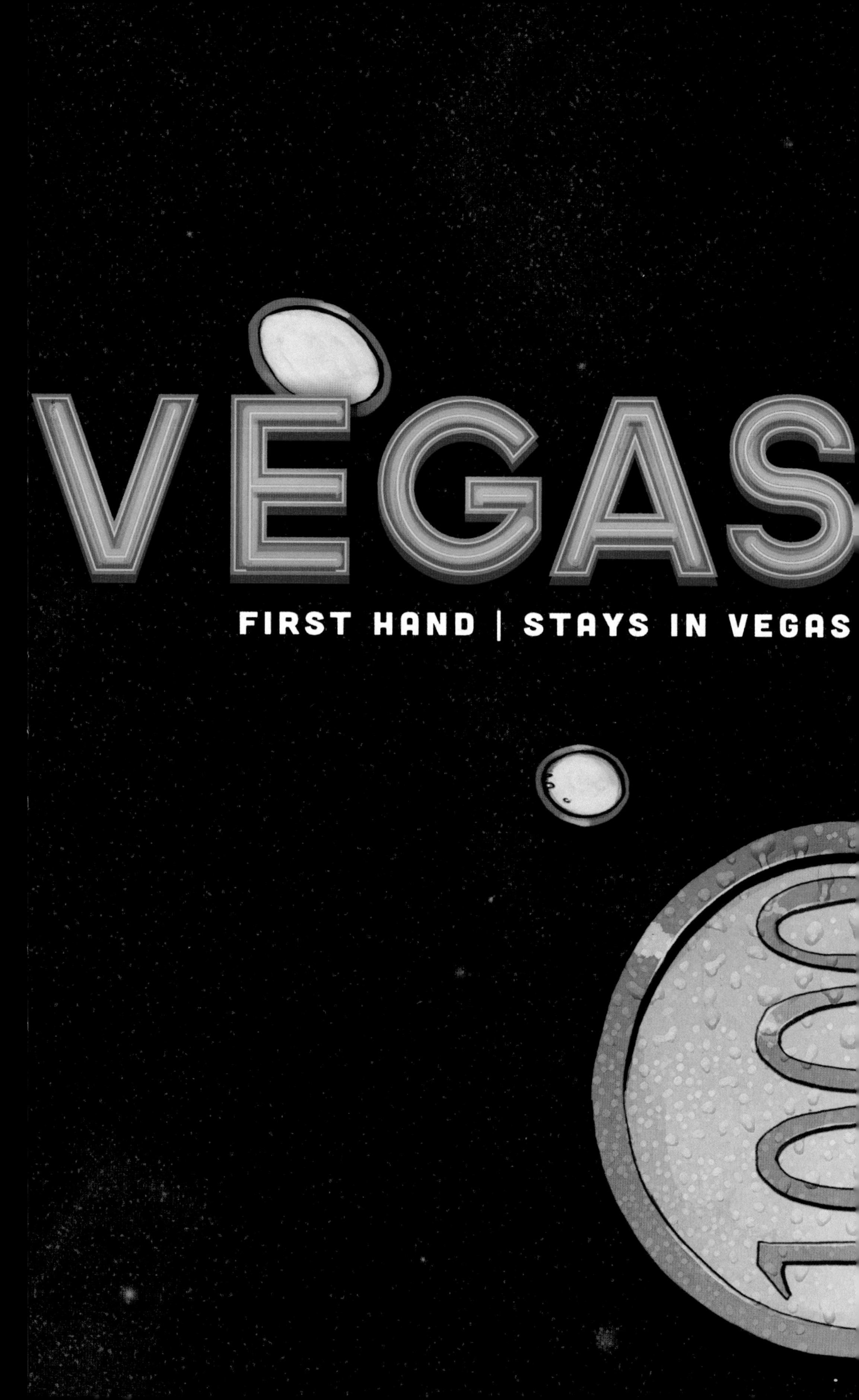
VEGAS
FIRST HAND | STAYS IN VEGAS

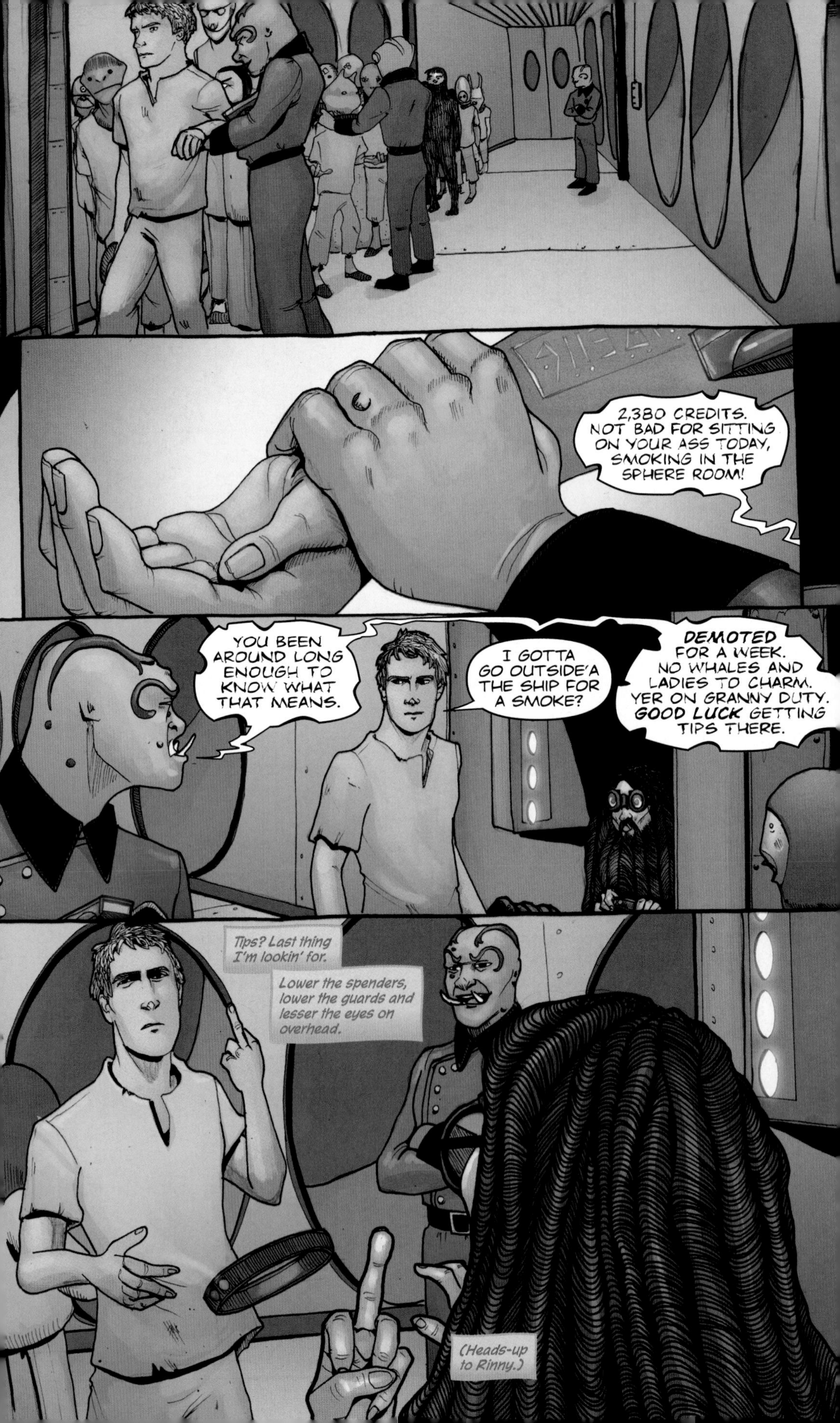
2,380 CREDITS. NOT BAD FOR SITTING ON YOUR ASS TODAY, SMOKING IN THE SPHERE ROOM!
YOU BEEN AROUND LONG ENOUGH TO KNOW WHAT THAT MEANS.
I GOTTA GO OUTSIDE'A THE SHIP FOR A SMOKE?
DEMOTED FOR A WEEK. NO WHALES AND LADIES TO CHARM. YER ON GRANNY DUTY. GOOD LUCK GETTING TIPS THERE.
Tips? Last thing I'm lookin' for.
Lower the spenders, lower the guards and lesser the eyes on overhead.
(Heads-up to Rinny.)

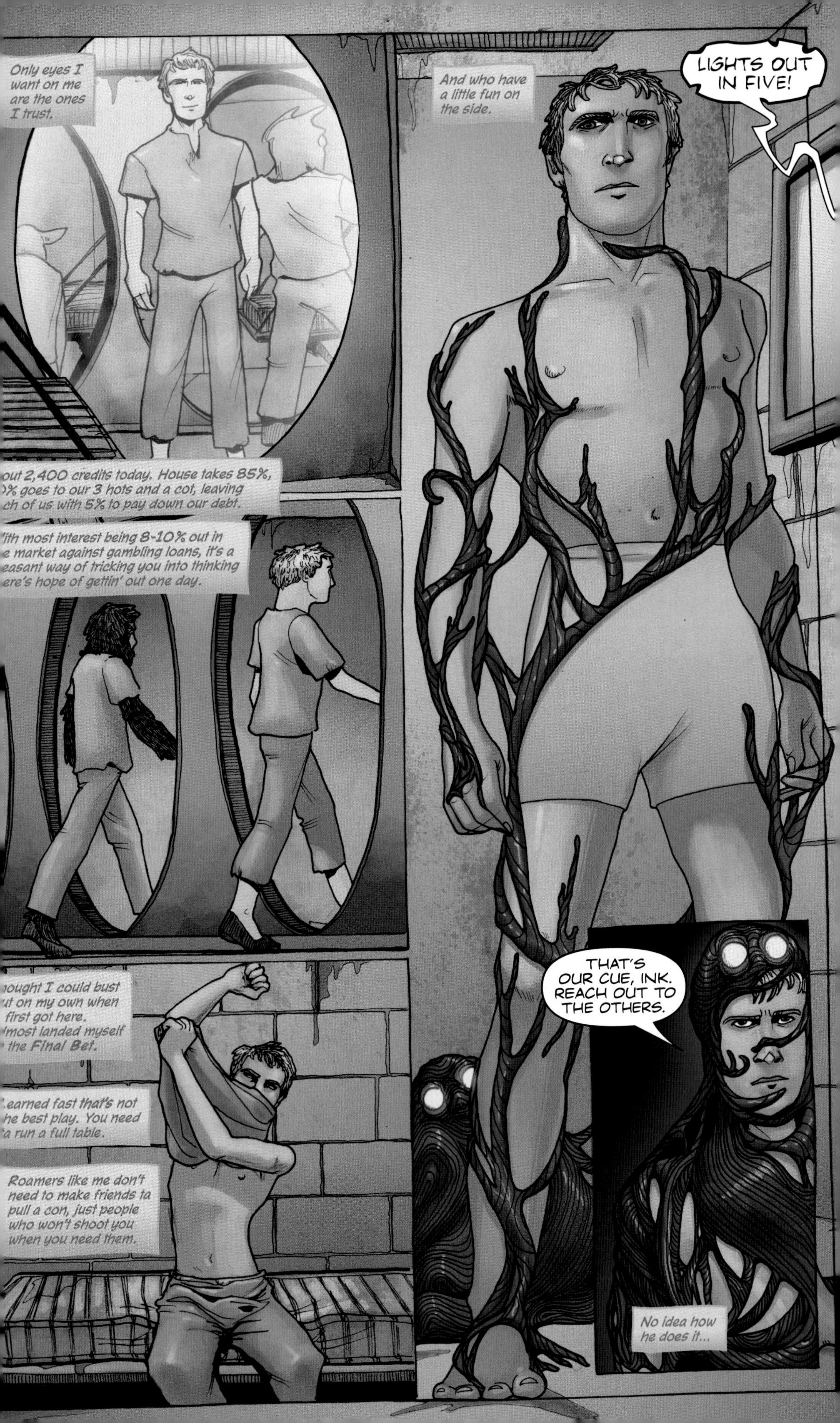
Only eyes I want on me are the ones I trust.
out 2,400 credits today. House takes 85%, 0% goes to our 3 hots and a cot, leaving ch of us with 5% to pay down our debt.
Vith most interest being 8-10% out in e market against gambling loans, it's a easant way of tricking you into thinking ere's hope of gettin' out one day.
hought I could bust ut on my own when first got here. lmost landed myself the Final Bet.
Learned fast that's not he best play. You need ta run a full table.
Roamers like me don't need to make friends ta pull a con, just people who won't shoot you when you need them.
And who have a little fun on the side.
LIGHTS OUT IN FIVE!
THAT'S OUR CUE, INK. REACH OUT TO THE OTHERS.
No idea how he does it...

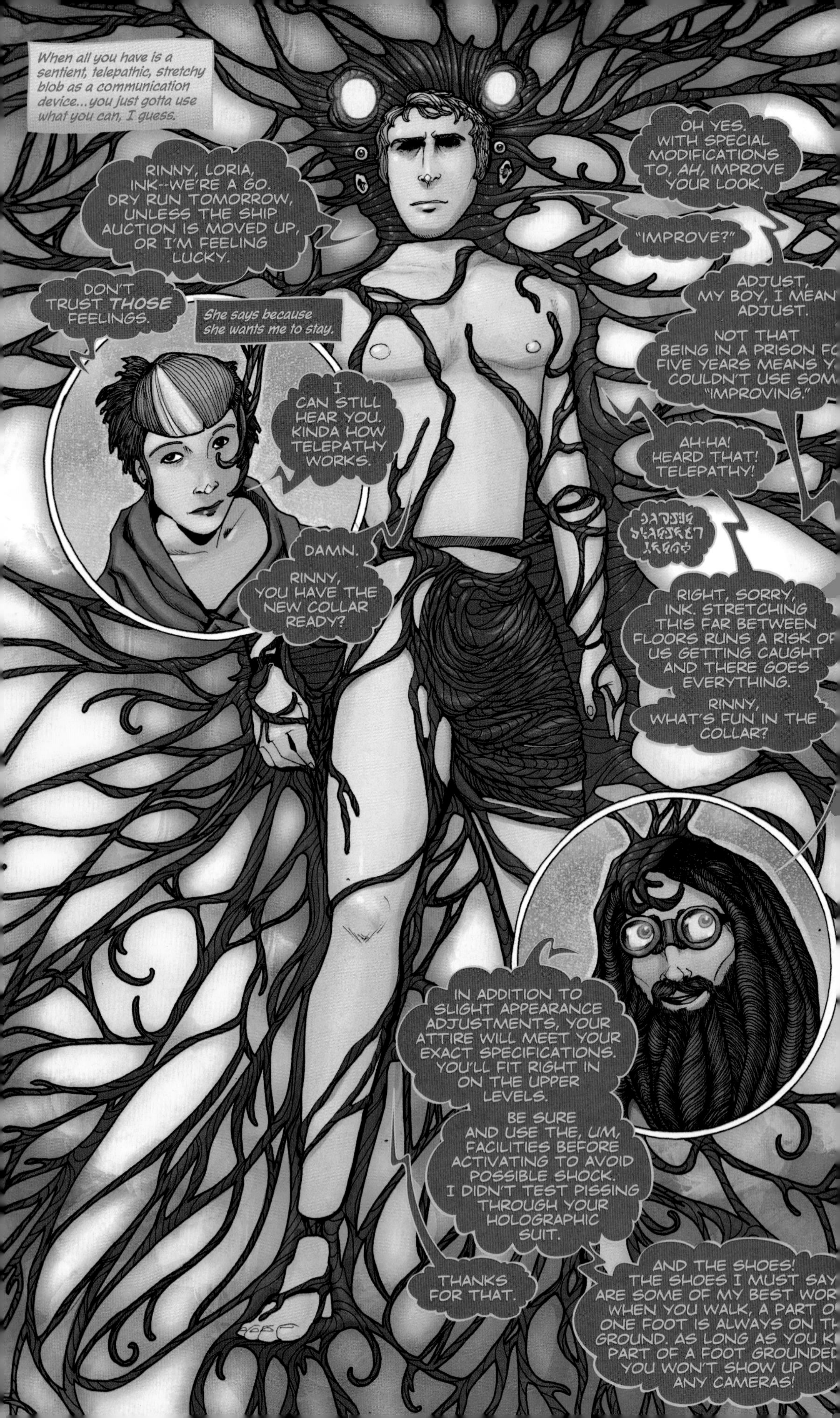
When all you have is a sentient, telepathic, stretchy blob as a communication device...you just gotta use what you can, I guess.
RINNY, LORIA, INK--WE'RE A GO. DRY RUN TOMORROW, UNLESS THE SHIP AUCTION IS MOVED UP, OR I'M FEELING LUCKY.
OH YES. WITH SPECIAL MODIFICATIONS TO, AH, IMPROVE YOUR LOOK.
"IMPROVE?"
ADJUST, MY BOY, I MEAN ADJUST.
NOT THAT BEING IN A PRISON FIVE YEARS MEANS COULDN'T USE "IMPROVING."
DON'T TRUST *THOSE* FEELINGS.
She says because she wants me to stay.
I CAN STILL HEAR YOU. KINDA HOW TELEPATHY WORKS.
AH-HA! HEARD THAT! TELEPATHY!
DAMN.
RINNY, YOU HAVE THE NEW COLLAR READY?
RIGHT, SORRY, INK. STRETCHING THIS FAR BETWEEN FLOORS RUNS A RISK US GETTING CAUGHT AND THERE GOES EVERYTHING.
RINNY, WHAT'S FUN IN THE COLLAR?
IN ADDITION TO SLIGHT APPEARANCE ADJUSTMENTS, YOUR ATTIRE WILL MEET YOUR EXACT SPECIFICATIONS. YOU'LL FIT RIGHT IN ON THE UPPER LEVELS.
BE SURE AND USE THE, UM, FACILITIES BEFORE ACTIVATING TO AVOID POSSIBLE SHOCK. I DIDN'T TEST PISSING THROUGH YOUR HOLOGRAPHIC SUIT.
THANKS FOR THAT.
AND THE SHOES! THE SHOES I MUST SAY ARE SOME OF MY BEST WHEN YOU WALK, A PART ONE FOOT IS ALWAYS ON GROUND. AS LONG AS YOU PART OF A FOOT YOU WON'T SHOW UP ON ANY CAMERAS!

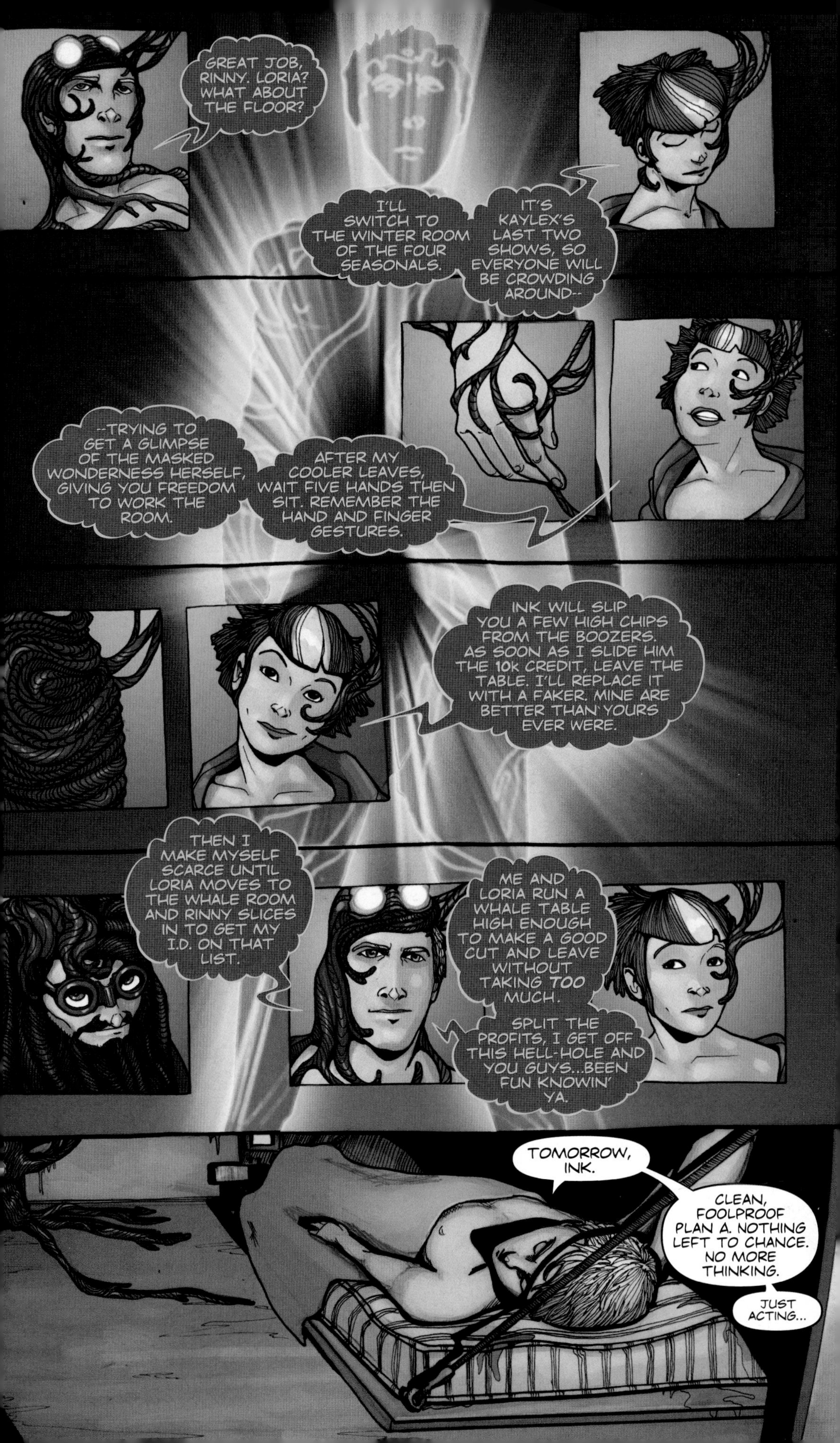
GREAT JOB, RINNY. LORIA? WHAT ABOUT THE FLOOR?
I'LL SWITCH TO THE WINTER ROOM OF THE FOUR SEASONALS.
IT'S KAYLEX'S LAST TWO SHOWS, SO EVERYONE WILL BE CROWDING AROUND--
--TRYING TO GET A GLIMPSE OF THE MASKED WONDERNESS HERSELF, GIVING YOU FREEDOM TO WORK THE ROOM.
AFTER MY COOLER LEAVES, WAIT FIVE HANDS THEN SIT. REMEMBER THE HAND AND FINGER GESTURES.
INK WILL SLIP YOU A FEW HIGH CHIPS FROM THE BOOZERS. AS SOON AS I SLIDE HIM THE 10k CREDIT, LEAVE THE TABLE. I'LL REPLACE IT WITH A FAKER. MINE ARE BETTER THAN YOURS EVER WERE.
THEN I MAKE MYSELF SCARCE UNTIL LORIA MOVES TO THE WHALE ROOM AND RINNY SLICES IN TO GET MY I.D. ON THAT LIST.
ME AND LORIA RUN A WHALE TABLE HIGH ENOUGH TO MAKE A GOOD CUT AND LEAVE WITHOUT TAKING *TOO* MUCH.
SPLIT THE PROFITS, I GET OFF THIS HELL-HOLE AND YOU GUYS...BEEN FUN KNOWIN' YA.
TOMORROW, INK.
CLEAN, FOOLPROOF PLAN A. NOTHING LEFT TO CHANCE. NO MORE THINKING.
JUST ACTING...

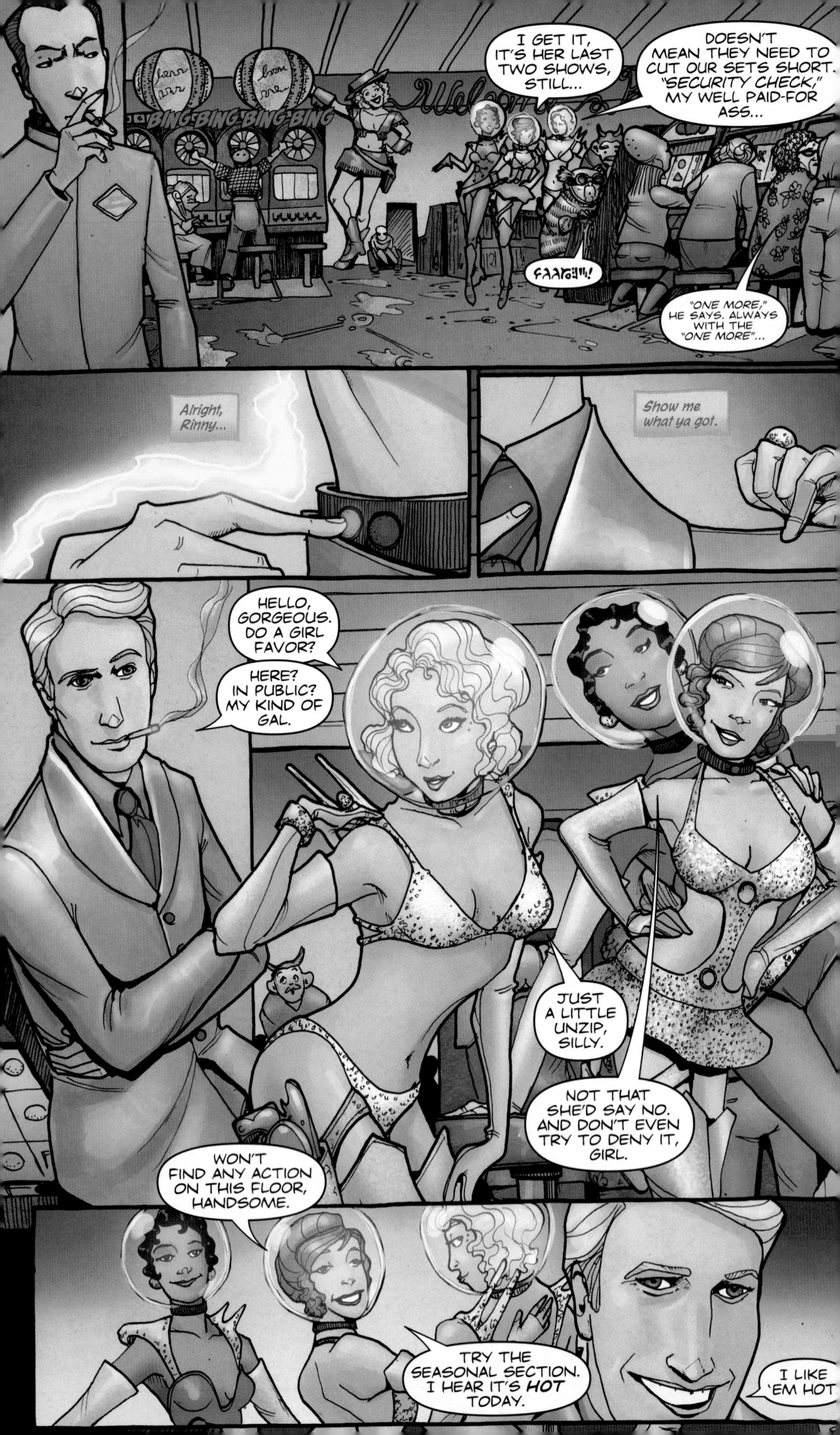

BING BING BING BING
I GET IT, IT'S HER LAST TWO SHOWS, STILL...
DOESN'T MEAN THEY NEED TO CUT OUR SETS SHORT. "SECURITY CHECK," MY WELL PAID-FOR ASS...
"ONE MORE," HE SAYS. ALWAYS WITH THE "ONE MORE"...
Alright, Rinny...
Show me what ya got.
HELLO, GORGEOUS. DO A GIRL FAVOR?
HERE? IN PUBLIC? MY KIND OF GAL.
JUST A LITTLE UNZIP, SILLY.
NOT THAT SHE'D SAY NO. AND DON'T EVEN TRY TO DENY IT, GIRL.
WON'T FIND ANY ACTION ON THIS FLOOR, HANDSOME.
TRY THE SEASONAL SECTION. I HEAR IT'S **HOT** TODAY.
I LIKE 'EM HOT

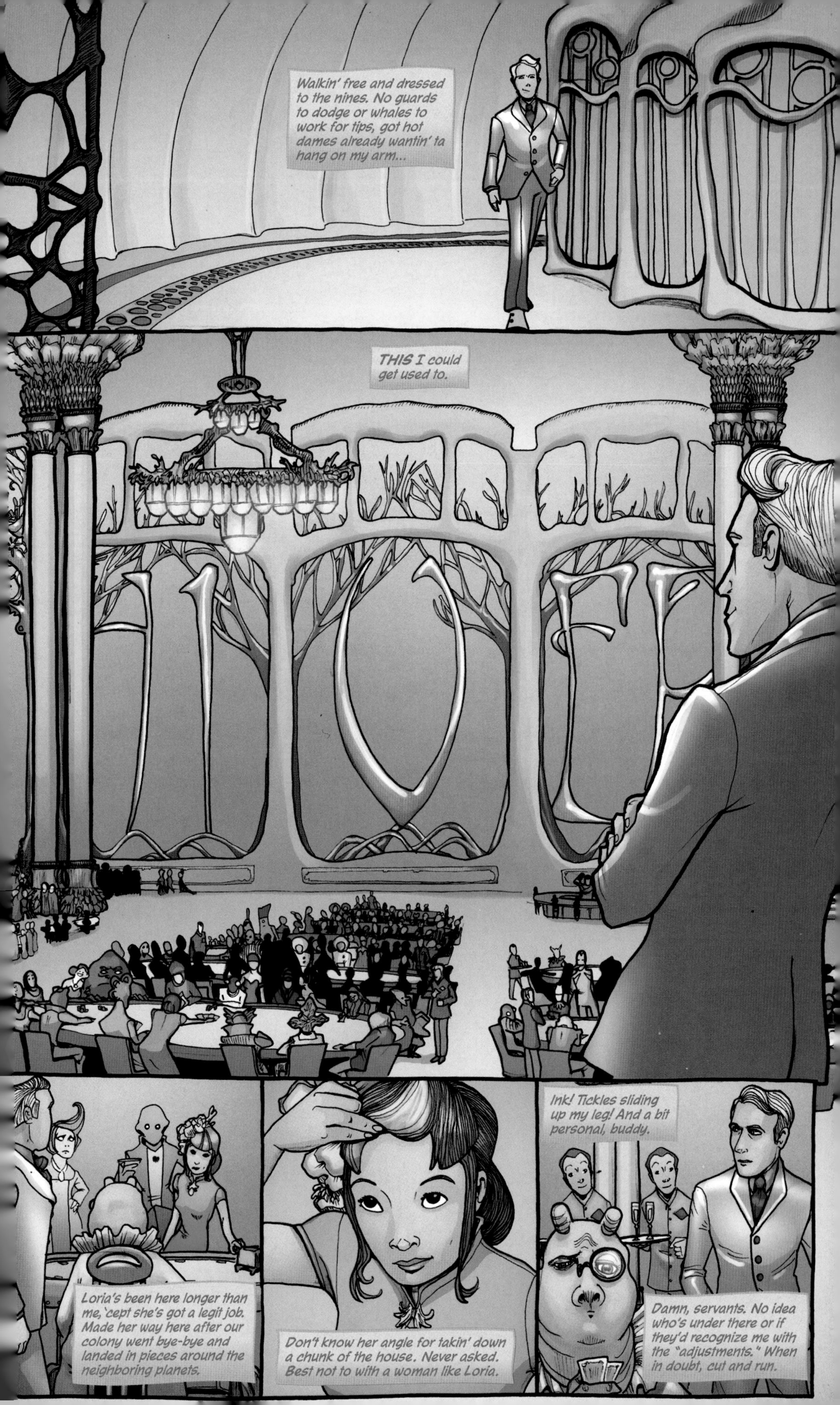

Walkin' free and dressed to the nines. No guards to dodge or whales to work for tips, got hot dames already wantin' ta hang on my arm...
THIS I could get used to.
Loria's been here longer than me, 'cept she's got a legit job. Made her way here after our colony went bye-bye and landed in pieces around the neighboring planets.
Don't know her angle for takin' down a chunk of the house. Never asked. Best not to with a woman like Loria.
Ink! Tickles sliding up my leg! And a bit personal, buddy.
Damn, servants. No idea who's under there or if they'd recognize me with the "adjustments." When in doubt, cut and run.

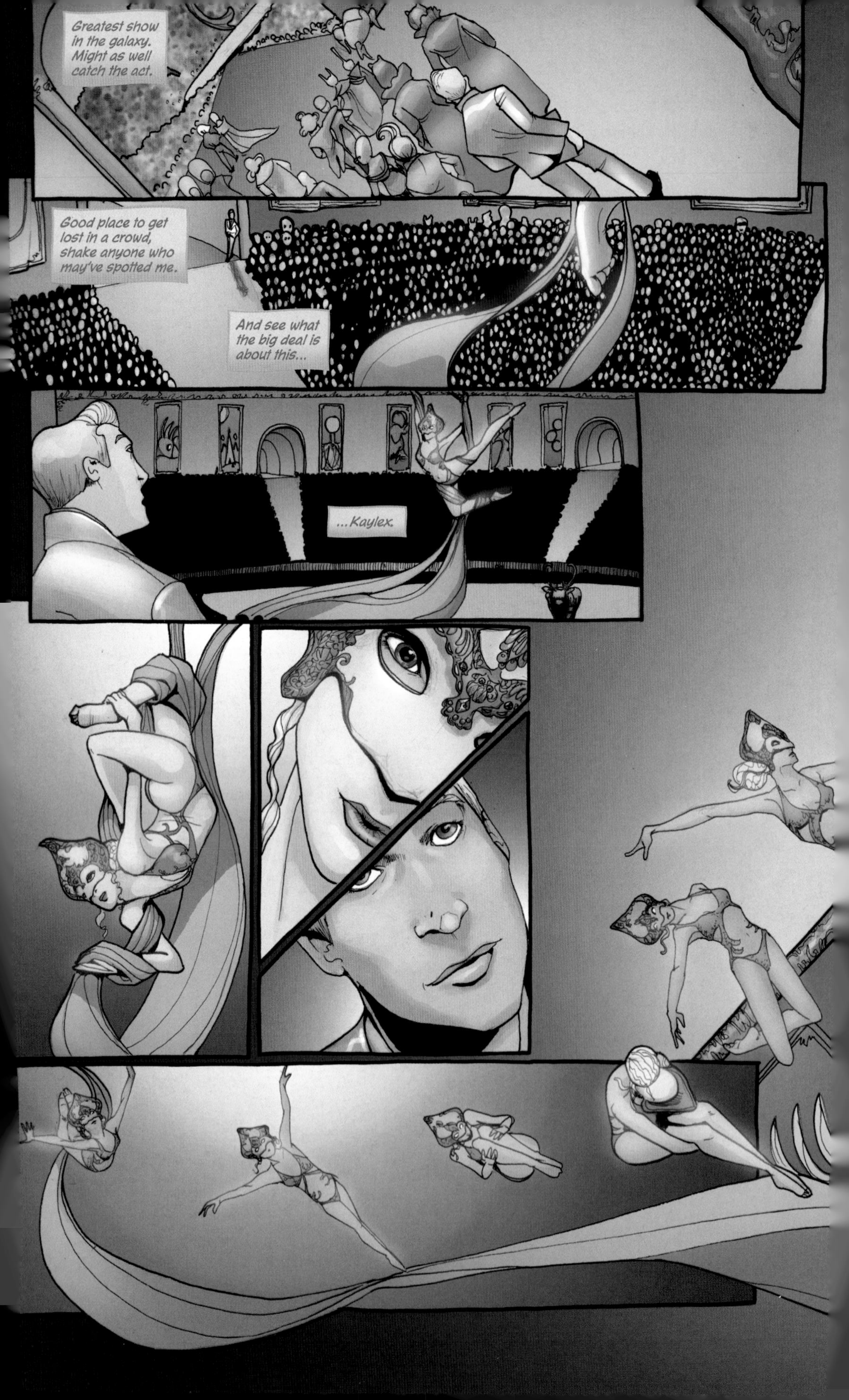

Greatest show in the galaxy. Might as well catch the act.
Good place to get lost in a crowd, shake anyone who may've spotted me.
And see what the big deal is about this...
...Kaylex.

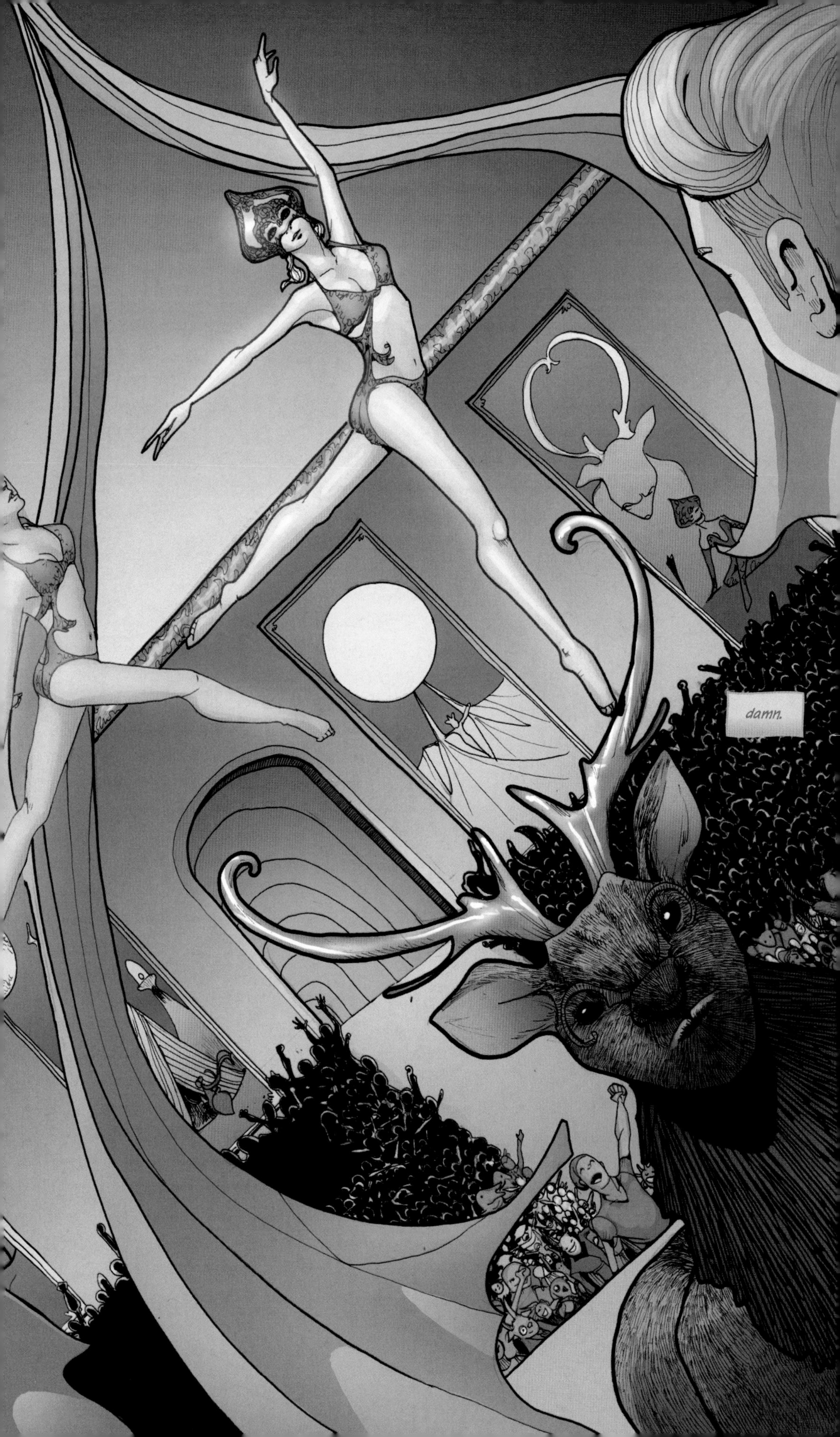
damn.

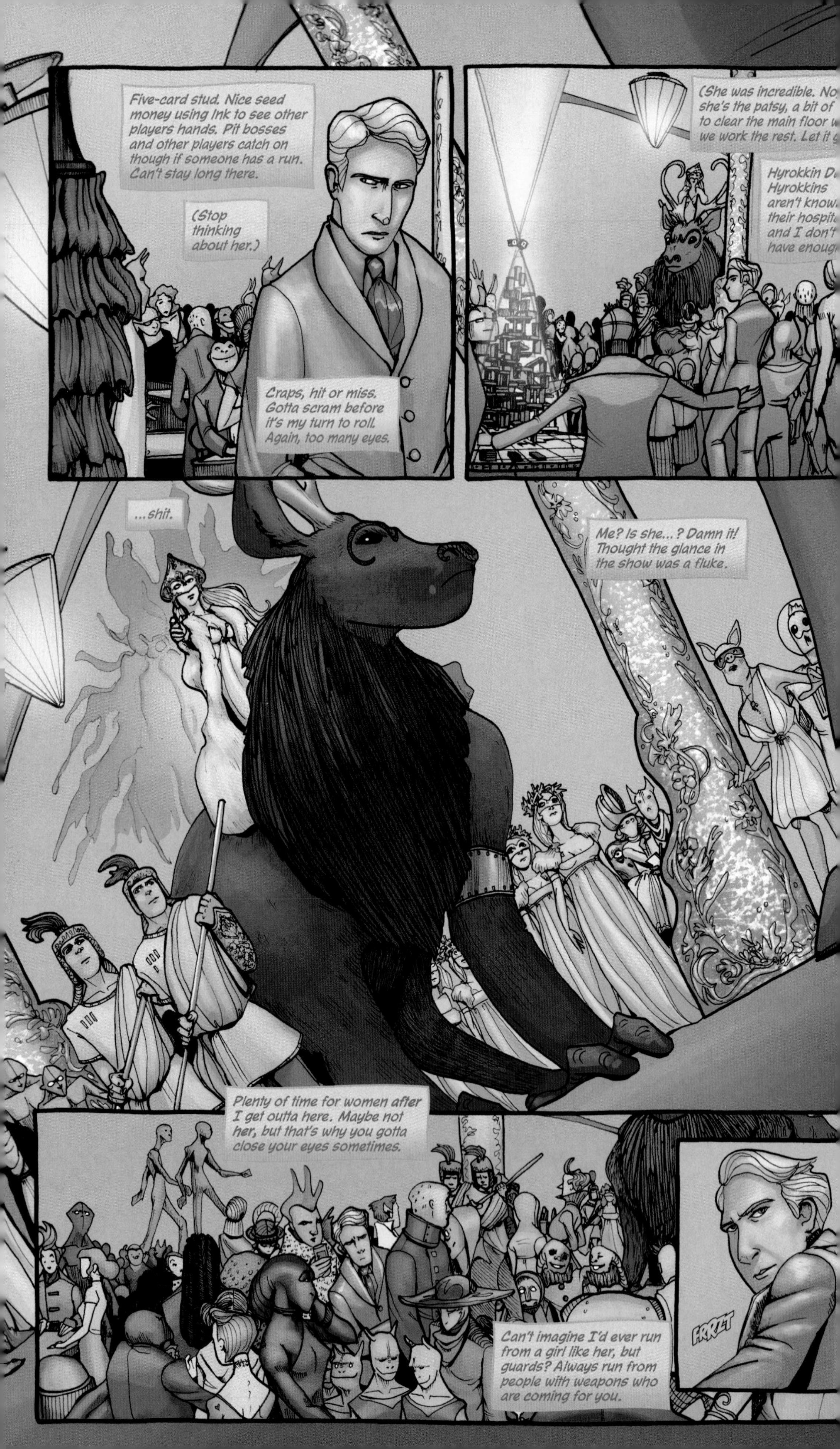
Five-card stud. Nice seed money using Ink to see other players hands. Pit bosses and other players catch on though if someone has a run. Can't stay long there.
(Stop thinking about her.)
Craps, hit or miss. Gotta scram before it's my turn to roll. Again, too many eyes.
(She was incredible. No
she's the patsy, a bit of
to clear the main floor w
we work the rest. Let it g
Hyrokkin D
Hyrokkins
aren't know
their hospit
and I don't
have enoug
...shit.
Me? Is she...? Damn it! Thought the glance in the show was a fluke.
Plenty of time for women after I get outta here. Maybe not her, but that's why you gotta close your eyes sometimes.
Can't imagine I'd ever run from a girl like her, but guards? Always run from people with weapons who are coming for you.
FRRZT

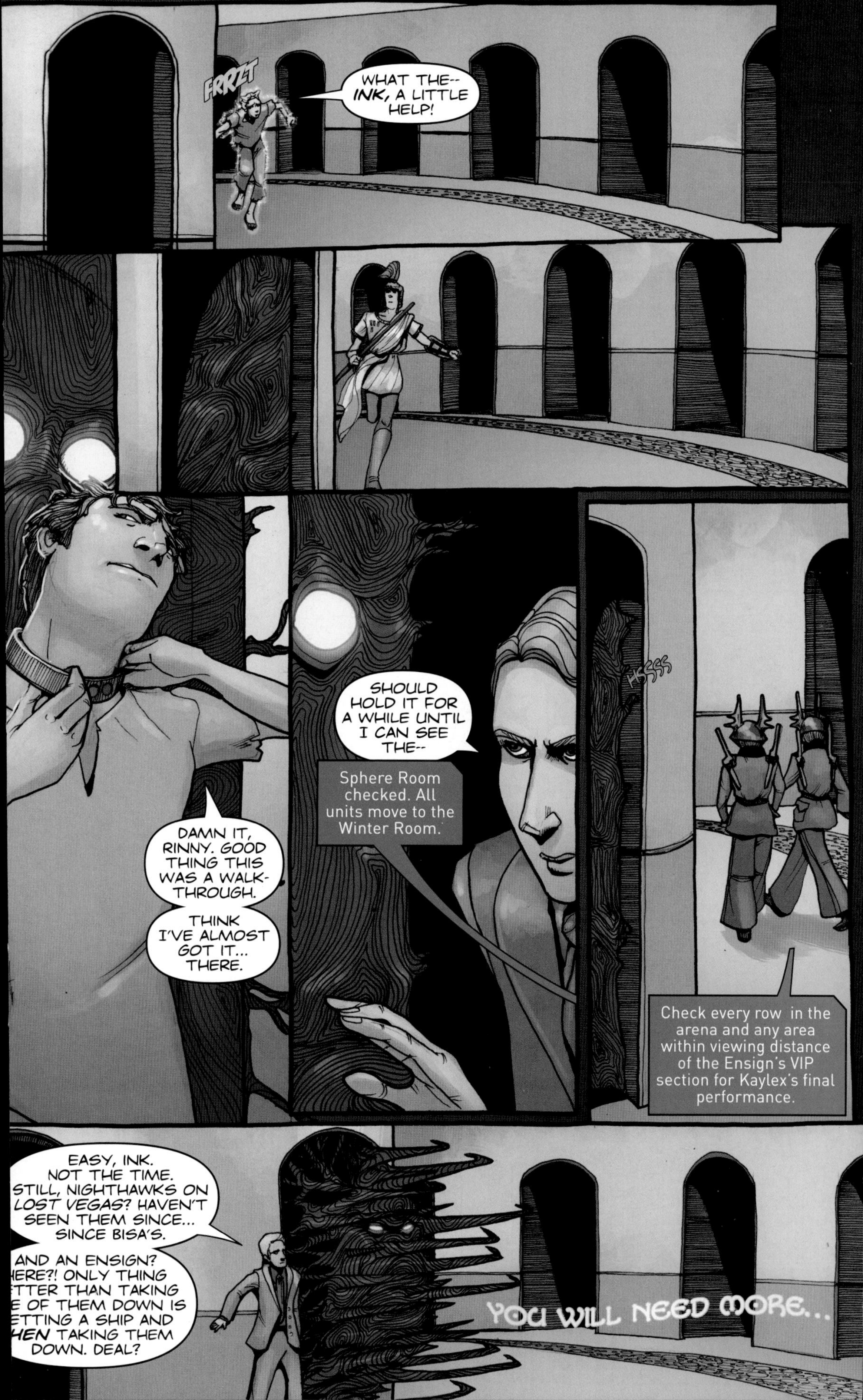
FRRZT
WHAT THE-- INK, A LITTLE HELP!
SHOULD HOLD IT FOR A WHILE UNTIL I CAN SEE THE--
Sphere Room checked. All units move to the Winter Room.
HSSSS
Check every row in the arena and any area within viewing distance of the Ensign's VIP section for Kaylex's final performance.
DAMN IT, RINNY. GOOD THING THIS WAS A WALK-THROUGH.
THINK I'VE ALMOST GOT IT... THERE.
EASY, INK. NOT THE TIME. STILL, NIGHTHAWKS ON LOST VEGAS? HAVEN'T SEEN THEM SINCE... SINCE BISA'S.
AND AN ENSIGN? HERE?! ONLY THING ETTER THAN TAKING E OF THEM DOWN IS ETTING A SHIP AND HEN TAKING THEM DOWN. DEAL?
YOU WILL NEED MORE...

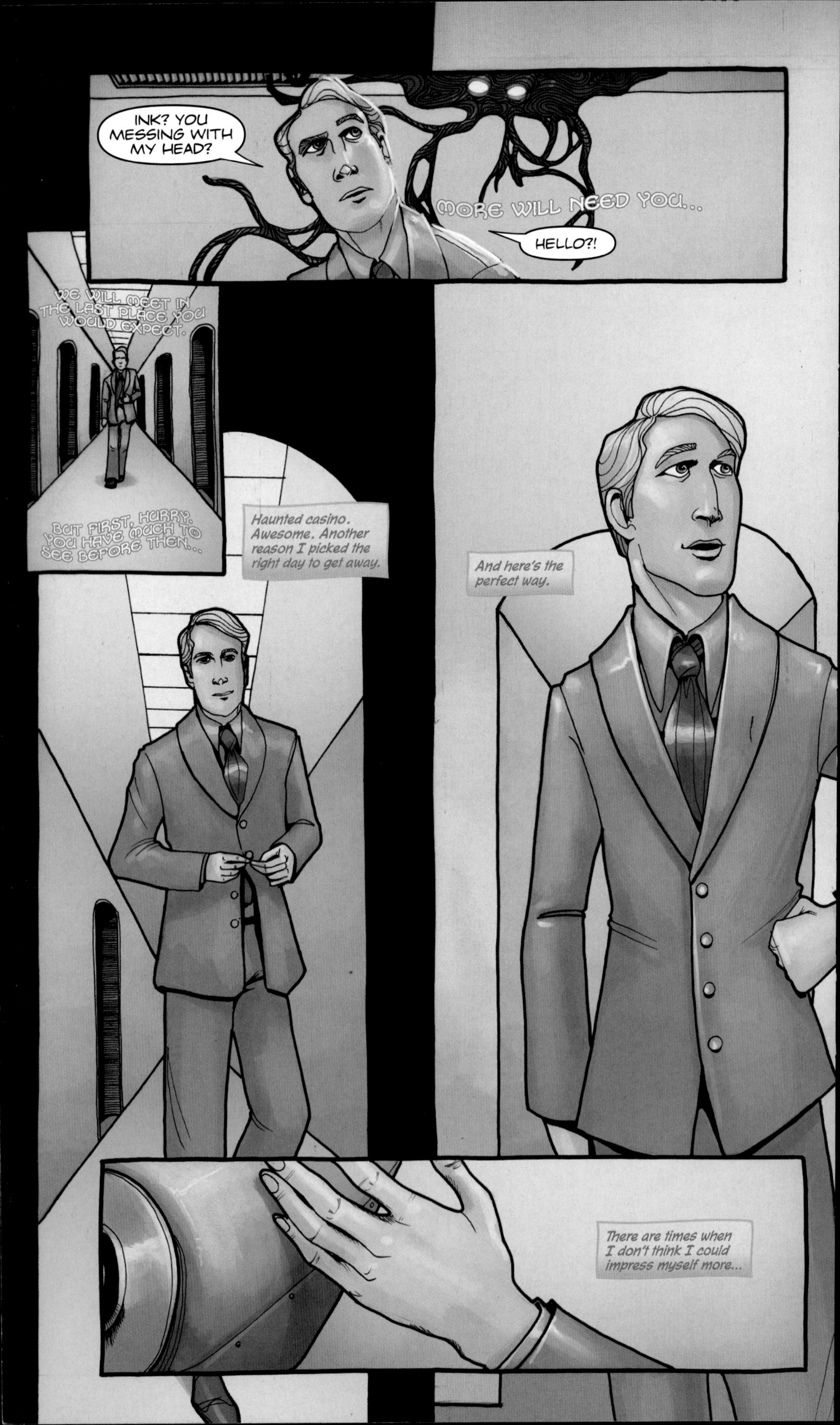

INK? YOU MESSING WITH MY HEAD?
MORE WILL NEED YOU...
HELLO?!
WE WILL MEET IN THE LAST PLACE YOU WOULD EXPECT.
BUT FIRST, HURRY. YOU HAVE MUCH TO SEE BEFORE THEN...
Haunted casino. Awesome. Another reason I picked the right day to get away.
And here's the perfect way.
There are times when I don't think I could impress myself more...

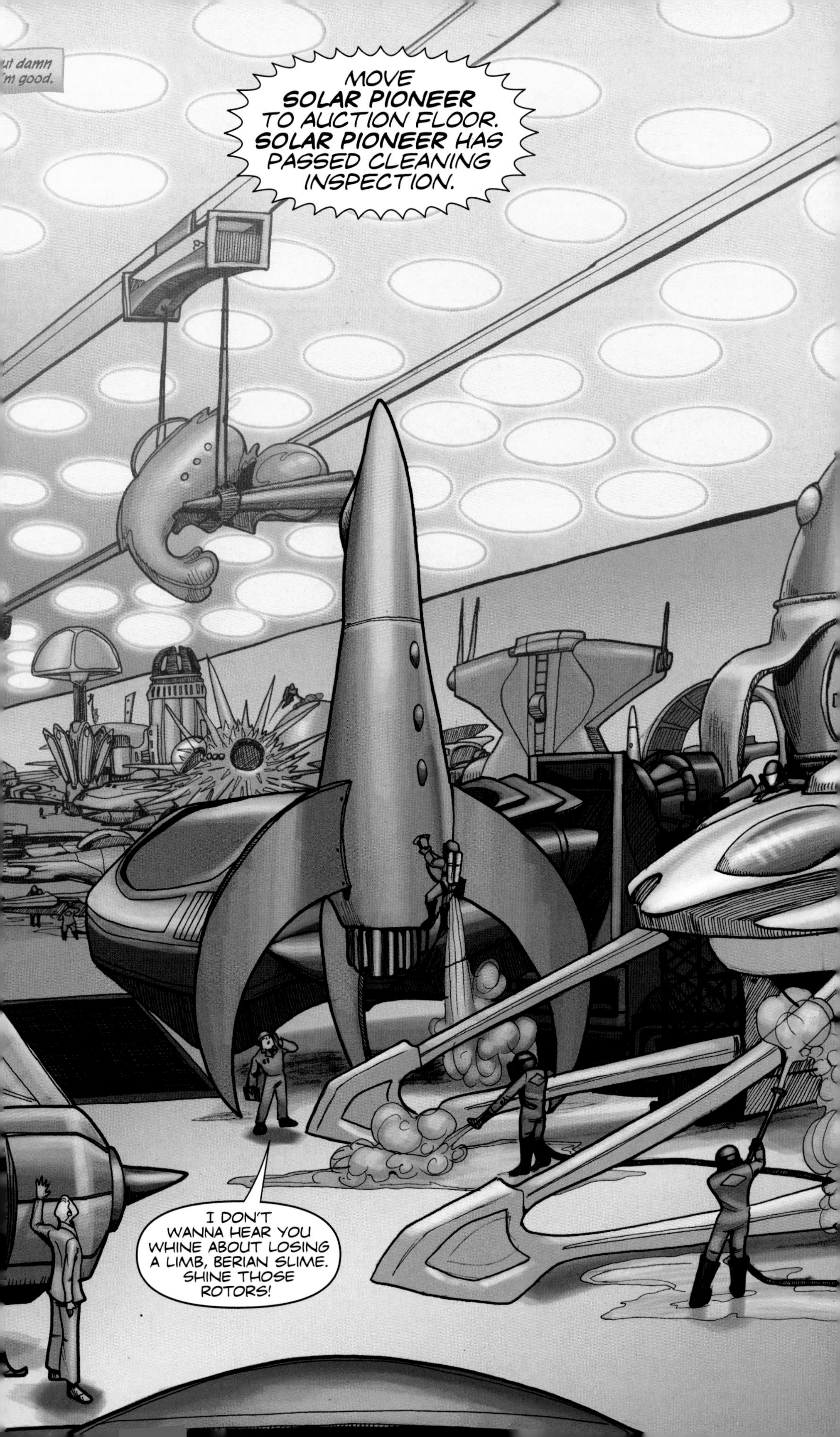
ut damn
'm good.
MOVE SOLAR PIONEER TO AUCTION FLOOR. SOLAR PIONEER HAS PASSED CLEANING INSPECTION.
I DON'T WANNA HEAR YOU WHINE ABOUT LOSING A LIMB, BERIAN SLIME. SHINE THOSE ROTORS!

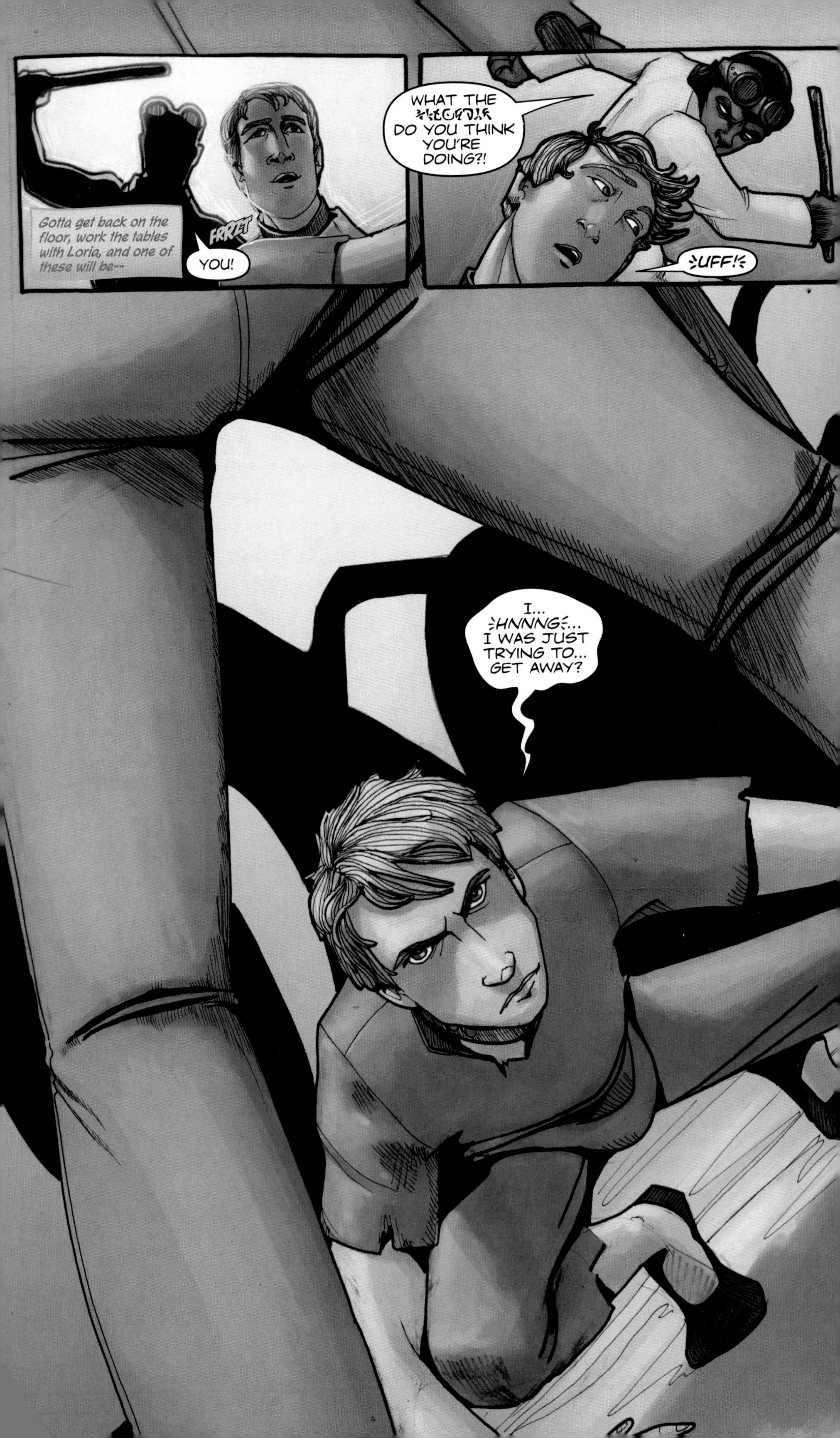
Gotta get back on the floor, work the tables with Loria, and one of these will be--
FRRZT
YOU!
WHAT THE ⁂⁂⁂ DO YOU THINK YOU'RE DOING?!
UFF!
I... HNNNG... I WAS JUST TRYING TO... GET AWAY?

END FIRST HAND

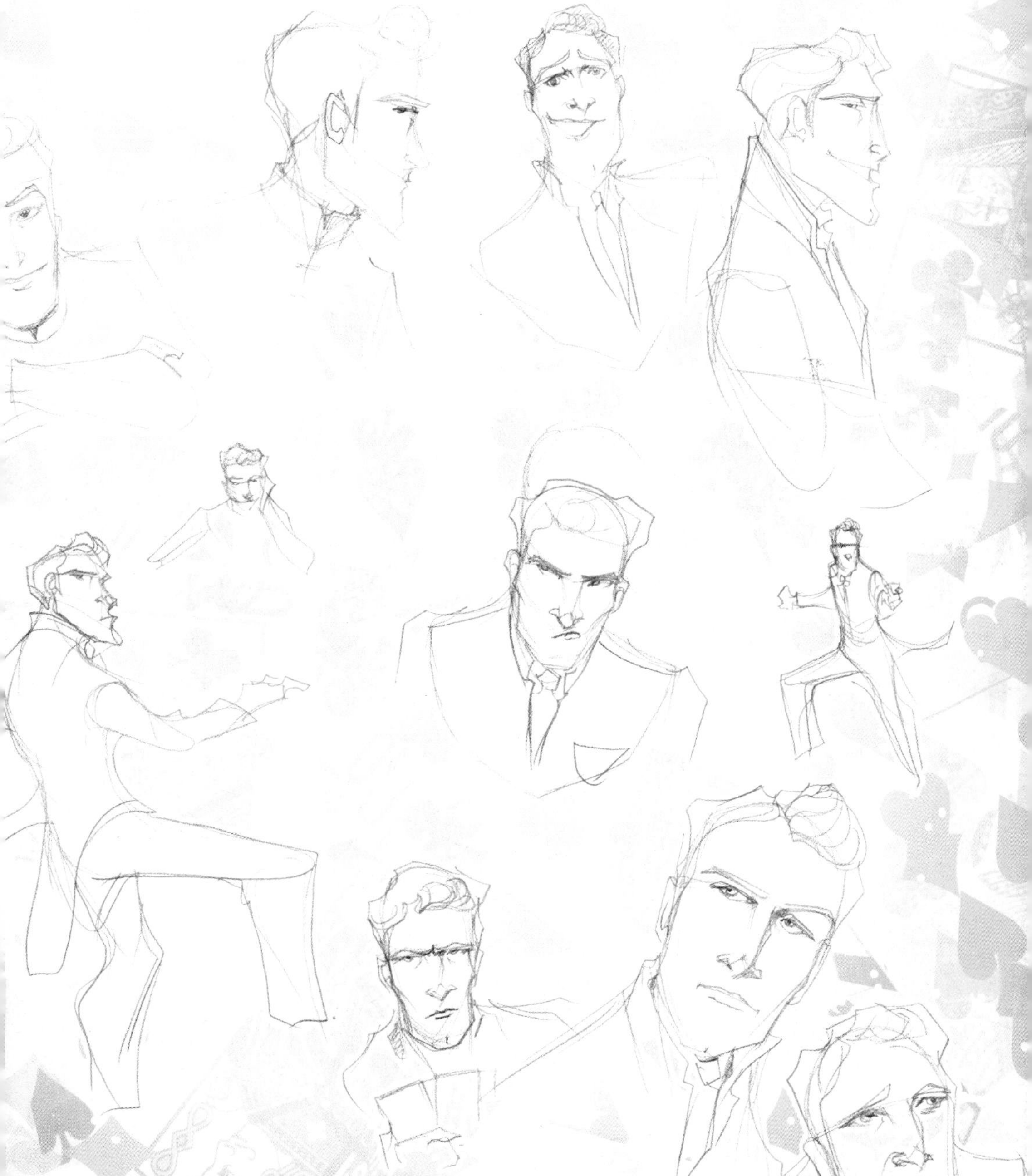

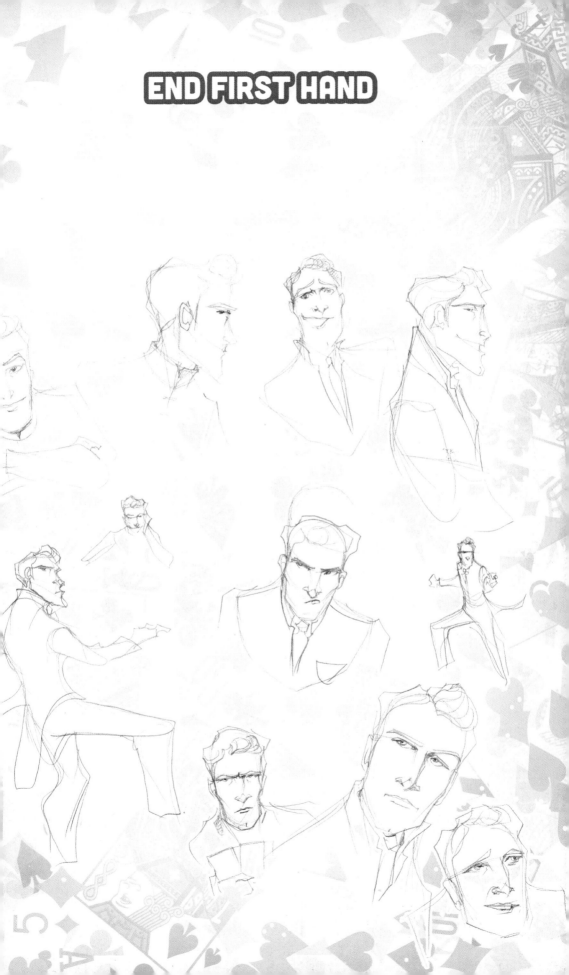

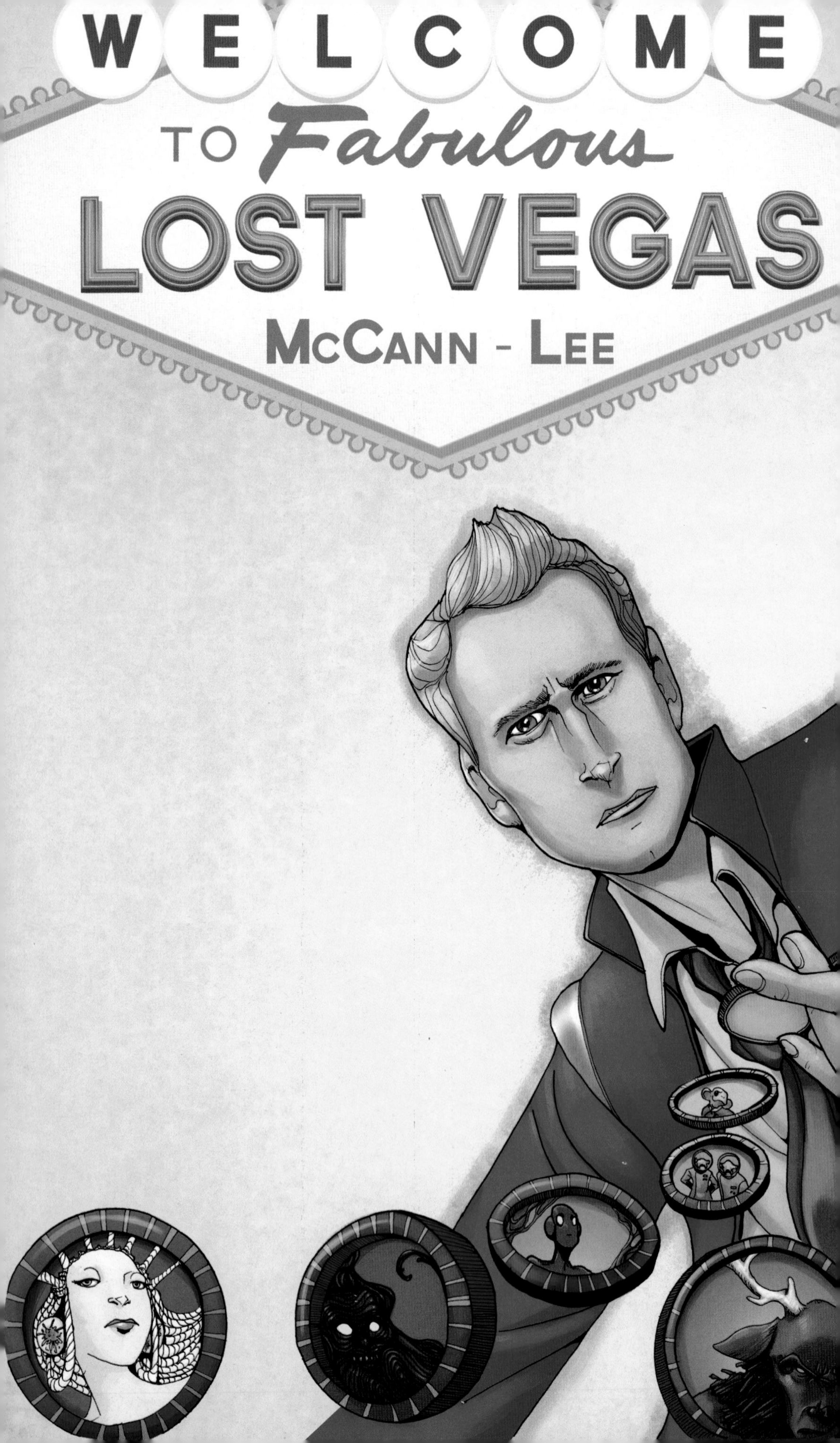
WELCOME
TO Fabulous
LOST VEGAS
McCANN - LEE

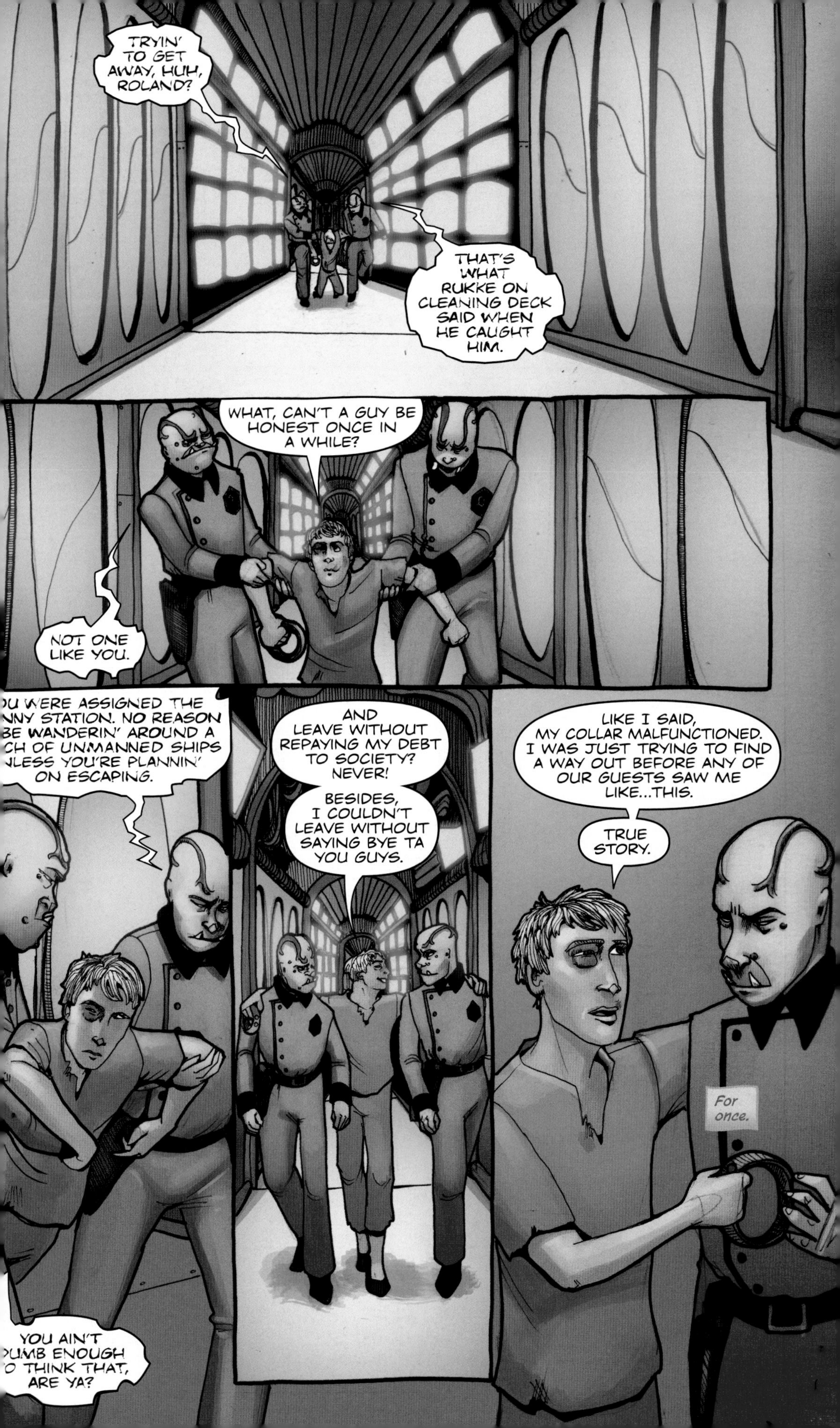
TRYIN' TO GET AWAY, HUH, ROLAND?
THAT'S WHAT RUKKE ON CLEANING DECK SAID WHEN HE CAUGHT HIM.
WHAT, CAN'T A GUY BE HONEST ONCE IN A WHILE?
NOT ONE LIKE YOU.
OU WERE ASSIGNED THE NNY STATION. NO REASON BE WANDERIN' AROUND A CH OF UNMANNED SHIPS NLESS YOU'RE PLANNIN' ON ESCAPING.
YOU AIN'T UMB ENOUGH O THINK THAT, ARE YA?
AND LEAVE WITHOUT REPAYING MY DEBT TO SOCIETY? NEVER!
BESIDES, I COULDN'T LEAVE WITHOUT SAYING BYE TA YOU GUYS.
LIKE I SAID, MY COLLAR MALFUNCTIONED. I WAS JUST TRYING TO FIND A WAY OUT BEFORE ANY OF OUR GUESTS SAW ME LIKE...THIS.
TRUE STORY.
For once.

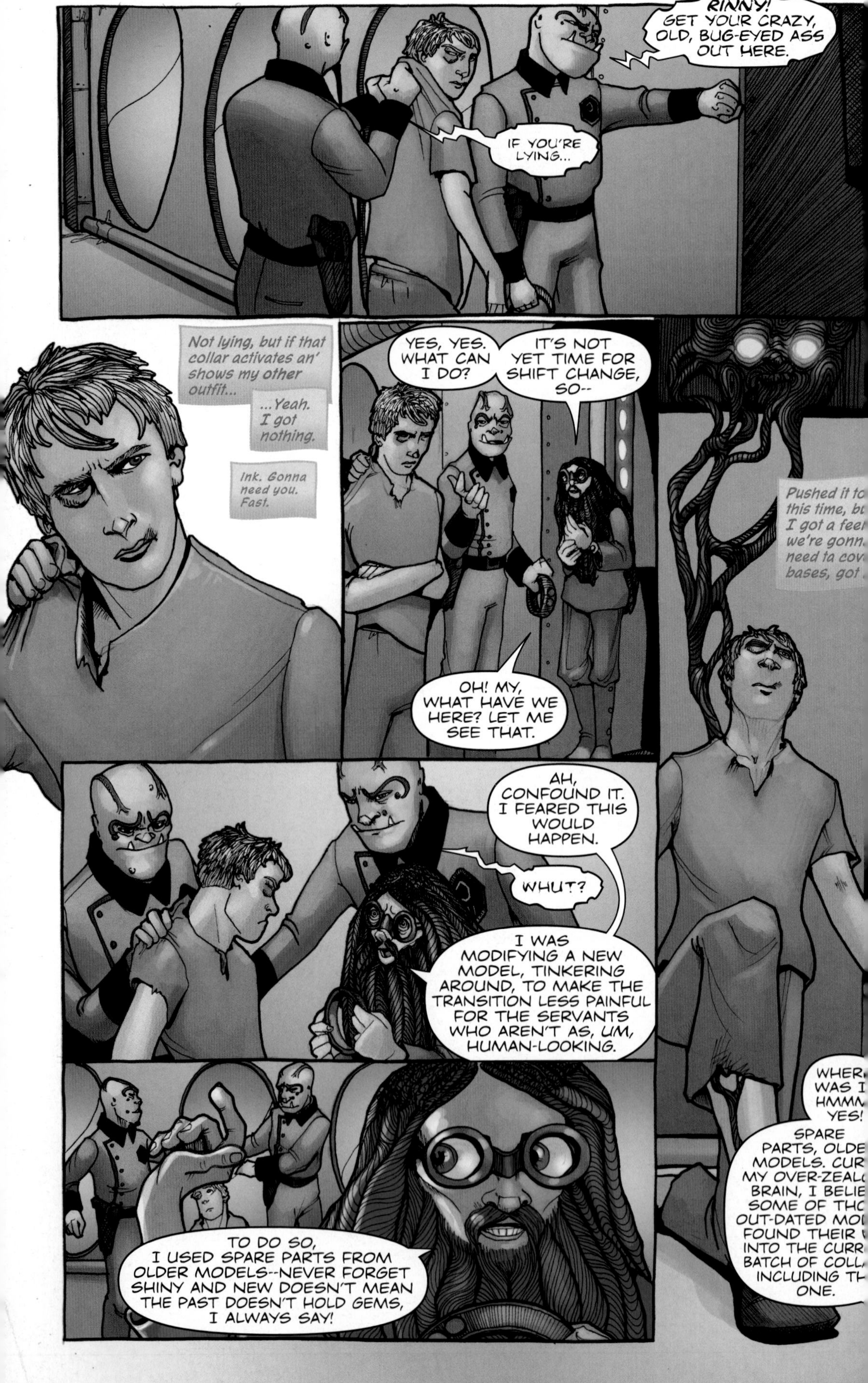
RINNY! GET YOUR CRAZY, OLD, BUG-EYED ASS OUT HERE.
IF YOU'RE LYING...
Not lying, but if that collar activates an' shows my other outfit...
...Yeah. I got nothing.
Ink. Gonna need you. Fast.
YES, YES. WHAT CAN I DO?
IT'S NOT YET TIME FOR SHIFT CHANGE, SO--
OH! MY, WHAT HAVE WE HERE? LET ME SEE THAT.
Pushed it to this time, bu I got a feel we're gonn need ta cov bases, got
AH, CONFOUND IT. I FEARED THIS WOULD HAPPEN.
WHUT?
I WAS MODIFYING A NEW MODEL, TINKERING AROUND, TO MAKE THE TRANSITION LESS PAINFUL FOR THE SERVANTS WHO AREN'T AS, UM, HUMAN-LOOKING.
TO DO SO, I USED SPARE PARTS FROM OLDER MODELS--NEVER FORGET SHINY AND NEW DOESN'T MEAN THE PAST DOESN'T HOLD GEMS, I ALWAYS SAY!
WHER WAS I HMMM YES!
SPARE PARTS, OLDE MODELS. CUR MY OVER-ZEAL BRAIN, I BELIE SOME OF TH OUT-DATED MO FOUND THEIR INTO THE CURR BATCH OF COLL INCLUDING T ONE.

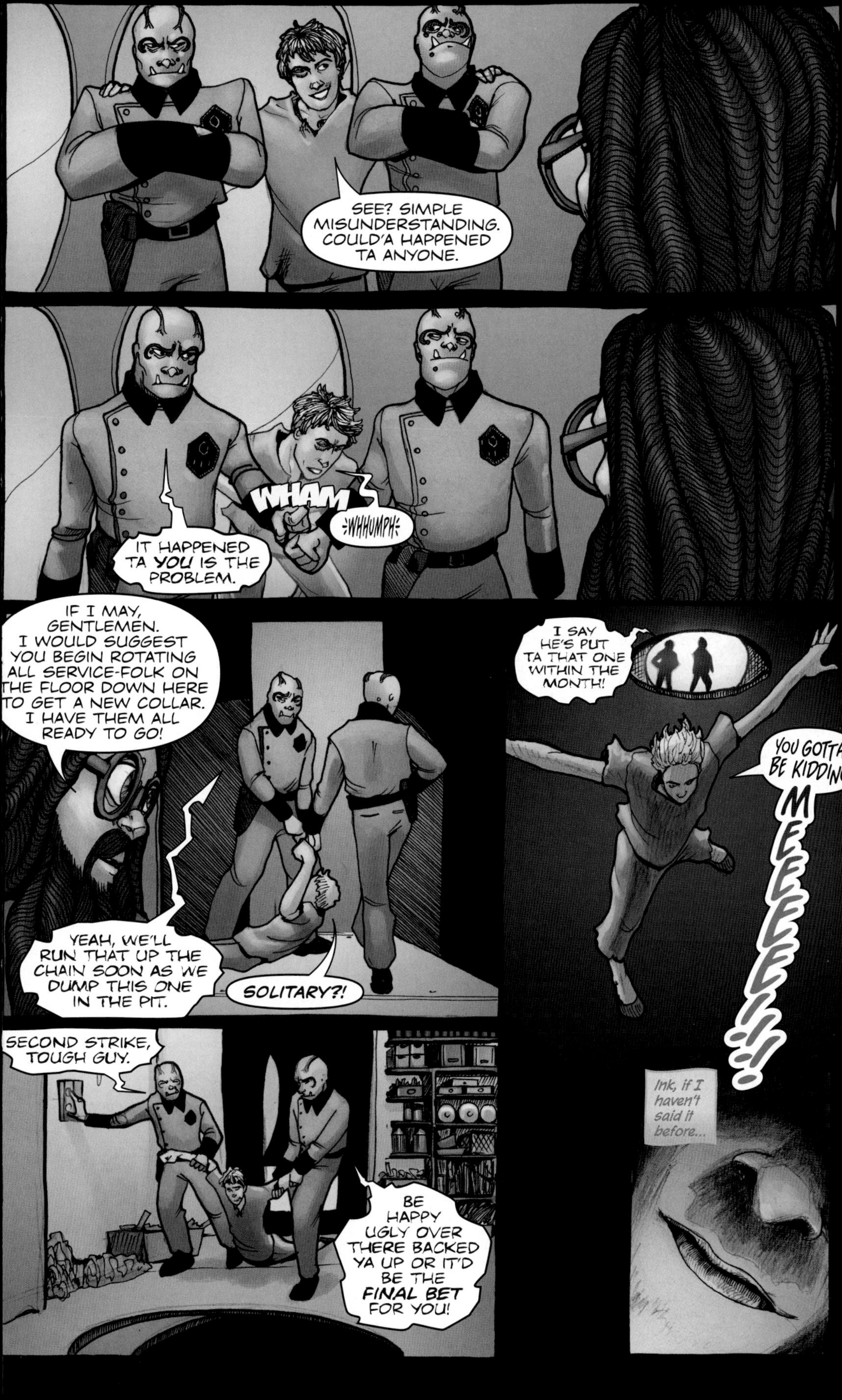
SEE? SIMPLE MISUNDERSTANDING. COULD'A HAPPENED TA ANYONE.
IT HAPPENED TA YOU IS THE PROBLEM.
WHAM
WHHUMPH
IF I MAY, GENTLEMEN. I WOULD SUGGEST YOU BEGIN ROTATING ALL SERVICE-FOLK ON THE FLOOR DOWN HERE TO GET A NEW COLLAR. I HAVE THEM ALL READY TO GO!
YEAH, WE'LL RUN THAT UP THE CHAIN SOON AS WE DUMP THIS ONE IN THE PIT.
SOLITARY?!
I SAY HE'S PUT TA THAT ONE WITHIN THE MONTH!
YOU GOTTA BE KIDDING MEEEEE!!!
SECOND STRIKE, TOUGH GUY.
BE HAPPY UGLY OVER THERE BACKED YA UP OR IT'D BE THE FINAL BET FOR YOU!
Ink, if I haven't said it before...

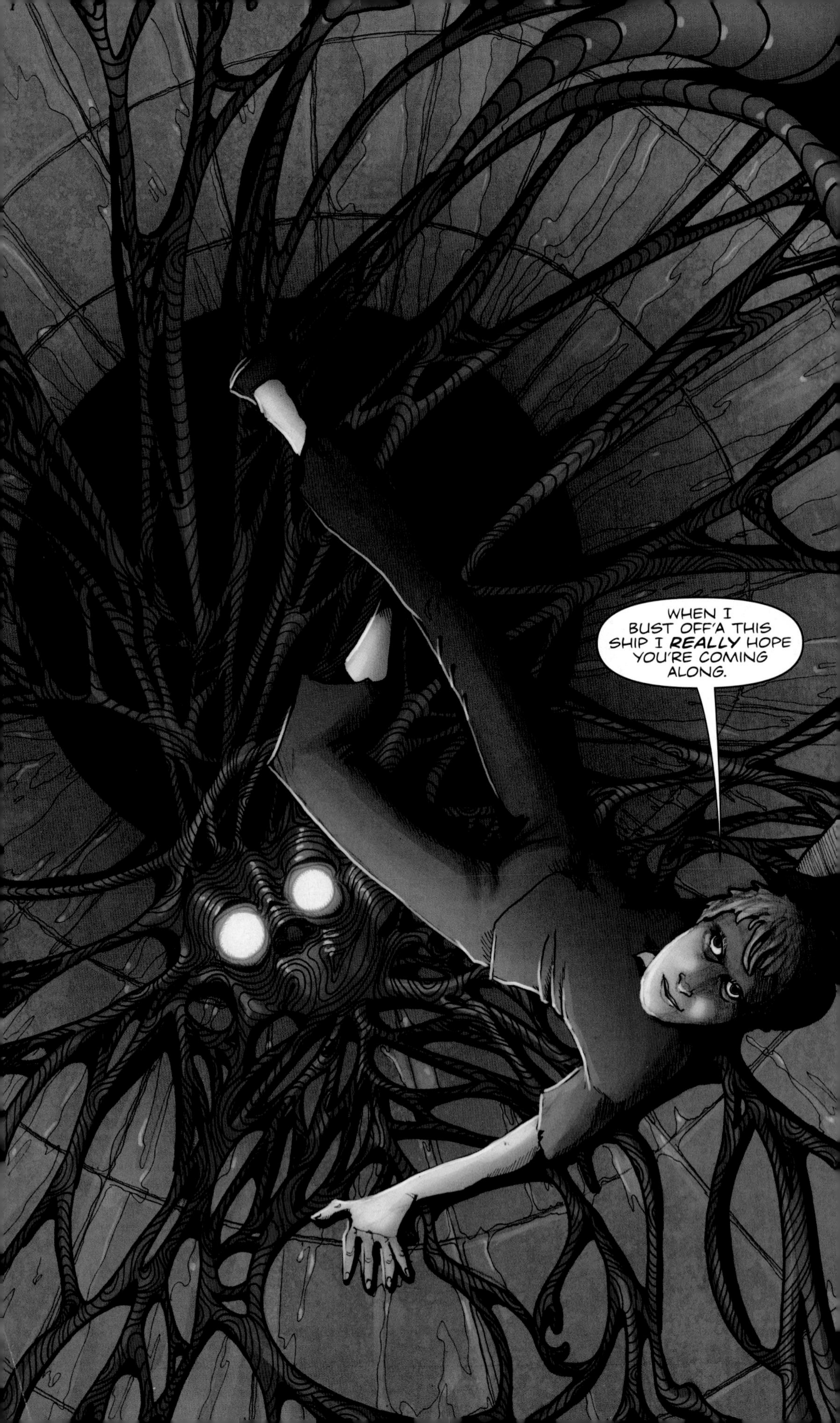
WHEN I BUST OFF'A THIS SHIP I **REALLY** HOPE YOU'RE COMING ALONG.

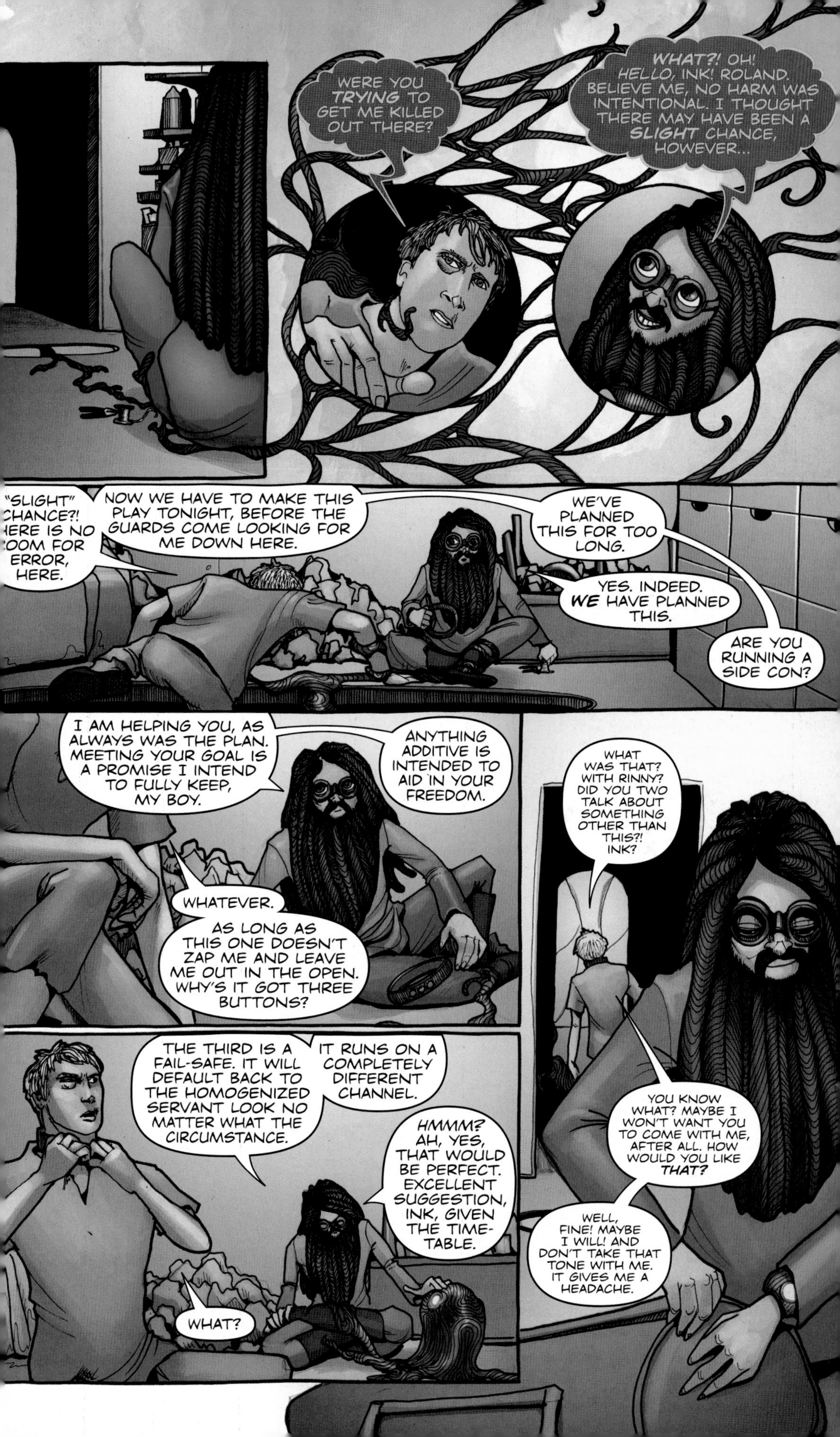
WERE YOU *TRYING* TO GET ME KILLED OUT THERE?
WHAT?! OH! HELLO, INK! ROLAND. BELIEVE ME, NO HARM WAS INTENTIONAL. I THOUGHT THERE MAY HAVE BEEN A *SLIGHT* CHANCE, HOWEVER...
"SLIGHT" CHANCE?! HERE IS NO OOM FOR ERROR, HERE.
NOW WE HAVE TO MAKE THIS PLAY TONIGHT, BEFORE THE GUARDS COME LOOKING FOR ME DOWN HERE.
WE'VE PLANNED THIS FOR TOO LONG.
YES. INDEED. **WE** HAVE PLANNED THIS.
ARE YOU RUNNING A SIDE CON?
I AM HELPING YOU, AS ALWAYS WAS THE PLAN. MEETING YOUR GOAL IS A PROMISE I INTEND TO FULLY KEEP, MY BOY.
ANYTHING ADDITIVE IS INTENDED TO AID IN YOUR FREEDOM.
WHATEVER.
AS LONG AS THIS ONE DOESN'T ZAP ME AND LEAVE ME OUT IN THE OPEN. WHY'S IT GOT THREE BUTTONS?
THE THIRD IS A FAIL-SAFE. IT WILL DEFAULT BACK TO THE HOMOGENIZED SERVANT LOOK NO MATTER WHAT THE CIRCUMSTANCE.
IT RUNS ON A COMPLETELY DIFFERENT CHANNEL.
HMMM? AH, YES, THAT WOULD BE PERFECT. EXCELLENT SUGGESTION, INK, GIVEN THE TIME-TABLE.
WHAT?
WHAT WAS THAT? WITH RINNY? DID YOU TWO TALK ABOUT SOMETHING OTHER THAN THIS?! INK?
YOU KNOW WHAT? MAYBE I WON'T WANT YOU TO COME WITH ME, AFTER ALL. HOW WOULD YOU LIKE *THAT?*
WELL, FINE! MAYBE I WILL! AND DON'T TAKE THAT TONE WITH ME. IT GIVES ME A HEADACHE.

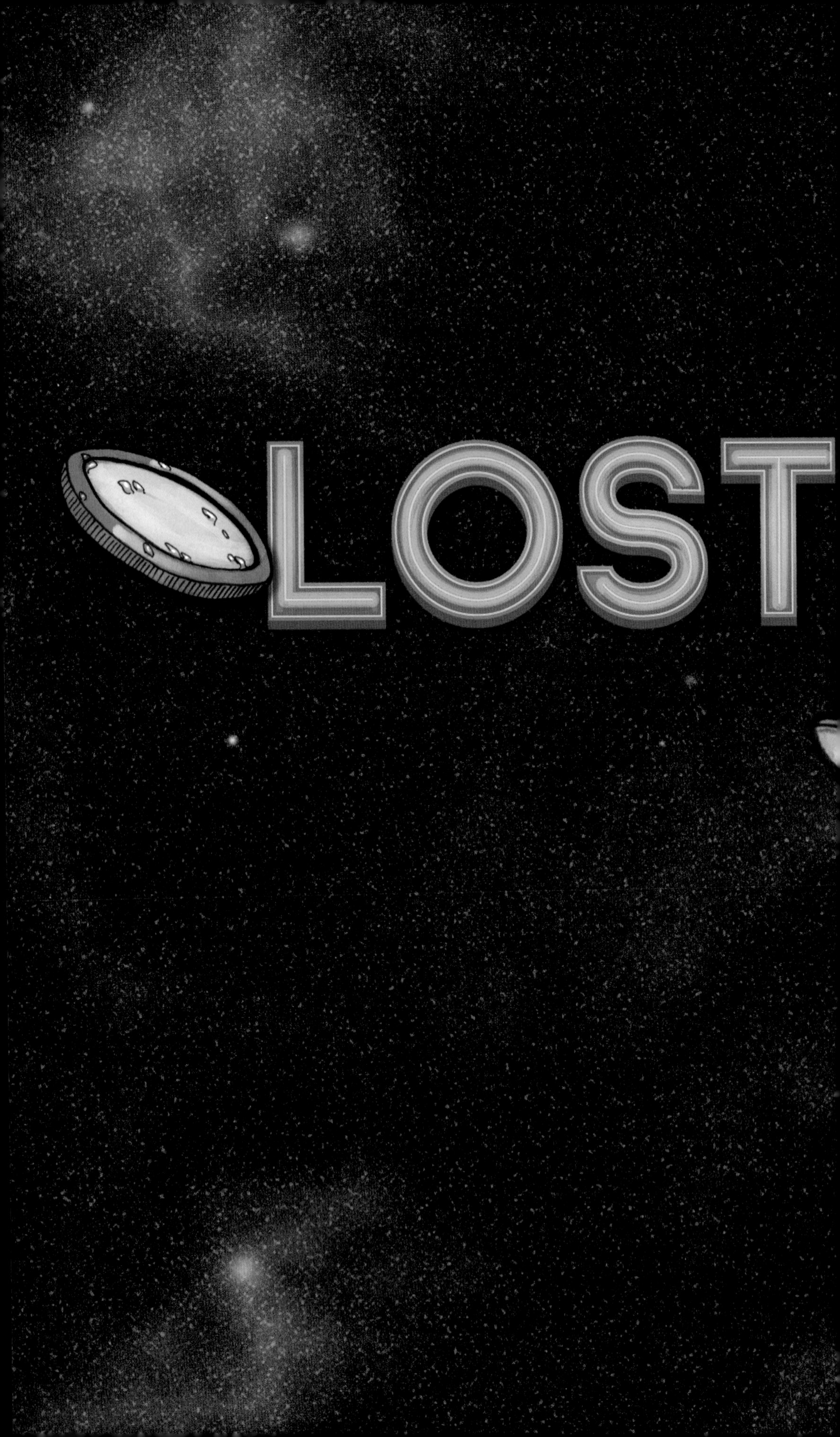
LOST

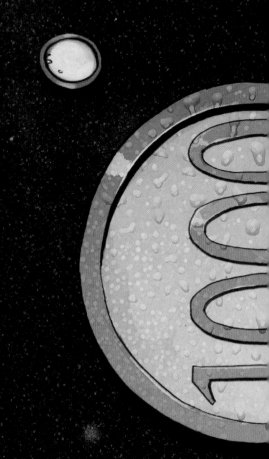

VEGAS

SECOND HAND | SHARKS AND WHALES

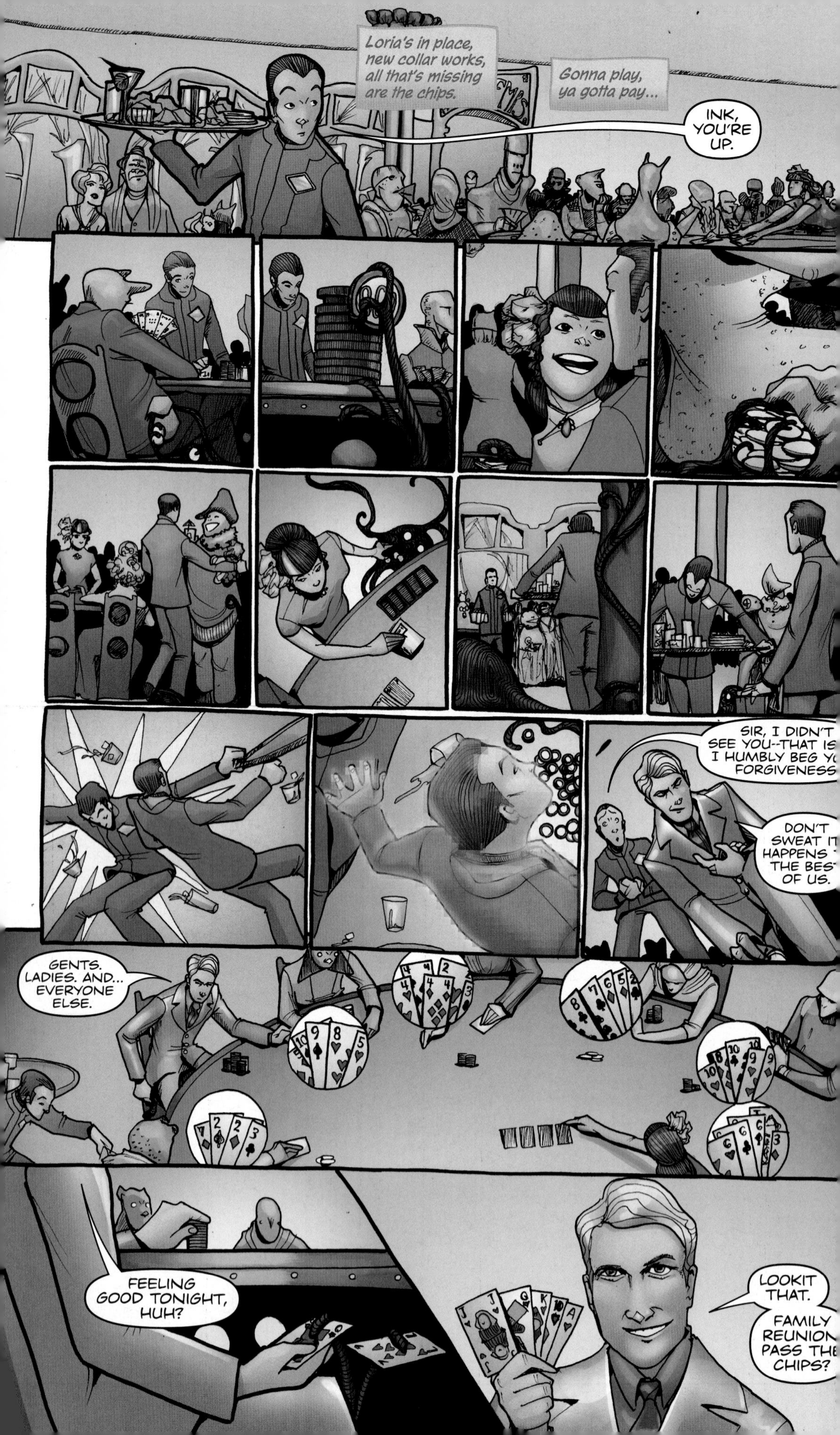
Loria's in place, new collar works, all that's missing are the chips.
Gonna play, ya gotta pay...
INK, YOU'RE UP.
SIR, I DIDN'T SEE YOU--THAT IS I HUMBLY BEG YO FORGIVENESS
DON'T SWEAT IT HAPPENS THE BEST OF US.
GENTS. LADIES. AND... EVERYONE ELSE.
FEELING GOOD TONIGHT, HUH?
LOOKIT THAT.
FAMILY REUNION PASS THE CHIPS?

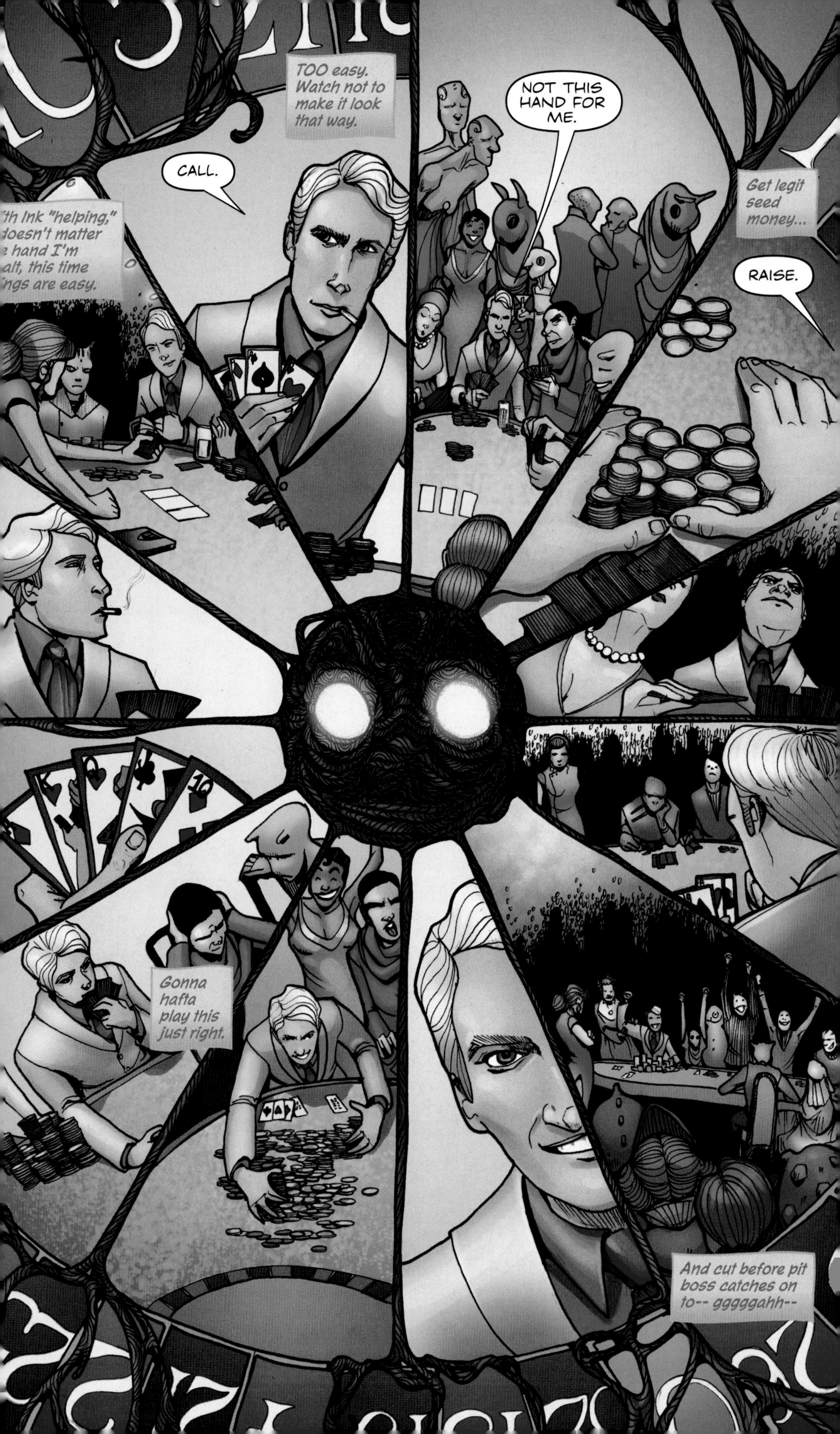
TOO easy. Watch not to make it look that way.
CALL.
...ith Ink "helping," ...doesn't matter ...e hand I'm ...alt, this time ...ngs are easy.
NOT THIS HAND FOR ME.
Get legit seed money...
RAISE.
Gonna hafta play this just right.
And cut before pit boss catches on to-- gggggahh--

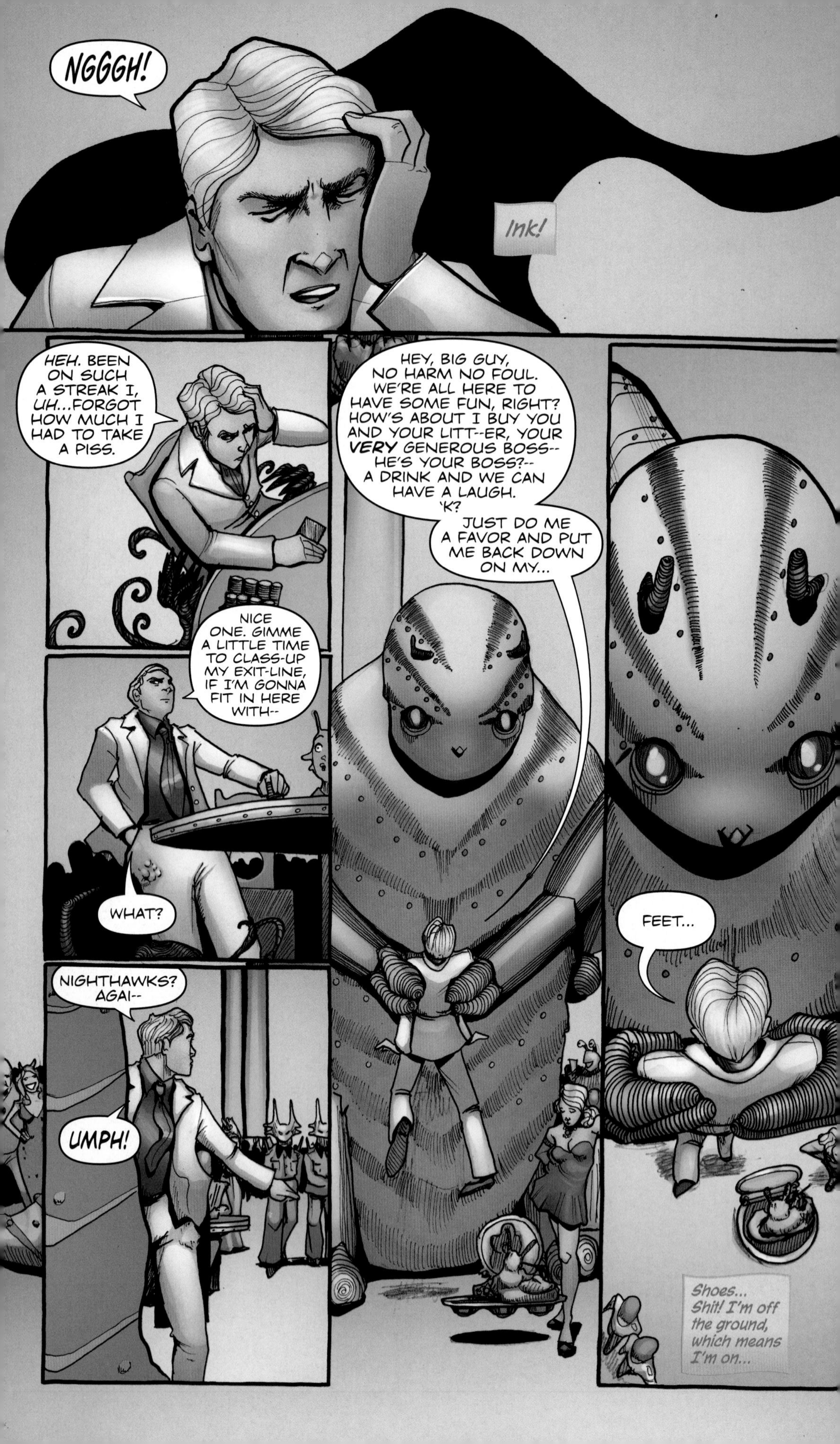
NGGGH!
Ink!
HEH. BEEN ON SUCH A STREAK I, UH...FORGOT HOW MUCH I HAD TO TAKE A PISS.
NICE ONE. GIMME A LITTLE TIME TO CLASS-UP MY EXIT-LINE, IF I'M GONNA FIT IN HERE WITH--
WHAT?
NIGHTHAWKS? AGAI--
UMPH!
HEY, BIG GUY, NO HARM NO FOUL. WE'RE ALL HERE TO HAVE SOME FUN, RIGHT? HOW'S ABOUT I BUY YOU AND YOUR LITT--ER, YOUR VERY GENEROUS BOSS-- HE'S YOUR BOSS?-- A DRINK AND WE CAN HAVE A LAUGH. 'K?
JUST DO ME A FAVOR AND PUT ME BACK DOWN ON MY...
FEET...
Shoes... Shit! I'm off the ground, which means I'm on...

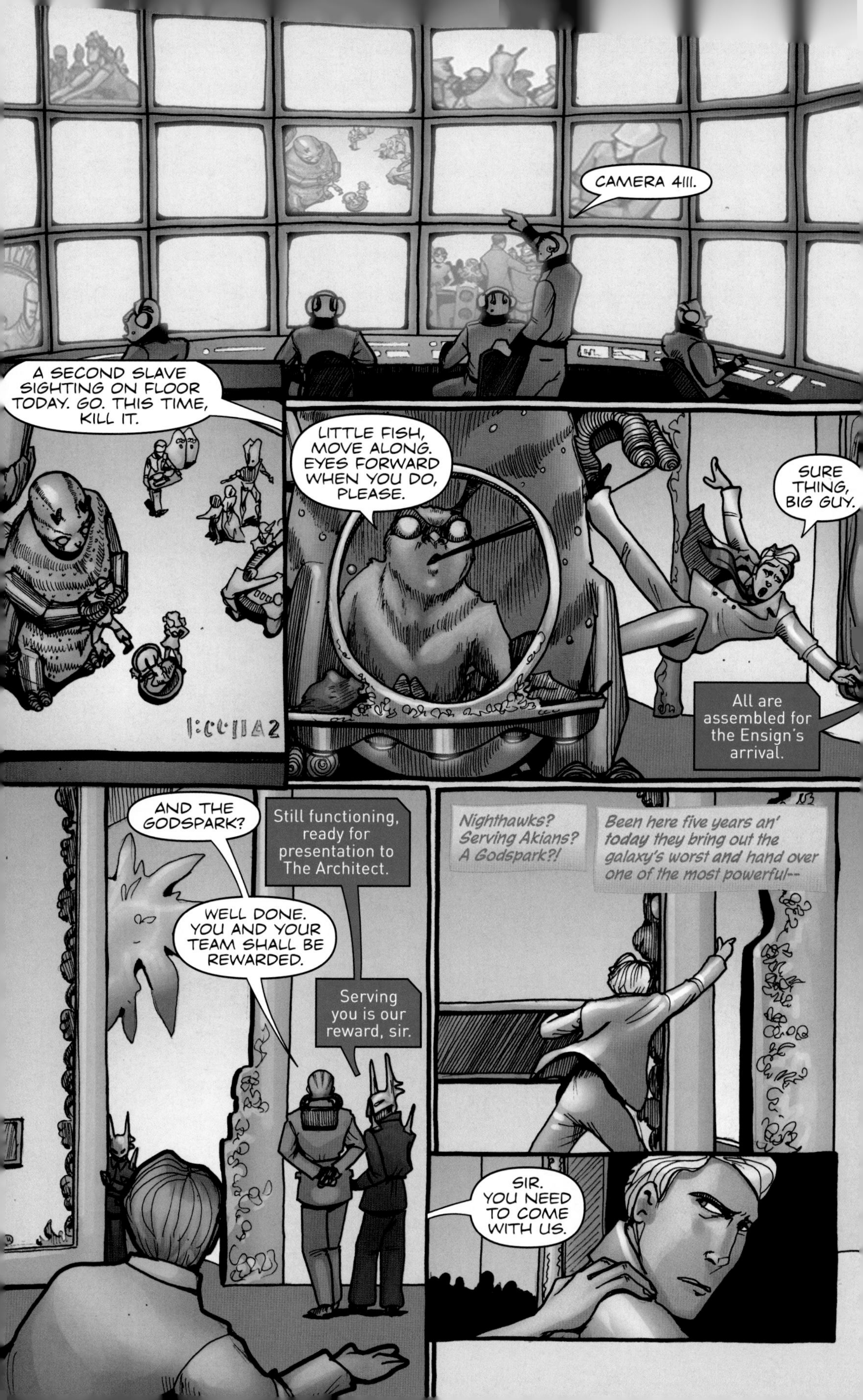

CAMERA 4III.
A SECOND SLAVE SIGHTING ON FLOOR TODAY. GO. THIS TIME, KILL IT.
LITTLE FISH, MOVE ALONG. EYES FORWARD WHEN YOU DO, PLEASE.
SURE THING, BIG GUY.
All are assembled for the Ensign's arrival.
AND THE GODSPARK?
Still functioning, ready for presentation to The Architect.
WELL DONE. YOU AND YOUR TEAM SHALL BE REWARDED.
Serving you is our reward, sir.
Nighthawks? Serving Akians? A Godspark?!
Been here five years an' today they bring out the galaxy's worst and hand over one of the most powerful--
SIR. YOU NEED TO COME WITH US.

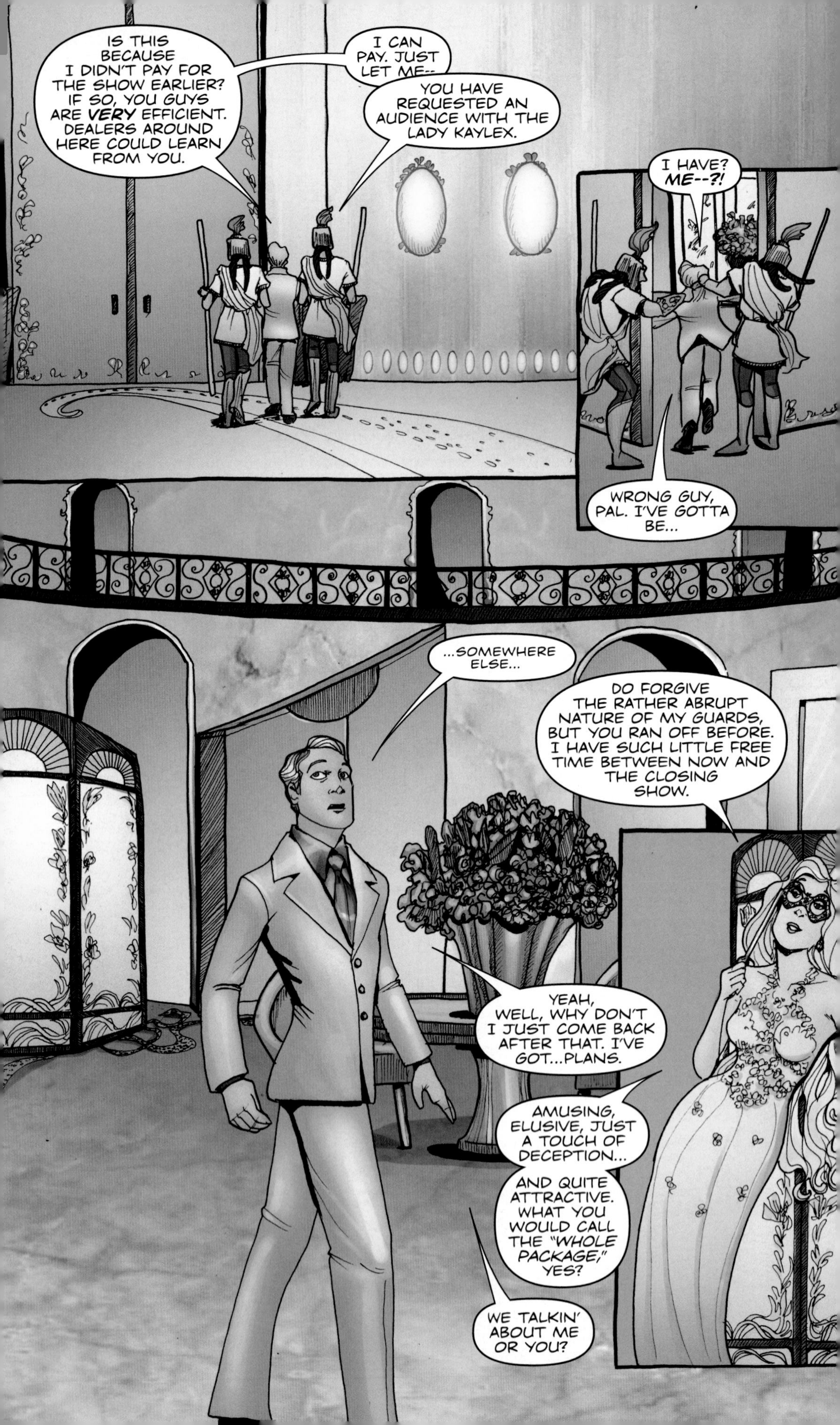
IS THIS BECAUSE I DIDN'T PAY FOR THE SHOW EARLIER? IF SO, YOU GUYS ARE **VERY** EFFICIENT. DEALERS AROUND HERE COULD LEARN FROM YOU.
I CAN PAY. JUST LET ME--
YOU HAVE REQUESTED AN AUDIENCE WITH THE LADY KAYLEX.
I HAVE? **ME--?!**
WRONG GUY, PAL. I'VE GOTTA BE...
...SOMEWHERE ELSE...
DO FORGIVE THE RATHER ABRUPT NATURE OF MY GUARDS, BUT YOU RAN OFF BEFORE. I HAVE SUCH LITTLE FREE TIME BETWEEN NOW AND THE CLOSING SHOW.
YEAH, WELL, WHY DON'T I JUST COME BACK AFTER THAT. I'VE GOT...PLANS.
AMUSING, ELUSIVE, JUST A TOUCH OF DECEPTION...
AND QUITE ATTRACTIVE. WHAT YOU WOULD CALL THE "WHOLE PACKAGE," YES?
WE TALKIN' ABOUT ME OR YOU?

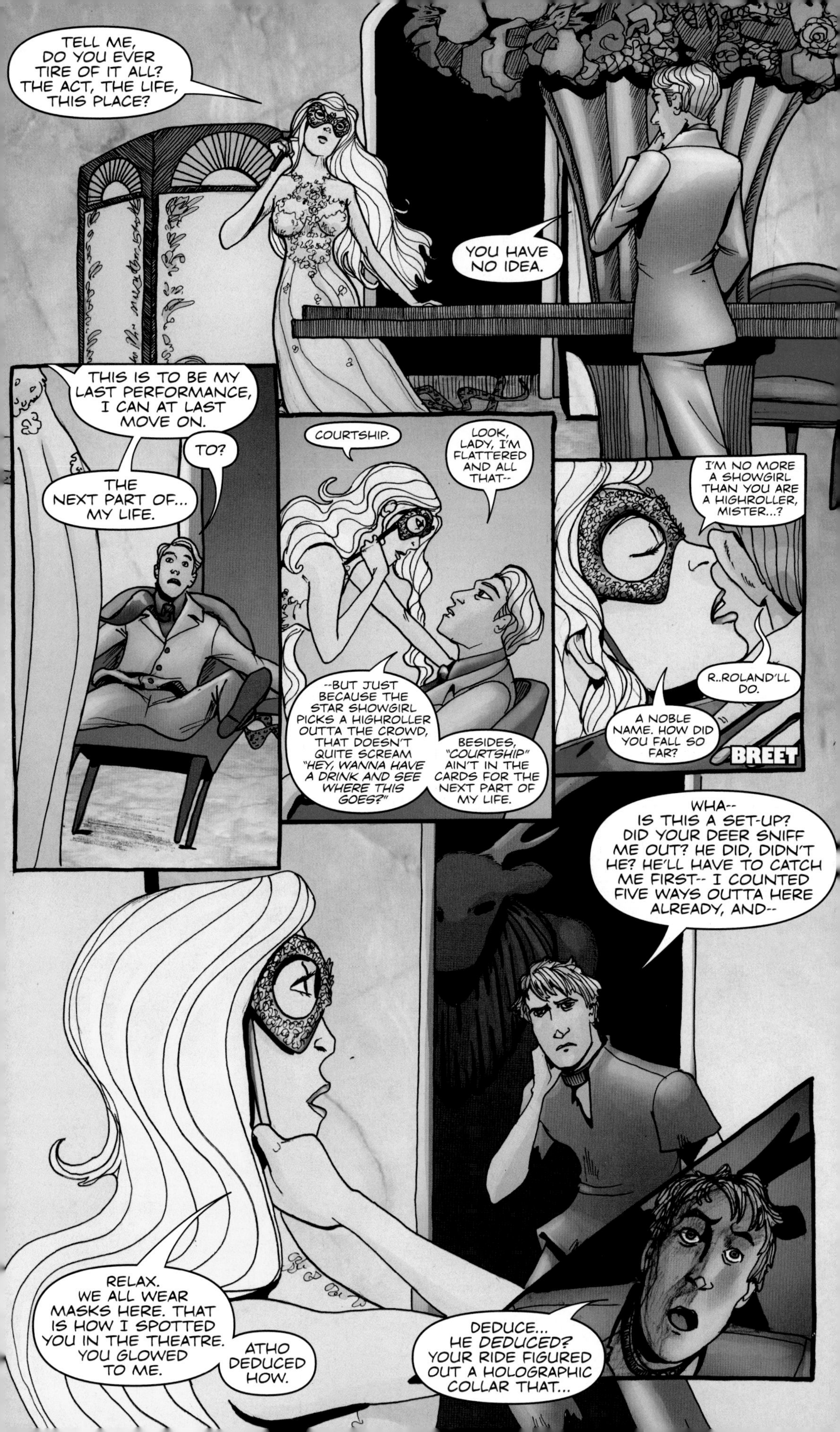
TELL ME, DO YOU EVER TIRE OF IT ALL? THE ACT, THE LIFE, THIS PLACE?
YOU HAVE NO IDEA.
THIS IS TO BE MY LAST PERFORMANCE, I CAN AT LAST MOVE ON.
TO?
THE NEXT PART OF... MY LIFE.
COURTSHIP.
LOOK, LADY, I'M FLATTERED AND ALL THAT--
--BUT JUST BECAUSE THE STAR SHOWGIRL PICKS A HIGHROLLER OUTTA THE CROWD, THAT DOESN'T QUITE SCREAM *"HEY, WANNA HAVE A DRINK AND SEE WHERE THIS GOES?"*
BESIDES, *"COURTSHIP"* AIN'T IN THE CARDS FOR THE NEXT PART OF MY LIFE.
I'M NO MORE A SHOWGIRL THAN YOU ARE A HIGHROLLER, MISTER...?
R..ROLAND'LL DO.
A NOBLE NAME. HOW DID YOU FALL SO FAR?
BREET
WHA-- IS THIS A SET-UP? DID YOUR DEER SNIFF ME OUT? HE DID, DIDN'T HE? HE'LL HAVE TO CATCH ME FIRST-- I COUNTED FIVE WAYS OUTTA HERE ALREADY, AND--
RELAX. WE ALL WEAR MASKS HERE. THAT IS HOW I SPOTTED YOU IN THE THEATRE. YOU GLOWED TO ME.
ATHO DEDUCED HOW.
DEDUCE... HE *DEDUCED*? YOUR RIDE FIGURED OUT A HOLOGRAPHIC COLLAR THAT...

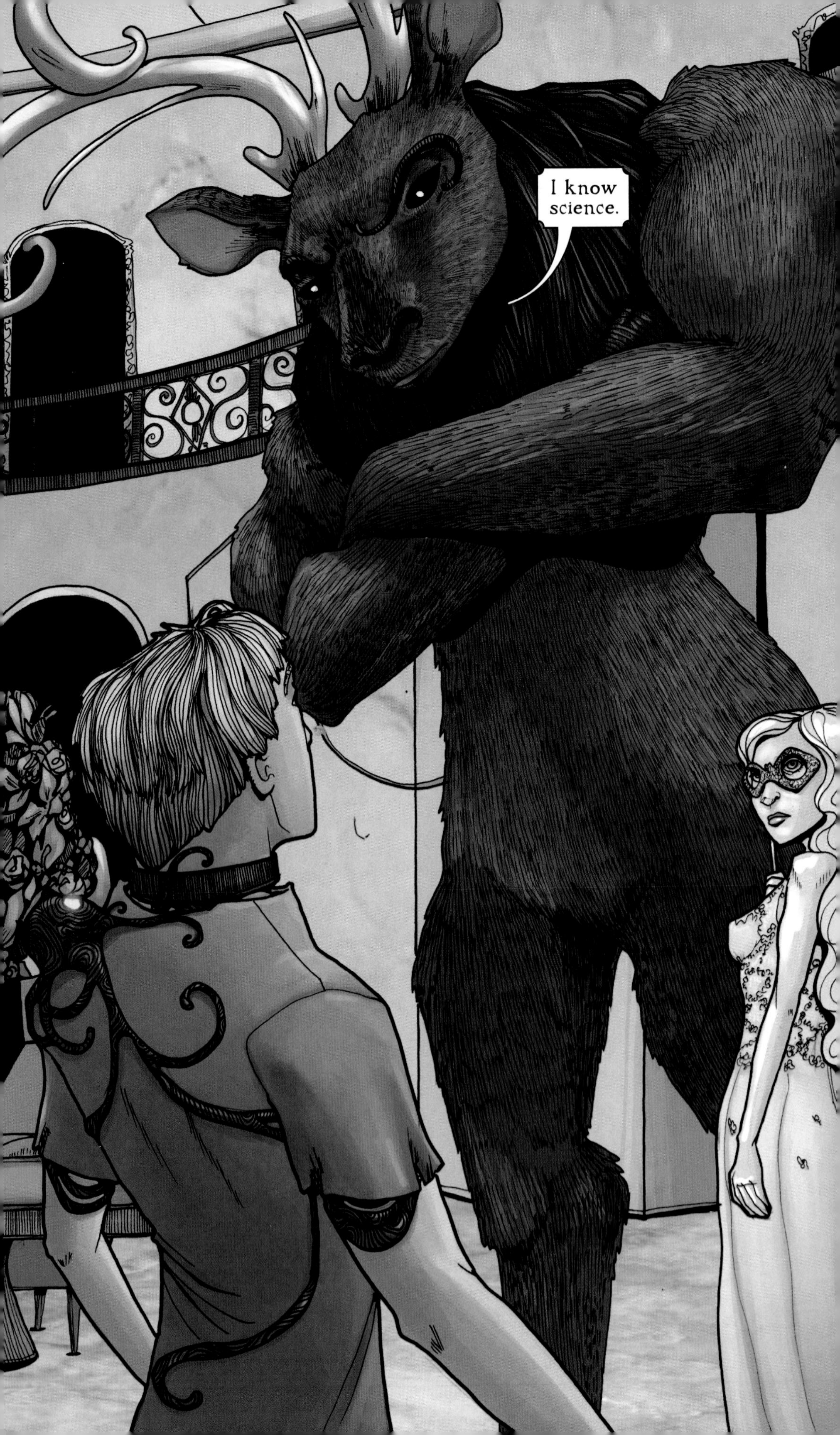
I know science.

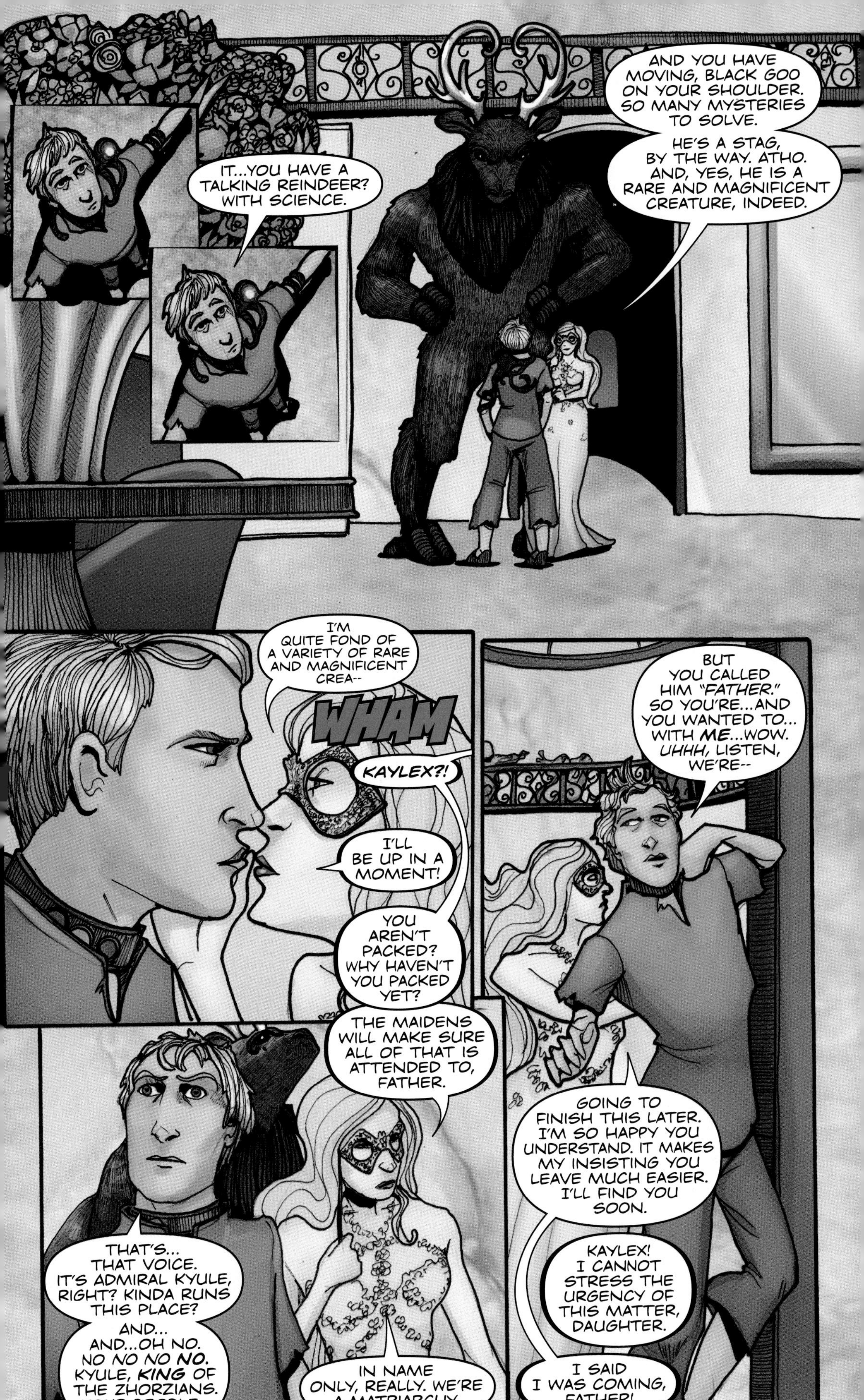
IT...YOU HAVE A TALKING REINDEER? WITH SCIENCE.
AND YOU HAVE MOVING, BLACK GOO ON YOUR SHOULDER. SO MANY MYSTERIES TO SOLVE.
HE'S A STAG, BY THE WAY. ATHO. AND, YES, HE IS A RARE AND MAGNIFICENT CREATURE, INDEED.
I'M QUITE FOND OF A VARIETY OF RARE AND MAGNIFICENT CREA--
WHAM
KAYLEX?!
I'LL BE UP IN A MOMENT!
YOU AREN'T PACKED? WHY HAVEN'T YOU PACKED YET?
THE MAIDENS WILL MAKE SURE ALL OF THAT IS ATTENDED TO, FATHER.
THAT'S... THAT VOICE. IT'S ADMIRAL KYULE, RIGHT? KINDA RUNS THIS PLACE?
AND... AND...OH NO. NO NO NO NO. KYULE, KING OF THE ZHORZIANS. YOUR PEOPLE--
IN NAME ONLY, REALLY. WE'RE A MATRIARCHY.
BUT YOU CALLED HIM "FATHER." SO YOU'RE...AND YOU WANTED TO... WITH ME...WOW. UHHH, LISTEN, WE'RE--
GOING TO FINISH THIS LATER. I'M SO HAPPY YOU UNDERSTAND. IT MAKES MY INSISTING YOU LEAVE MUCH EASIER. I'LL FIND YOU SOON.
KAYLEX! I CANNOT STRESS THE URGENCY OF THIS MATTER, DAUGHTER.
I SAID I WAS COMING, FATHER!

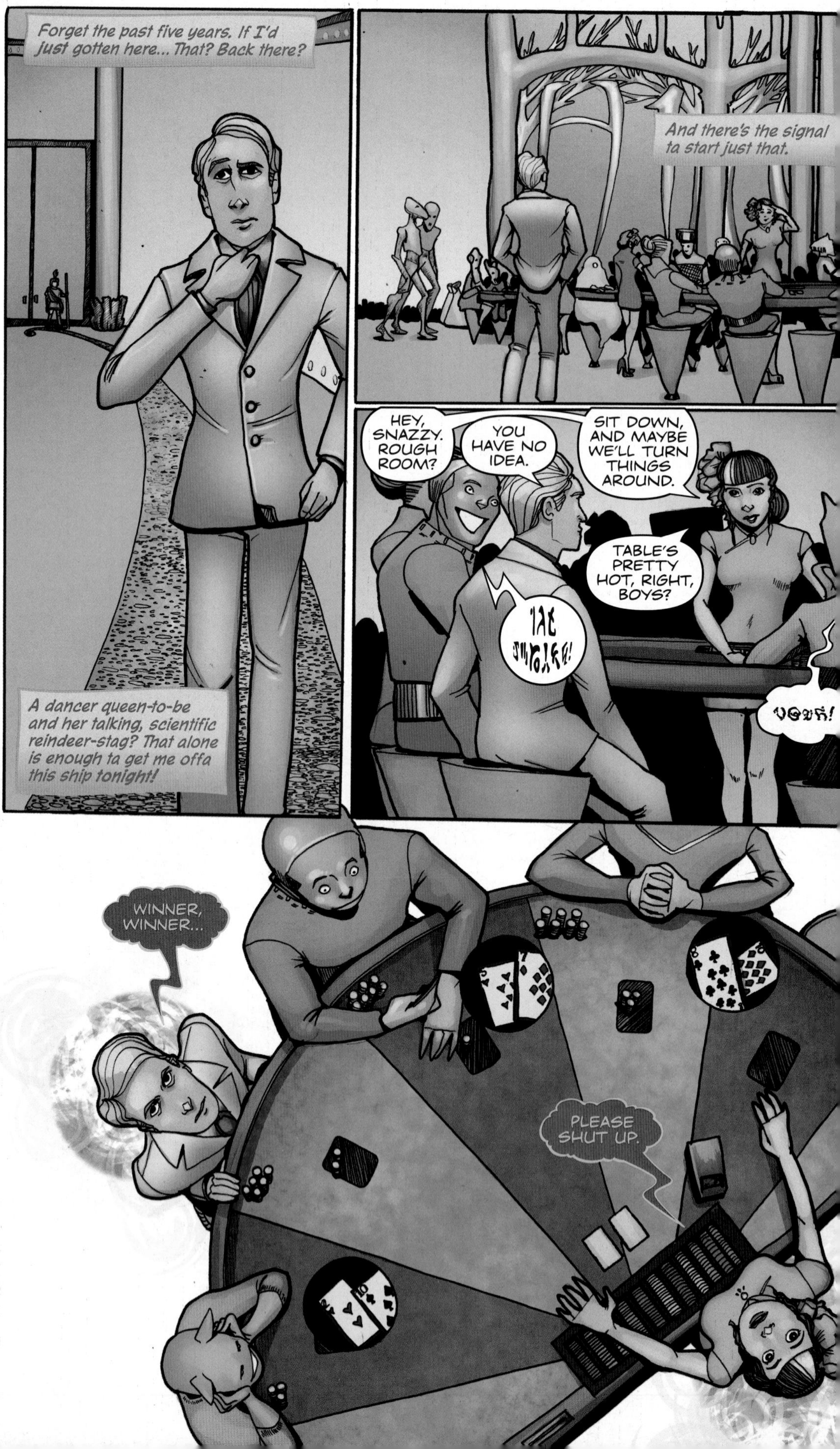
Forget the past five years. If I'd just gotten here... That? Back there?
A dancer queen-to-be and her talking, scientific reindeer-stag? That alone is enough ta get me offa this ship tonight!
And there's the signal ta start just that.
HEY, SNAZZY. ROUGH ROOM?
YOU HAVE NO IDEA.
SIT DOWN, AND MAYBE WE'LL TURN THINGS AROUND.
TABLE'S PRETTY HOT, RIGHT, BOYS?
WINNER, WINNER...
PLEASE SHUT UP.

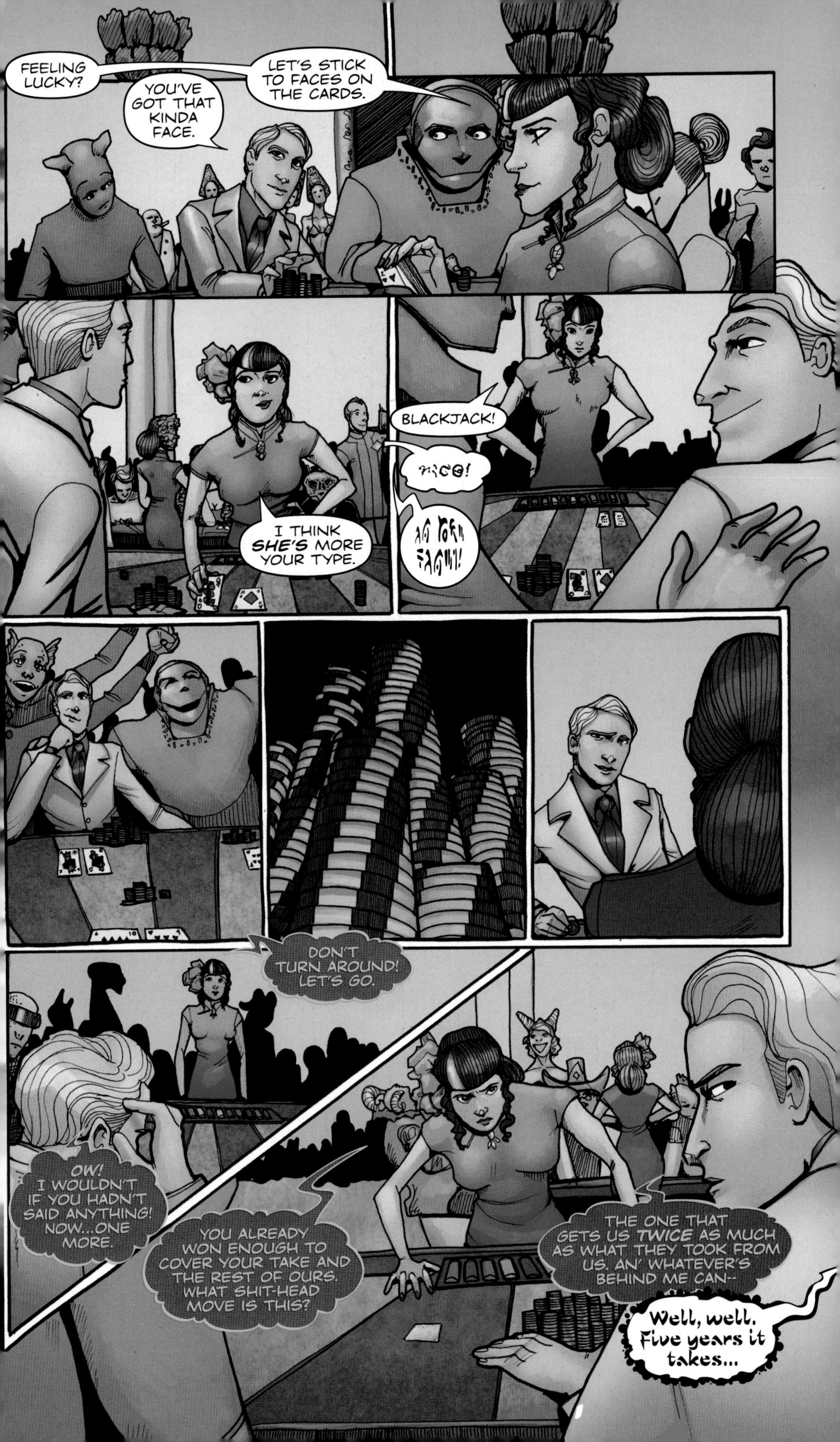
FEELING LUCKY?
YOU'VE GOT THAT KINDA FACE.
LET'S STICK TO FACES ON THE CARDS.
I THINK SHE'S MORE YOUR TYPE.
BLACKJACK!
DON'T TURN AROUND! LET'S GO.
OW! I WOULDN'T IF YOU HADN'T SAID ANYTHING! NOW...ONE MORE.
YOU ALREADY WON ENOUGH TO COVER YOUR TAKE AND THE REST OF OURS. WHAT SHIT-HEAD MOVE IS THIS?
THE ONE THAT GETS US TWICE AS MUCH AS WHAT THEY TOOK FROM US. AN' WHATEVER'S BEHIND ME CAN--
Well, well. Five years it takes...

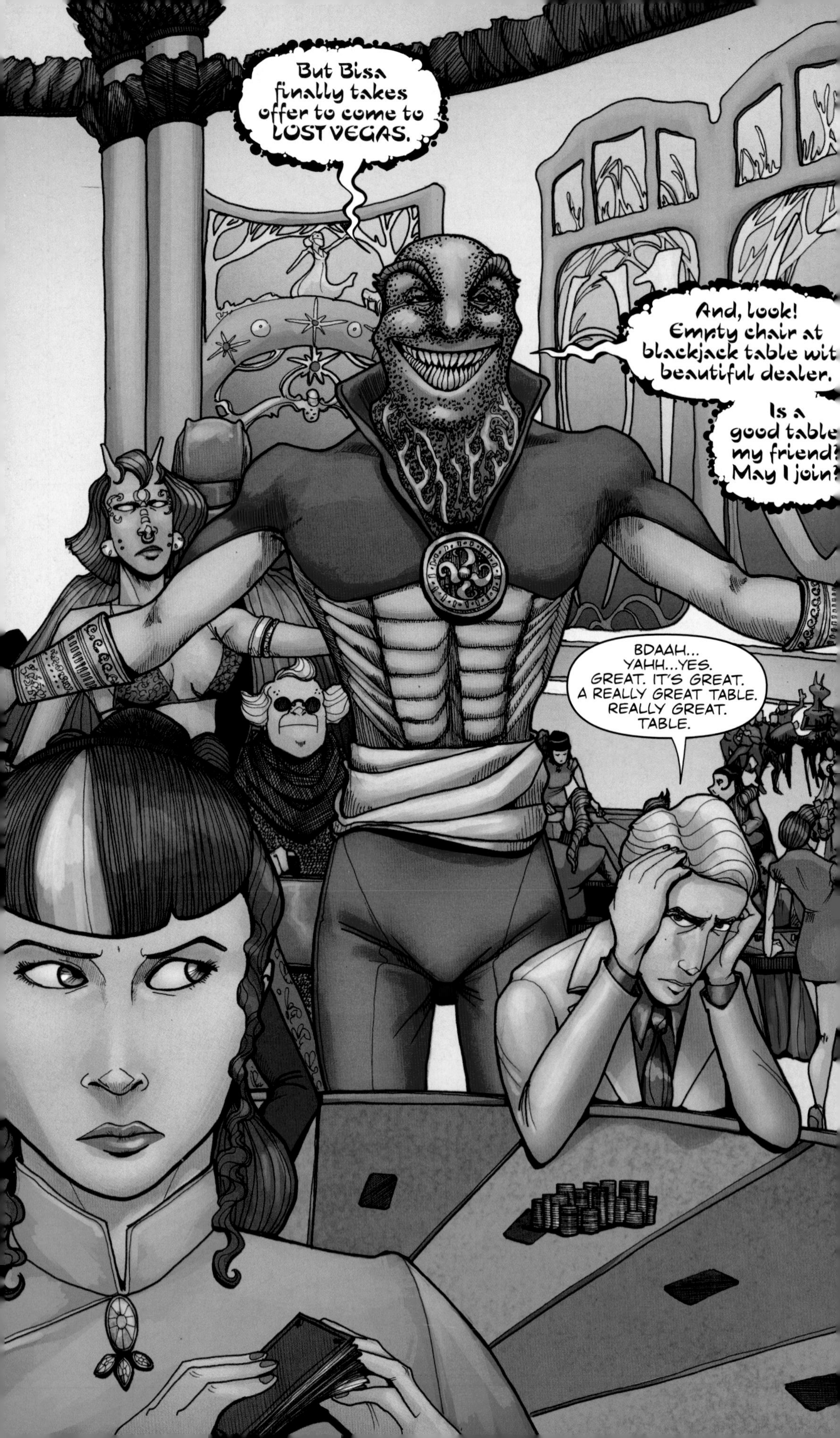

But Bisa finally takes offer to come to LOST VEGAS.
And, look! Empty chair at blackjack table wit beautiful dealer.
Is a good table my friend? May I join?
BDAAH... YAHH...YES. GREAT. IT'S GREAT. A REALLY GREAT TABLE. REALLY GREAT. TABLE.

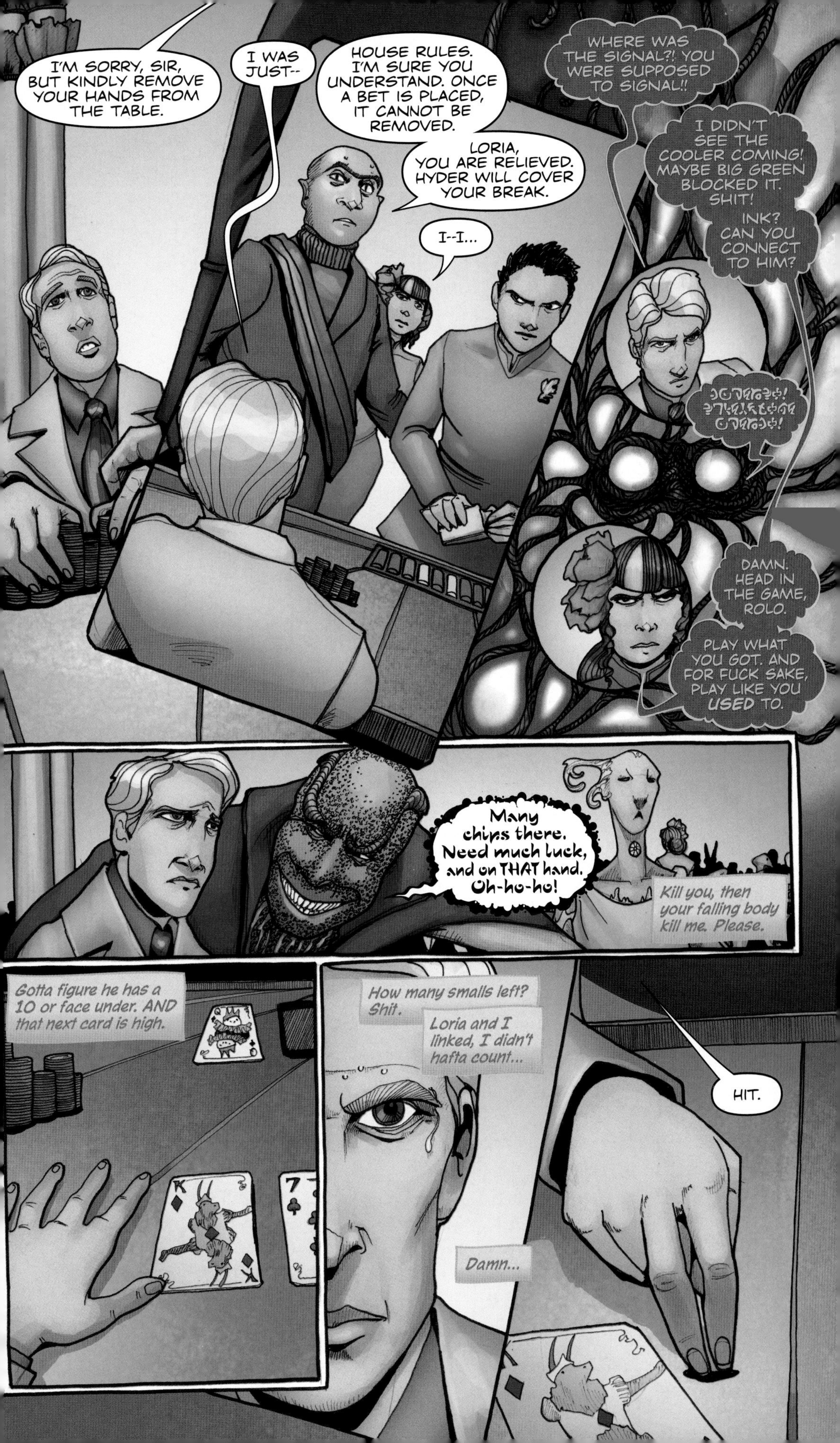
I'M SORRY, SIR, BUT KINDLY REMOVE YOUR HANDS FROM THE TABLE.
I WAS JUST--
HOUSE RULES. I'M SURE YOU UNDERSTAND. ONCE A BET IS PLACED, IT CANNOT BE REMOVED.
LORIA, YOU ARE RELIEVED. HYDER WILL COVER YOUR BREAK.
I--I...
WHERE WAS THE SIGNAL?! YOU WERE SUPPOSED TO SIGNAL!!
I DIDN'T SEE THE COOLER COMING! MAYBE BIG GREEN BLOCKED IT. SHIT!
INK? CAN YOU CONNECT TO HIM?
DAMN. HEAD IN THE GAME, ROLO.
PLAY WHAT YOU GOT. AND FOR FUCK SAKE, PLAY LIKE YOU USED TO.
Many chips there. Need much luck, and on THAT hand. Oh-ho-ho!
Kill you, then your falling body kill me. Please.
Gotta figure he has a 10 or face under. AND that next card is high.
How many smalls left? Shit.
Loria and I linked, I didn't hafta count...
HIT.
Damn...

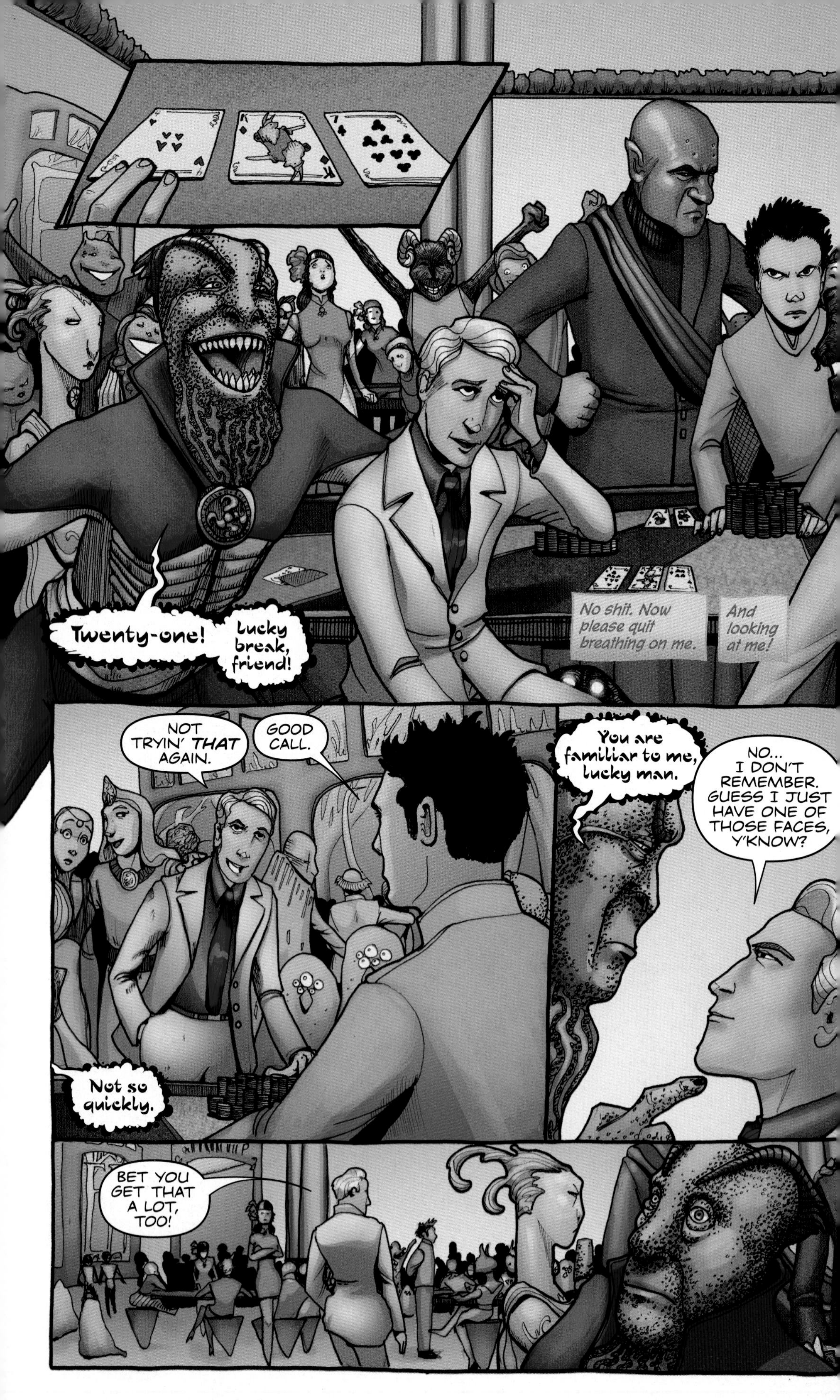
Twenty-one!
Lucky break, friend!
No shit. Now please quit breathing on me.
And looking at me!
NOT TRYIN' THAT AGAIN.
GOOD CALL.
Not so quickly.
You are familiar to me, lucky man.
NO... I DON'T REMEMBER. GUESS I JUST HAVE ONE OF THOSE FACES, Y'KNOW?
BET YOU GET THAT A LOT, TOO!

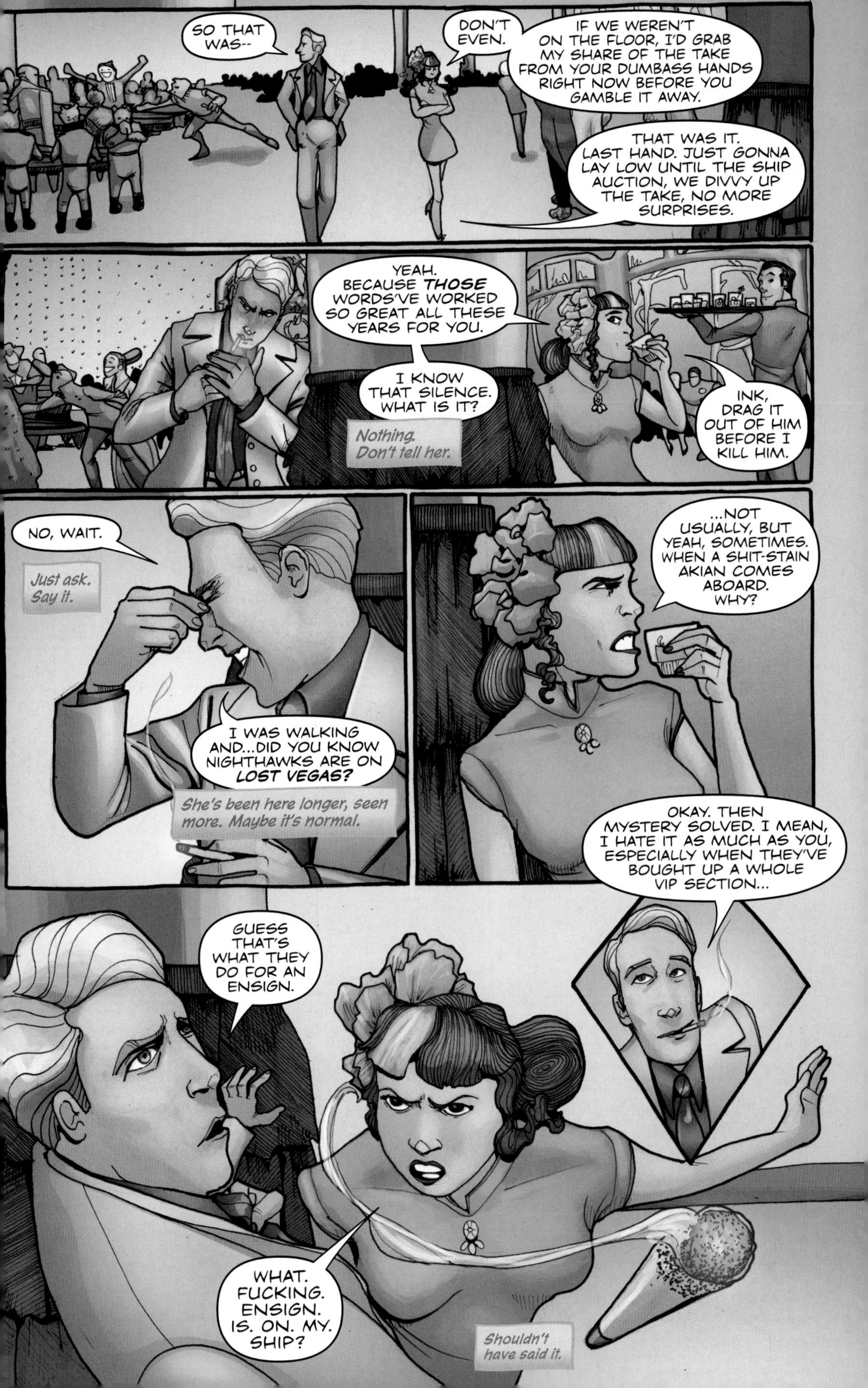
SO THAT WAS--
DON'T EVEN.
IF WE WEREN'T ON THE FLOOR, I'D GRAB MY SHARE OF THE TAKE FROM YOUR DUMBASS HANDS RIGHT NOW BEFORE YOU GAMBLE IT AWAY.
THAT WAS IT. LAST HAND. JUST GONNA LAY LOW UNTIL THE SHIP AUCTION, WE DIVVY UP THE TAKE, NO MORE SURPRISES.
YEAH. BECAUSE THOSE WORDS'VE WORKED SO GREAT ALL THESE YEARS FOR YOU.
I KNOW THAT SILENCE. WHAT IS IT?
Nothing. Don't tell her.
INK, DRAG IT OUT OF HIM BEFORE I KILL HIM.
NO, WAIT.
Just ask. Say it.
I WAS WALKING AND...DID YOU KNOW NIGHTHAWKS ARE ON LOST VEGAS?
She's been here longer, seen more. Maybe it's normal.
...NOT USUALLY, BUT YEAH, SOMETIMES. WHEN A SHIT-STAIN AKIAN COMES ABOARD. WHY?
OKAY. THEN MYSTERY SOLVED. I MEAN, I HATE IT AS MUCH AS YOU, ESPECIALLY WHEN THEY'VE BOUGHT UP A WHOLE VIP SECTION...
GUESS THAT'S WHAT THEY DO FOR AN ENSIGN.
WHAT. FUCKING. ENSIGN. IS. ON. MY. SHIP?
Shouldn't have said it.

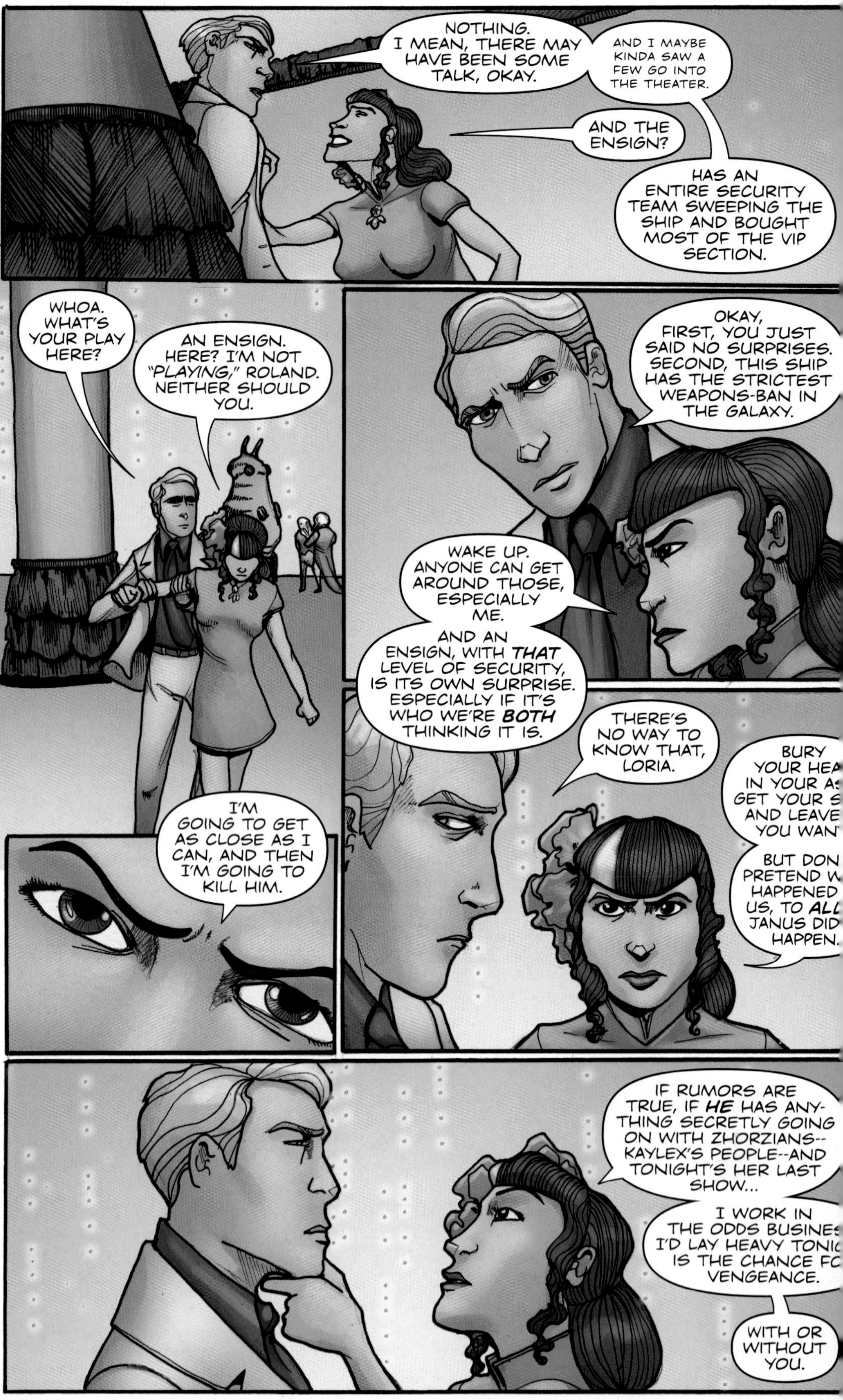
NOTHING. I MEAN, THERE MAY HAVE BEEN SOME TALK, OKAY.
AND I MAYBE KINDA SAW A FEW GO INTO THE THEATER.
AND THE ENSIGN?
HAS AN ENTIRE SECURITY TEAM SWEEPING THE SHIP AND BOUGHT MOST OF THE VIP SECTION.
WHOA. WHAT'S YOUR PLAY HERE?
AN ENSIGN. HERE? I'M NOT "PLAYING," ROLAND. NEITHER SHOULD YOU.
OKAY, FIRST, YOU JUST SAID NO SURPRISES. SECOND, THIS SHIP HAS THE STRICTEST WEAPONS-BAN IN THE GALAXY.
WAKE UP. ANYONE CAN GET AROUND THOSE, ESPECIALLY ME.
AND AN ENSIGN, WITH ***THAT*** LEVEL OF SECURITY, IS ITS OWN SURPRISE. ESPECIALLY IF IT'S WHO WE'RE ***BOTH*** THINKING IT IS.
THERE'S NO WAY TO KNOW THAT, LORIA.
BURY YOUR HEA IN YOUR A GET YOUR AND LEAVE YOU WAN
BUT DON PRETEND W HAPPENED US, TO ***ALL*** JANUS DID HAPPEN.
I'M GOING TO GET AS CLOSE AS I CAN, AND THEN I'M GOING TO KILL HIM.
IF RUMORS ARE TRUE, IF ***HE*** HAS ANY-THING SECRETLY GOING ON WITH ZHORZIANS-- KAYLEX'S PEOPLE--AND TONIGHT'S HER LAST SHOW...
I WORK IN THE ODDS BUSINES I'D LAY HEAVY TONIG IS THE CHANCE FO VENGEANCE.
WITH OR WITHOUT YOU.

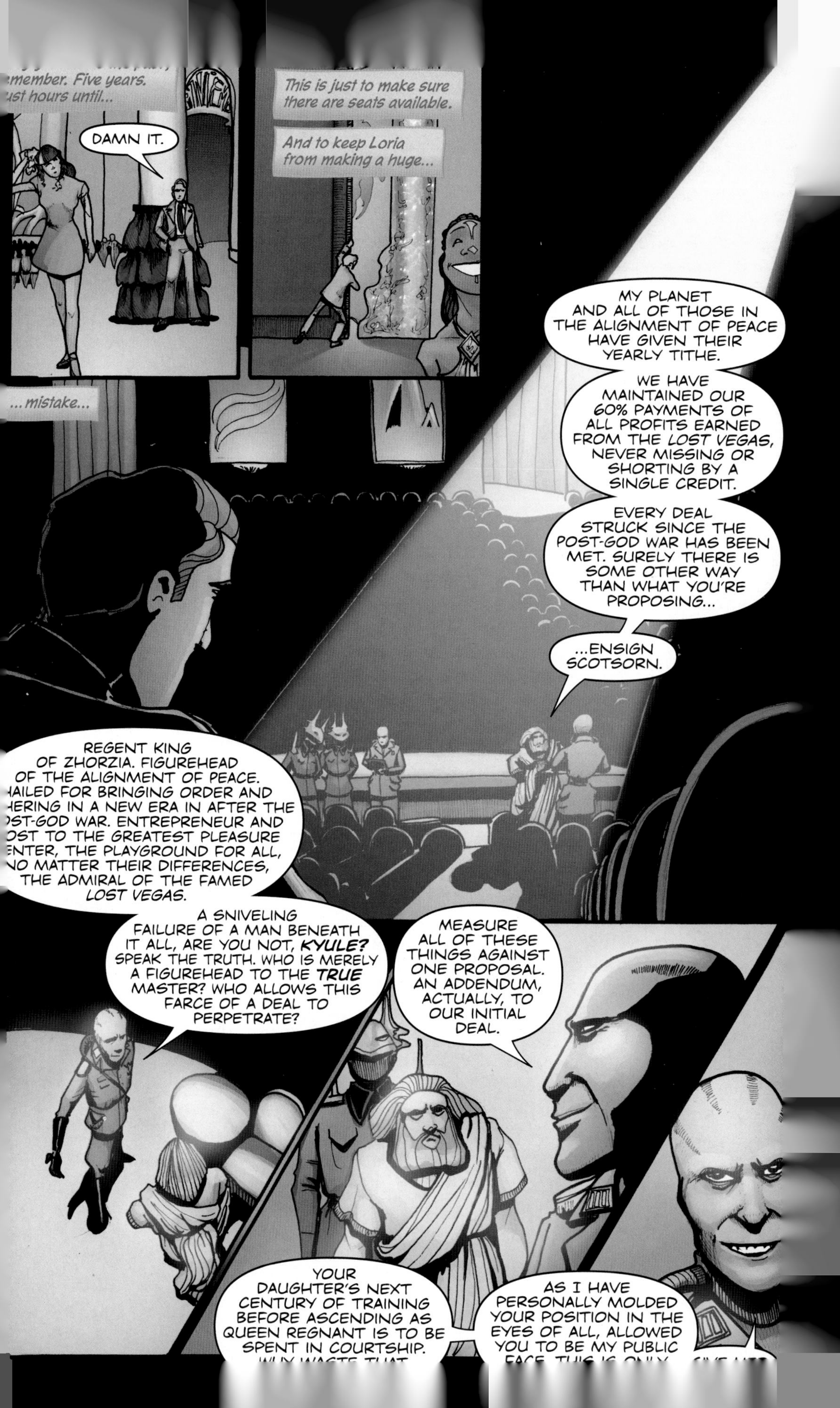
emember. Five years.
ust hours until...
DAMN IT.
This is just to make sure there are seats available.
And to keep Loria from making a huge...
...mistake...
MY PLANET AND ALL OF THOSE IN THE ALIGNMENT OF PEACE HAVE GIVEN THEIR YEARLY TITHE.
WE HAVE MAINTAINED OUR 60% PAYMENTS OF ALL PROFITS EARNED FROM THE LOST VEGAS, NEVER MISSING OR SHORTING BY A SINGLE CREDIT.
EVERY DEAL STRUCK SINCE THE POST-GOD WAR HAS BEEN MET. SURELY THERE IS SOME OTHER WAY THAN WHAT YOU'RE PROPOSING...
...ENSIGN SCOTSORN.
REGENT KING OF ZHORZIA. FIGUREHEAD OF THE ALIGNMENT OF PEACE. AILED FOR BRINGING ORDER AND HERING IN A NEW ERA IN AFTER THE ST-GOD WAR. ENTREPRENEUR AND OST TO THE GREATEST PLEASURE ENTER, THE PLAYGROUND FOR ALL, NO MATTER THEIR DIFFERENCES, THE ADMIRAL OF THE FAMED LOST VEGAS.
A SNIVELING FAILURE OF A MAN BENEATH IT ALL, ARE YOU NOT, KYULE? SPEAK THE TRUTH. WHO IS MERELY A FIGUREHEAD TO THE TRUE MASTER? WHO ALLOWS THIS FARCE OF A DEAL TO PERPETRATE?
MEASURE ALL OF THESE THINGS AGAINST ONE PROPOSAL. AN ADDENDUM, ACTUALLY, TO OUR INITIAL DEAL.
YOUR DAUGHTER'S NEXT CENTURY OF TRAINING BEFORE ASCENDING AS QUEEN REGNANT IS TO BE SPENT IN COURTSHIP.
AS I HAVE PERSONALLY MOLDED YOUR POSITION IN THE EYES OF ALL, ALLOWED YOU TO BE MY PUBLIC

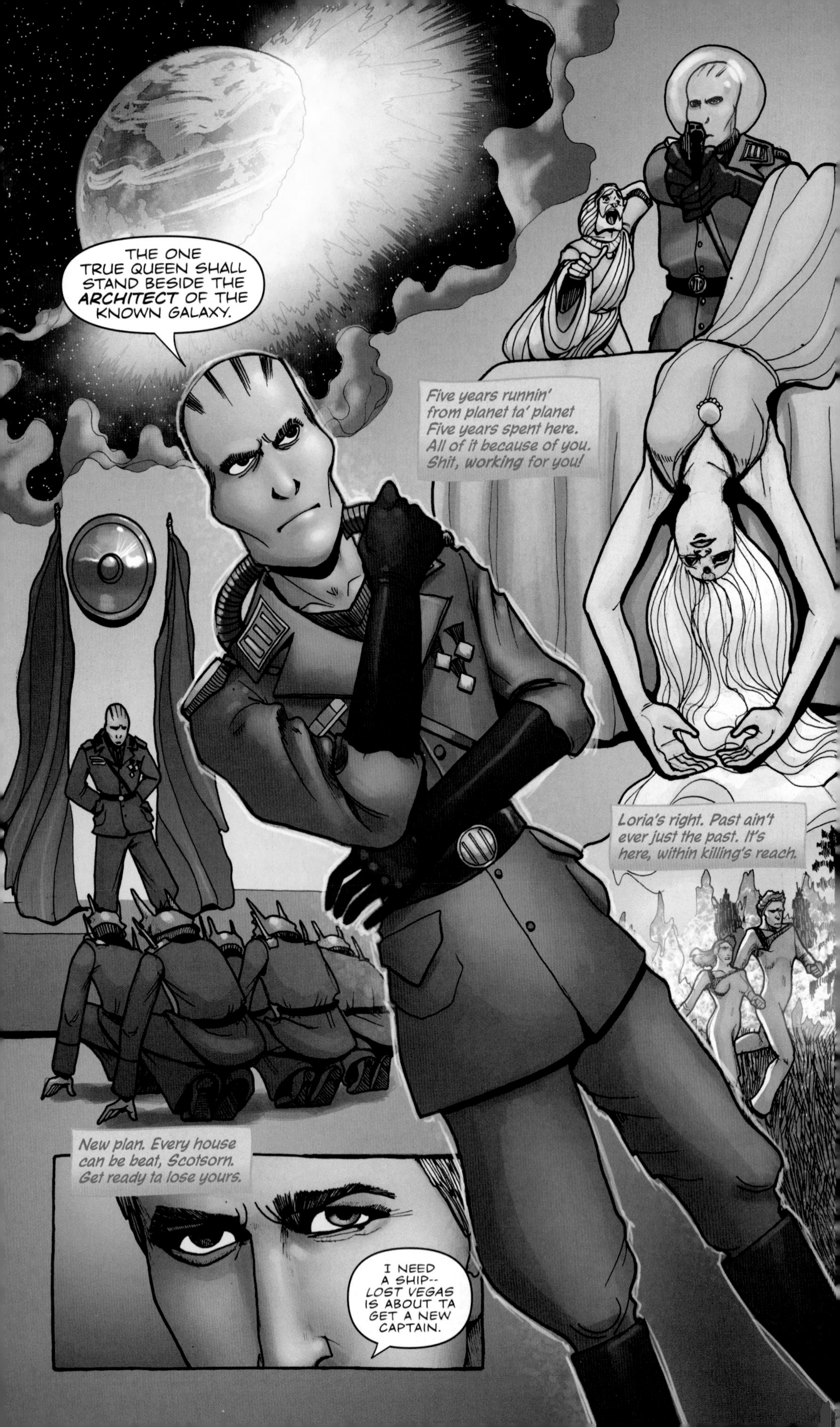
THE ONE TRUE QUEEN SHALL STAND BESIDE THE ARCHITECT OF THE KNOWN GALAXY.
Five years runnin' from planet ta' planet Five years spent here. All of it because of you. Shit, working for you!
Loria's right. Past ain't ever just the past. It's here, within killing's reach.
New plan. Every house can be beat, Scotsorn. Get ready ta lose yours.
I NEED A SHIP-- LOST VEGAS IS ABOUT TA GET A NEW CAPTAIN.

END SECOND HAND

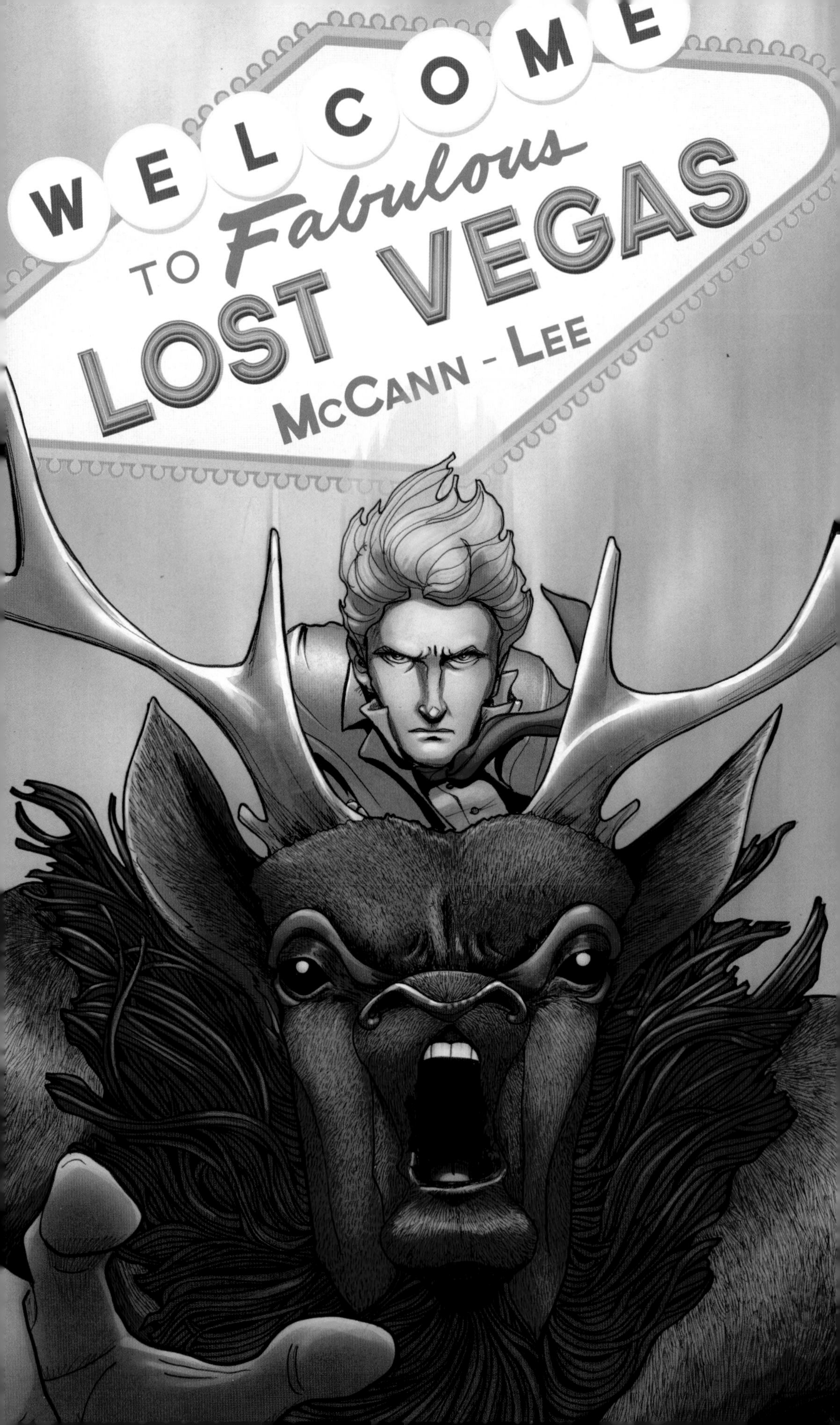
WELCOME
TO Fabulous
LOST VEGAS
McCANN - LEE

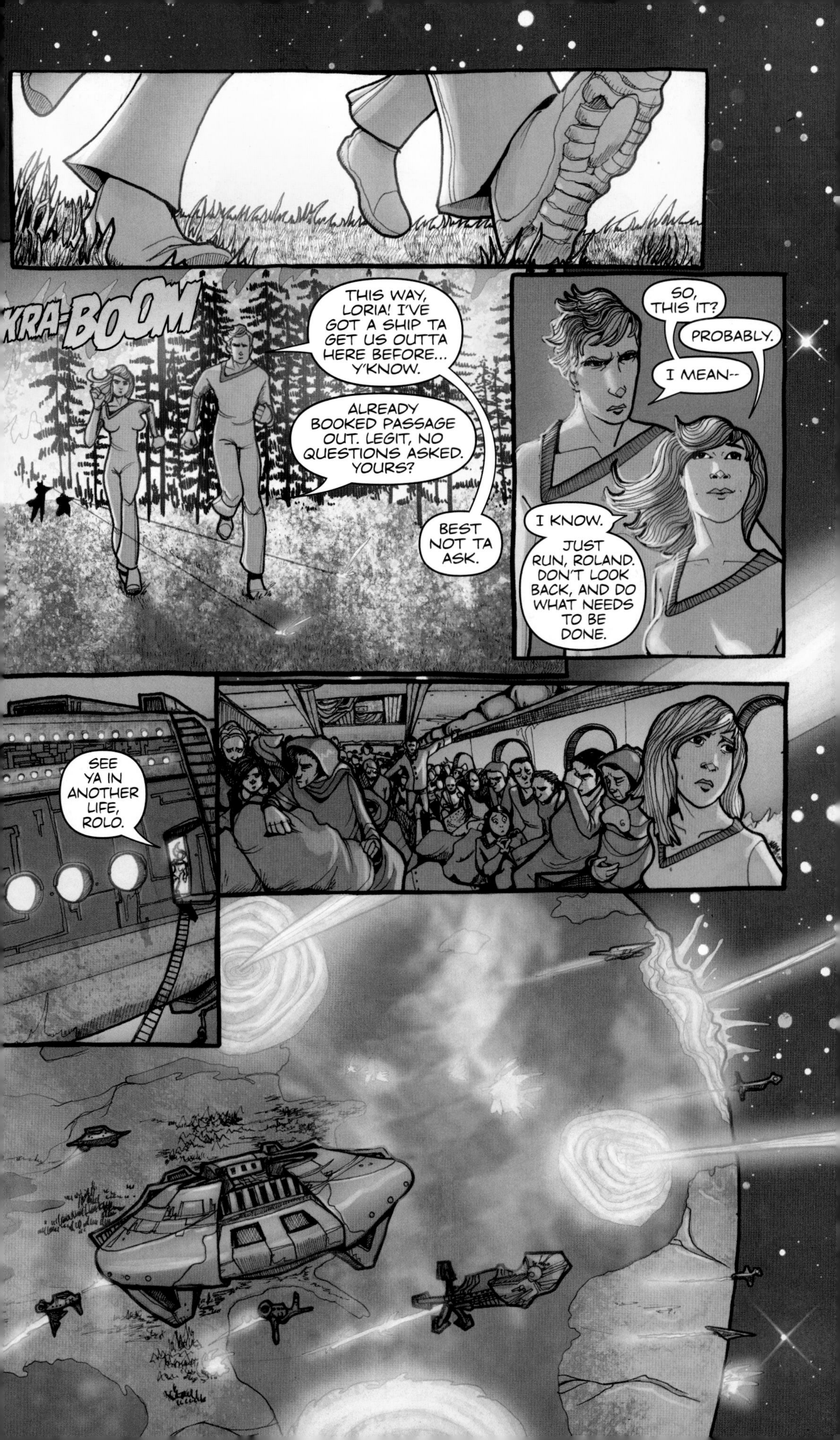
KRA-BOOM
THIS WAY, LORIA! I'VE GOT A SHIP TA GET US OUTTA HERE BEFORE... Y'KNOW.
ALREADY BOOKED PASSAGE OUT. LEGIT, NO QUESTIONS ASKED. YOURS?
BEST NOT TA ASK.
SO, THIS IT?
PROBABLY.
I MEAN--
I KNOW.
JUST RUN, ROLAND. DON'T LOOK BACK, AND DO WHAT NEEDS TO BE DONE.
SEE YA IN ANOTHER LIFE, ROLO.

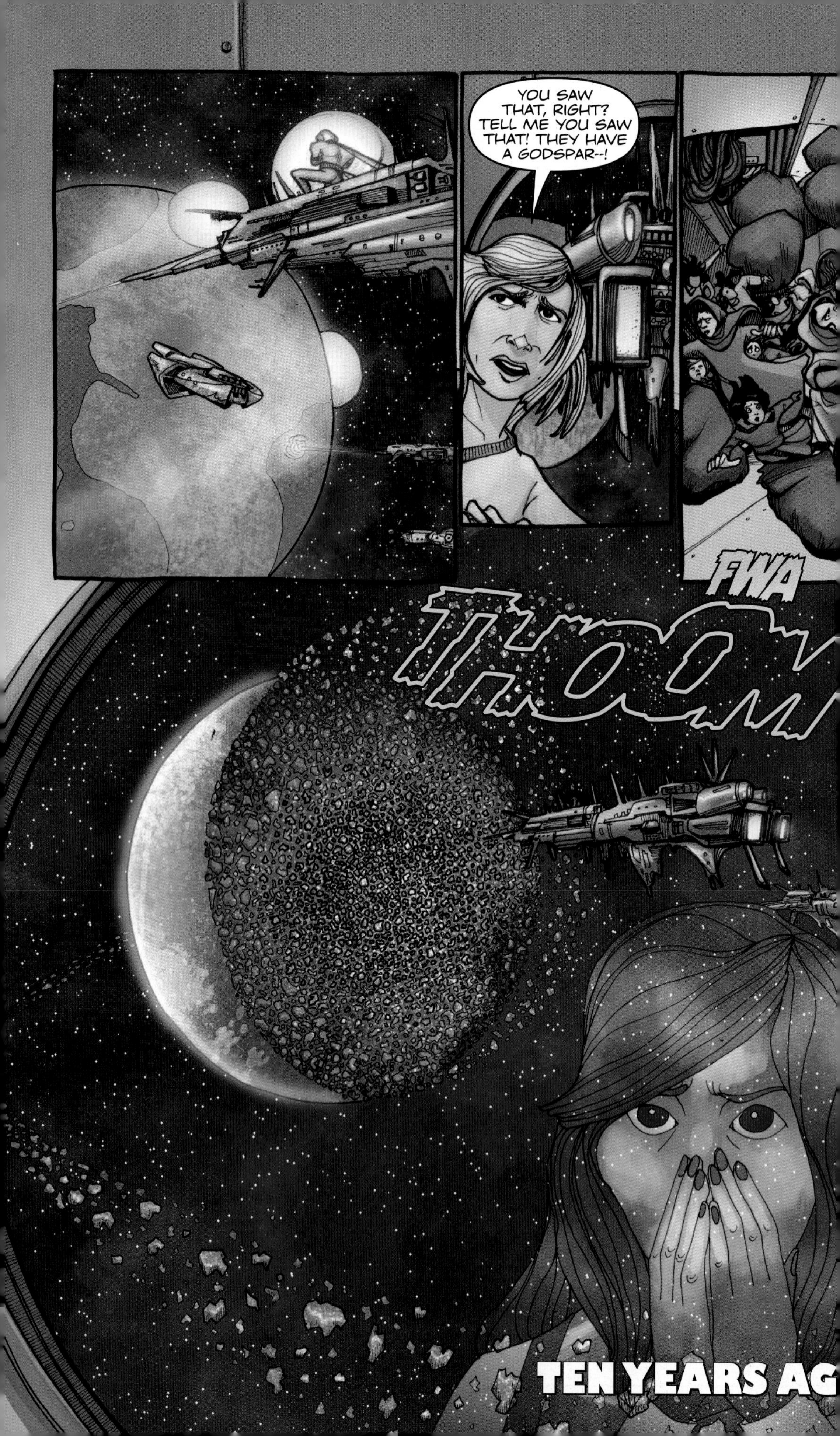
YOU SAW THAT, RIGHT? TELL ME YOU SAW THAT! THEY HAVE A GODSPAR--!
FWA
THOOM
TEN YEARS AG

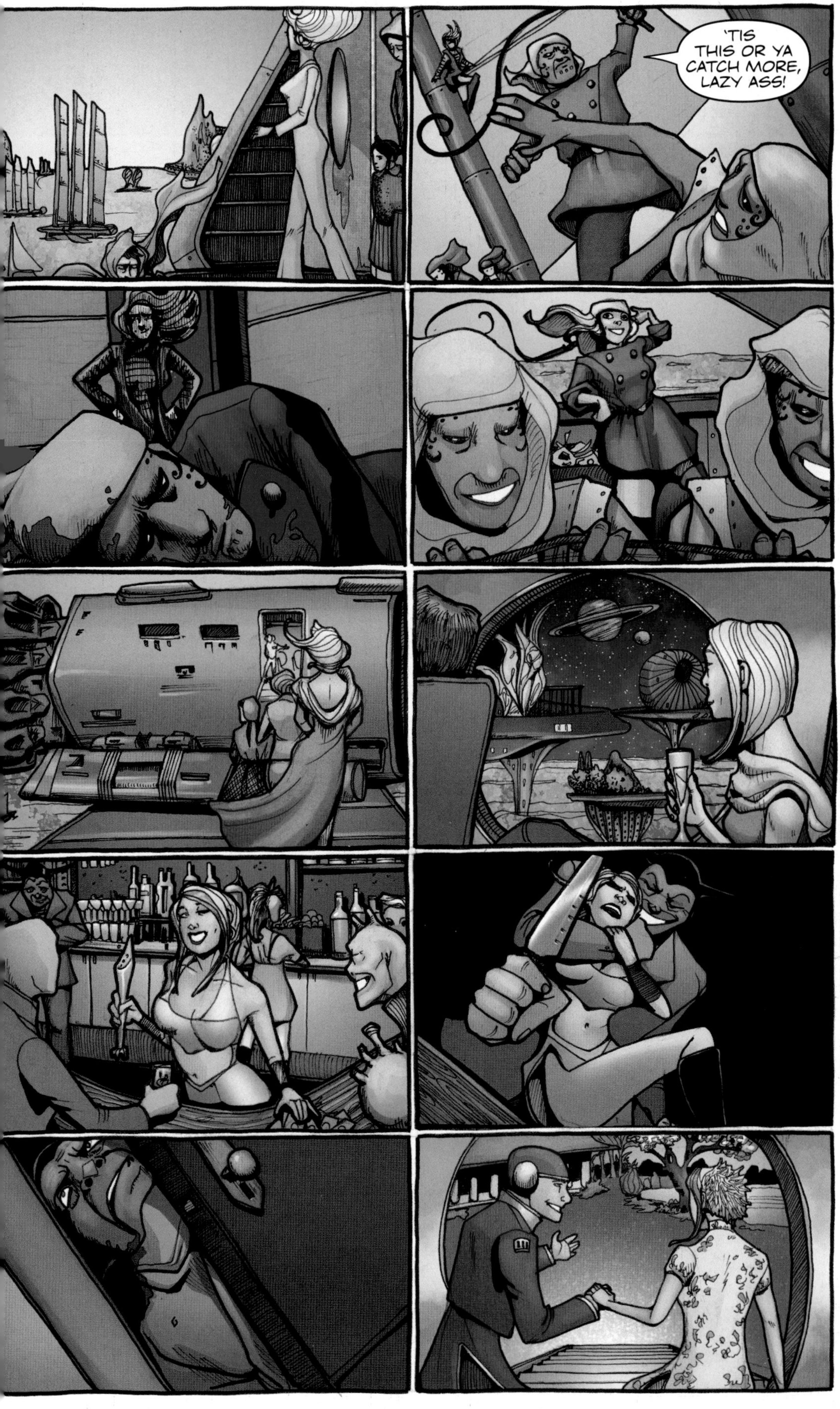
'TIS THIS OR YA CATCH MORE, LAZY ASS!

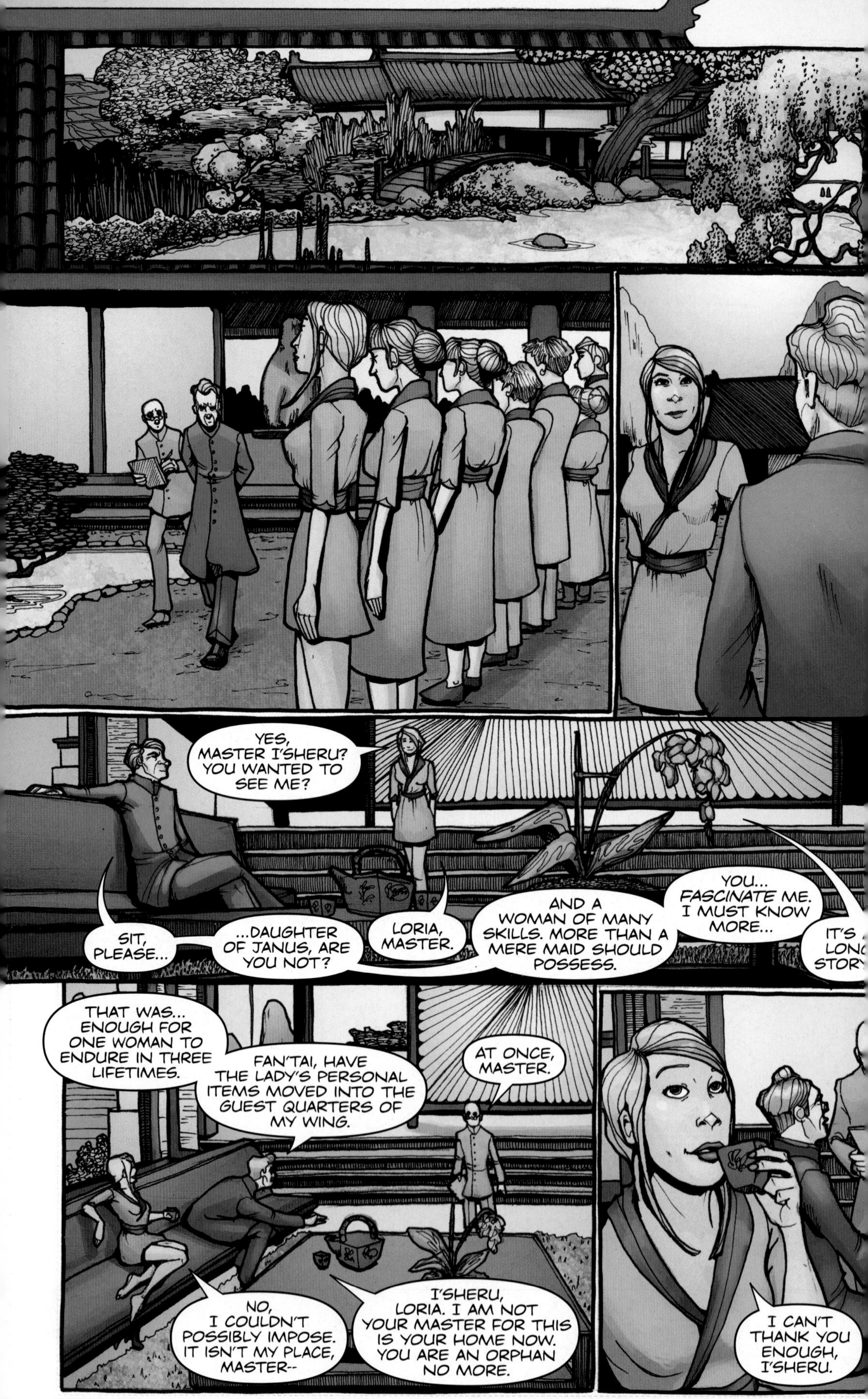
YES, MASTER I'SHERU? YOU WANTED TO SEE ME?
SIT, PLEASE...
...DAUGHTER OF JANUS, ARE YOU NOT?
LORIA, MASTER.
AND A WOMAN OF MANY SKILLS. MORE THAN A MERE MAID SHOULD POSSESS.
YOU... FASCINATE ME. I MUST KNOW MORE...
IT'S LONG STORY
THAT WAS... ENOUGH FOR ONE WOMAN TO ENDURE IN THREE LIFETIMES.
FAN'TAI, HAVE THE LADY'S PERSONAL ITEMS MOVED INTO THE GUEST QUARTERS OF MY WING.
AT ONCE, MASTER.
NO, I COULDN'T POSSIBLY IMPOSE. IT ISN'T MY PLACE, MASTER--
I'SHERU, LORIA. I AM NOT YOUR MASTER FOR THIS IS YOUR HOME NOW. YOU ARE AN ORPHAN NO MORE.
I CAN'T THANK YOU ENOUGH, I'SHERU.

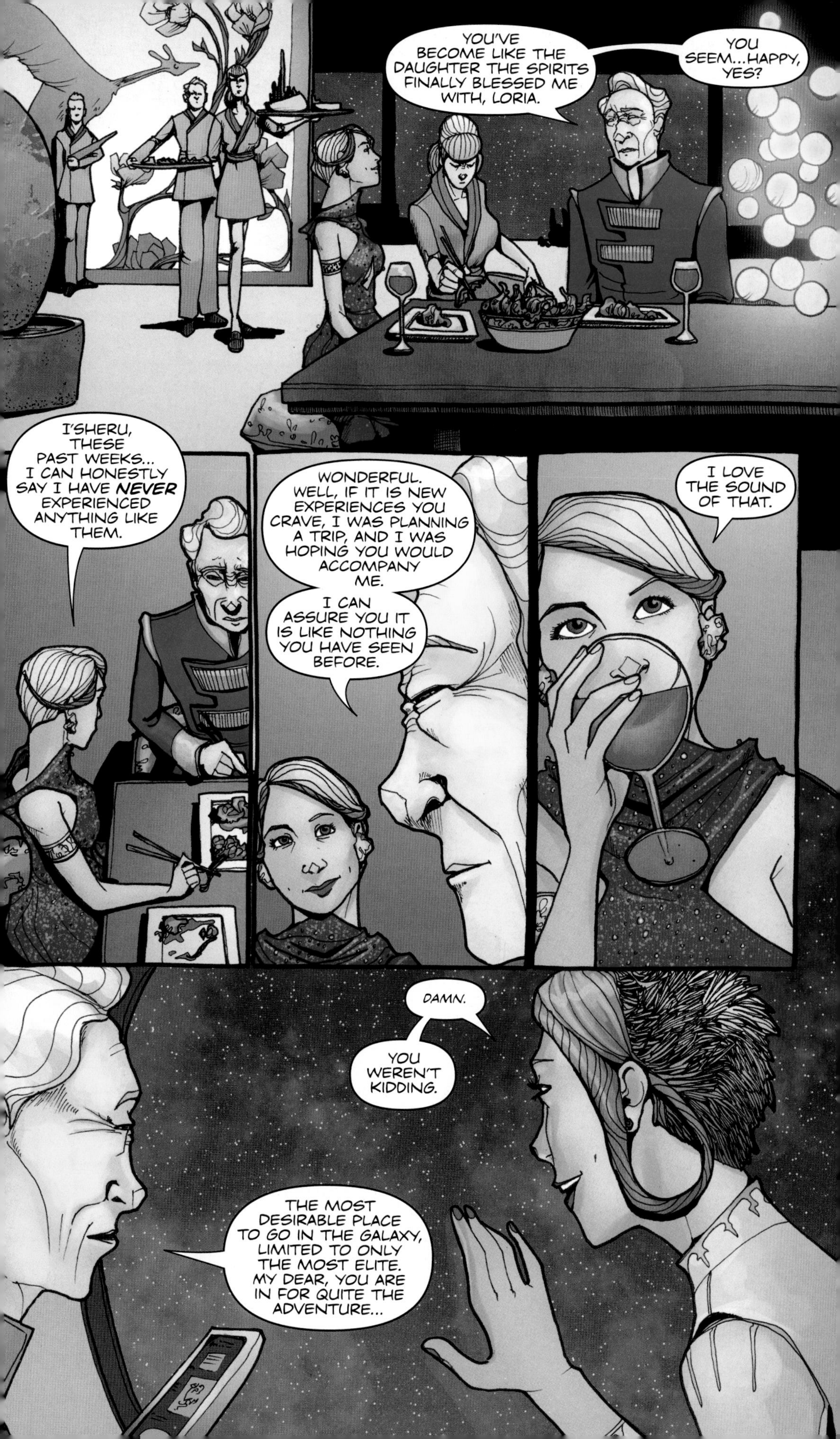
YOU'VE BECOME LIKE THE DAUGHTER THE SPIRITS FINALLY BLESSED ME WITH, LORIA.
YOU SEEM...HAPPY, YES?
I'SHERU, THESE PAST WEEKS... I CAN HONESTLY SAY I HAVE **NEVER** EXPERIENCED ANYTHING LIKE THEM.
WONDERFUL. WELL, IF IT IS NEW EXPERIENCES YOU CRAVE, I WAS PLANNING A TRIP, AND I WAS HOPING YOU WOULD ACCOMPANY ME.
I CAN ASSURE YOU IT IS LIKE NOTHING YOU HAVE SEEN BEFORE.
I LOVE THE SOUND OF THAT.
DAMN.
YOU WEREN'T KIDDING.
THE MOST DESIRABLE PLACE TO GO IN THE GALAXY, LIMITED TO ONLY THE MOST ELITE. MY DEAR, YOU ARE IN FOR QUITE THE ADVENTURE...

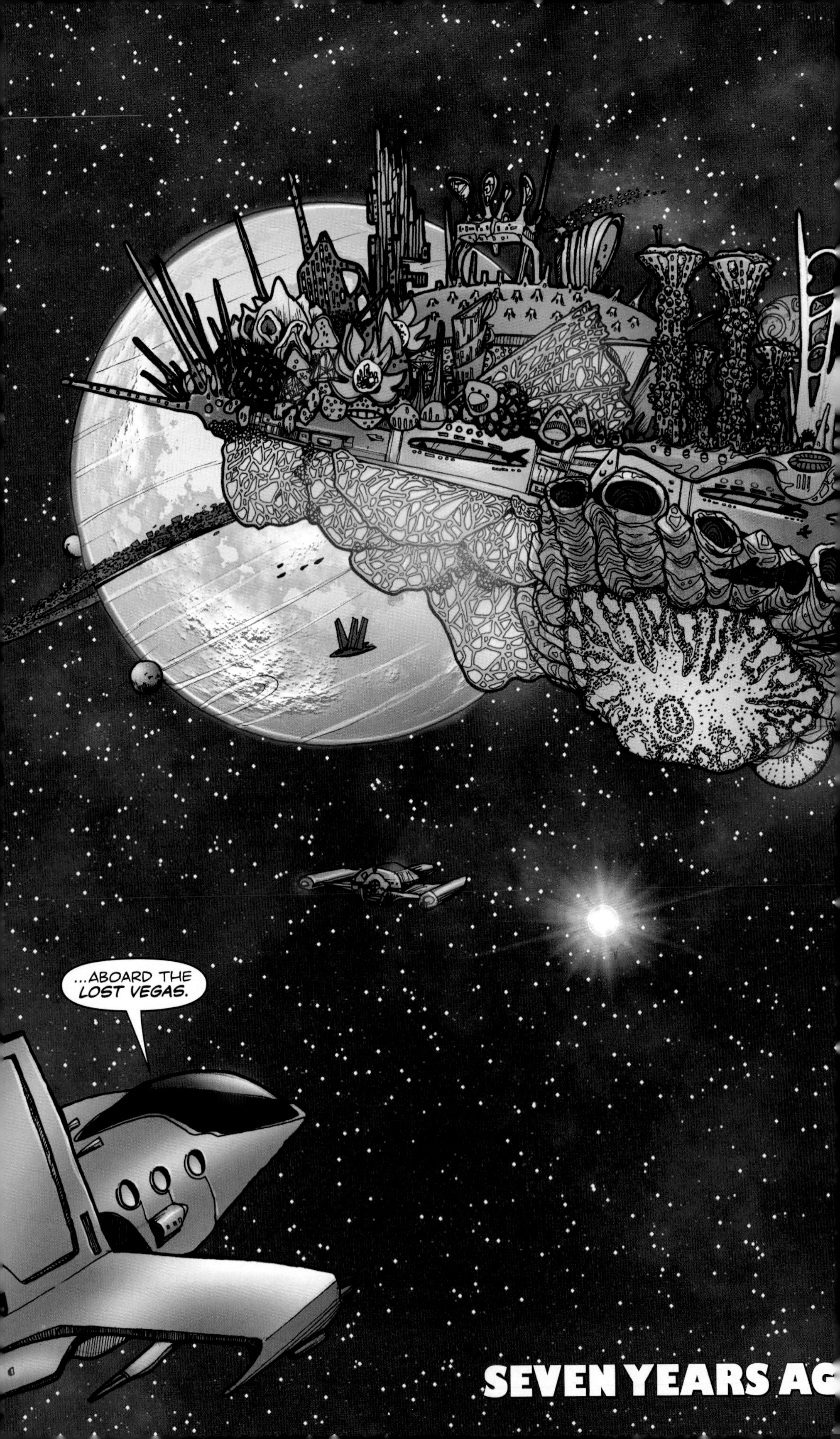
...ABOARD THE LOST VEGAS.
SEVEN YEARS AG

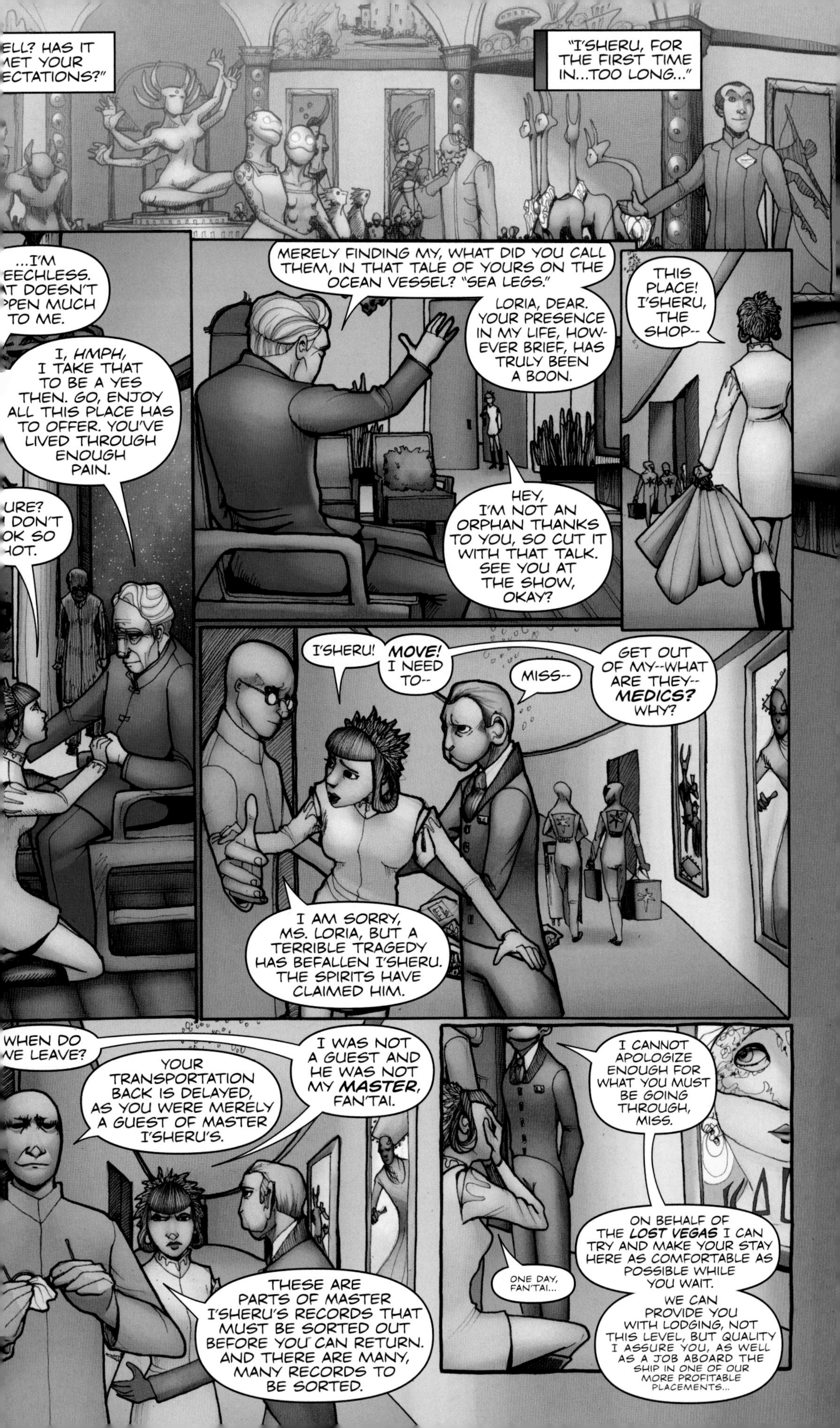

ELL? HAS IT MET YOUR ECTATIONS?"
"I'SHERU, FOR THE FIRST TIME IN...TOO LONG..."
...I'M EECHLESS. AT DOESN'T PPEN MUCH TO ME.
I, HMPH, I TAKE THAT TO BE A YES THEN. GO, ENJOY ALL THIS PLACE HAS TO OFFER. YOU'VE LIVED THROUGH ENOUGH PAIN.
URE? I DON'T OK SO HOT.
MERELY FINDING MY, WHAT DID YOU CALL THEM, IN THAT TALE OF YOURS ON THE OCEAN VESSEL? "SEA LEGS."
LORIA, DEAR. YOUR PRESENCE IN MY LIFE, HOW-EVER BRIEF, HAS TRULY BEEN A BOON.
HEY, I'M NOT AN ORPHAN THANKS TO YOU, SO CUT IT WITH THAT TALK. SEE YOU AT THE SHOW, OKAY?
THIS PLACE! I'SHERU, THE SHOP--
I'SHERU!
MOVE! I NEED TO--
MISS--
GET OUT OF MY--WHAT ARE THEY-- MEDICS? WHY?
I AM SORRY, MS. LORIA, BUT A TERRIBLE TRAGEDY HAS BEFALLEN I'SHERU. THE SPIRITS HAVE CLAIMED HIM.
WHEN DO VE LEAVE?
YOUR TRANSPORTATION BACK IS DELAYED, AS YOU WERE MERELY A GUEST OF MASTER I'SHERU'S.
I WAS NOT A GUEST AND HE WAS NOT MY MASTER, FAN'TAI.
THESE ARE PARTS OF MASTER I'SHERU'S RECORDS THAT MUST BE SORTED OUT BEFORE YOU CAN RETURN. AND THERE ARE MANY, MANY RECORDS TO BE SORTED.
I CANNOT APOLOGIZE ENOUGH FOR WHAT YOU MUST BE GOING THROUGH, MISS.
ON BEHALF OF THE LOST VEGAS I CAN TRY AND MAKE YOUR STAY HERE AS COMFORTABLE AS POSSIBLE WHILE YOU WAIT.
ONE DAY, FAN'TAI...
WE CAN PROVIDE YOU WITH LODGING, NOT THIS LEVEL, BUT QUALITY I ASSURE YOU, AS WELL AS A JOB ABOARD THE SHIP IN ONE OF OUR MORE PROFITABLE PLACEMENTS...

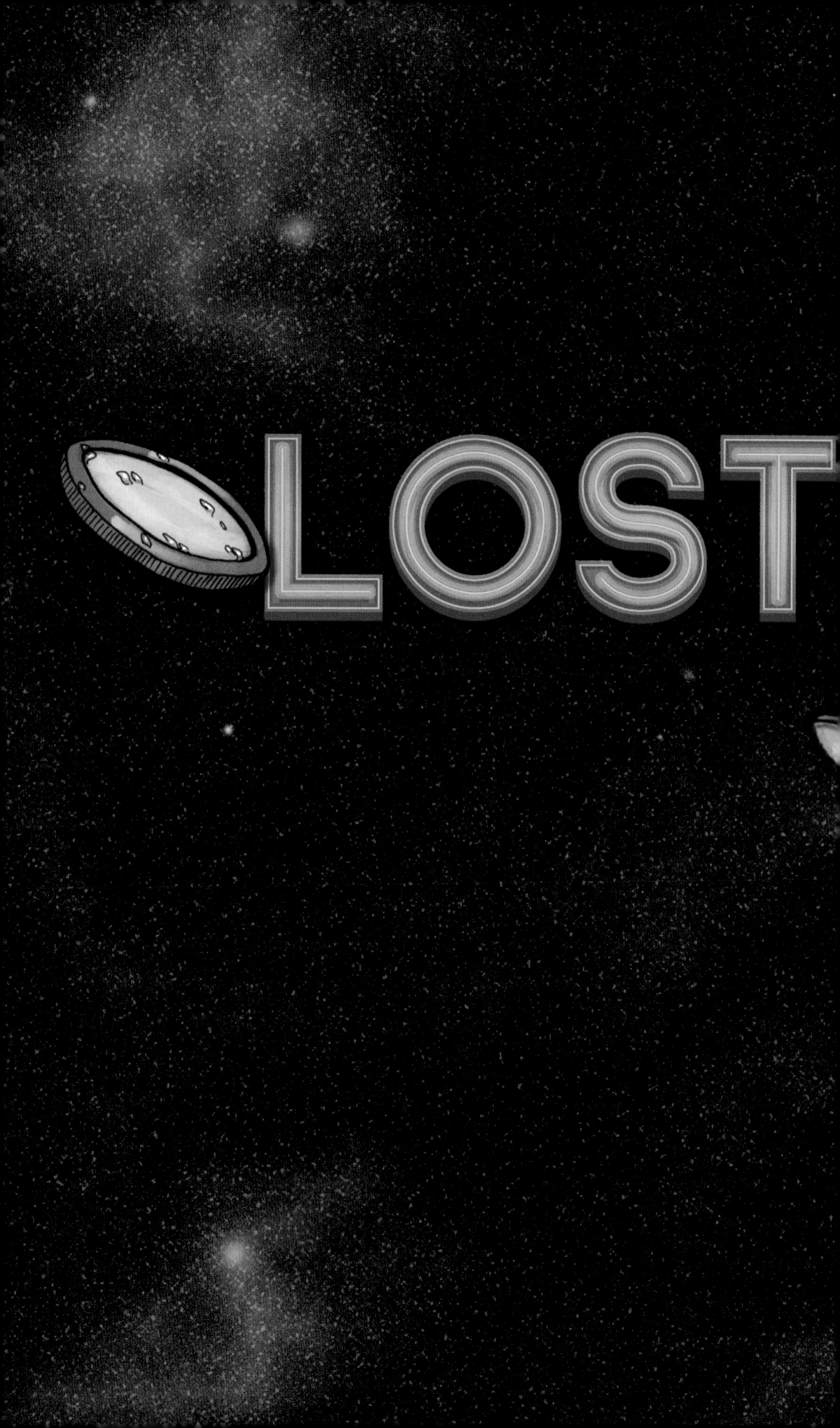
LOST

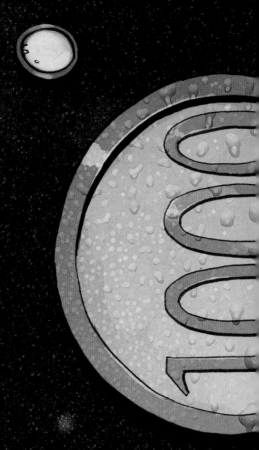

VEGAS

THIRD HAND | DOWN TO THE FELT

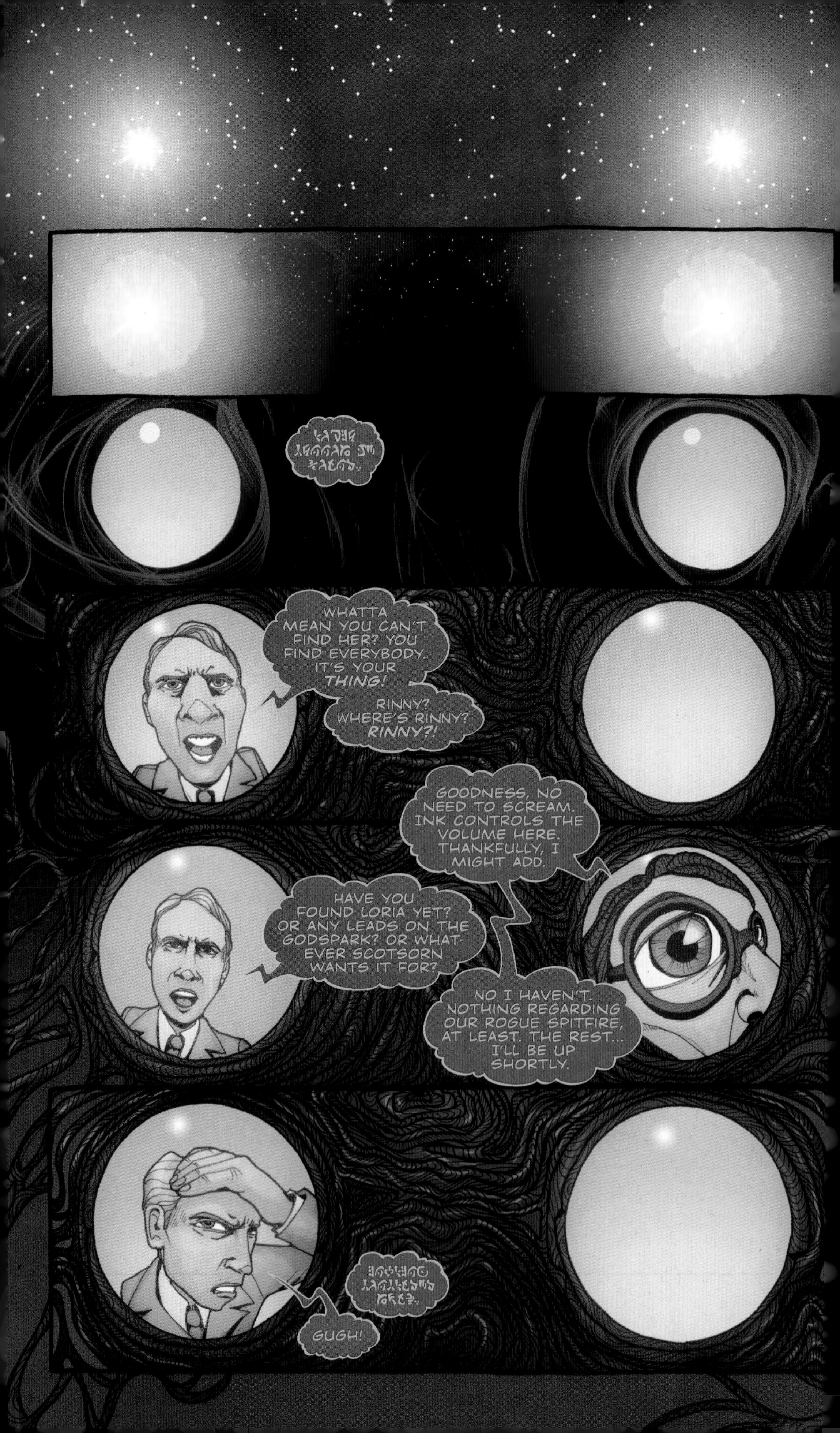
WHATTA MEAN YOU CAN'T FIND HER? YOU FIND EVERYBODY. IT'S YOUR THING!
RINNY? WHERE'S RINNY? RINNY?!
GOODNESS, NO NEED TO SCREAM. INK CONTROLS THE VOLUME HERE. THANKFULLY, I MIGHT ADD.
HAVE YOU FOUND LORIA YET? OR ANY LEADS ON THE GODSPARK? OR WHAT-EVER SCOTSORN WANTS IT FOR?
NO I HAVEN'T. NOTHING REGARDING OUR ROGUE SPITFIRE, AT LEAST. THE REST... I'LL BE UP SHORTLY.
GUGH!

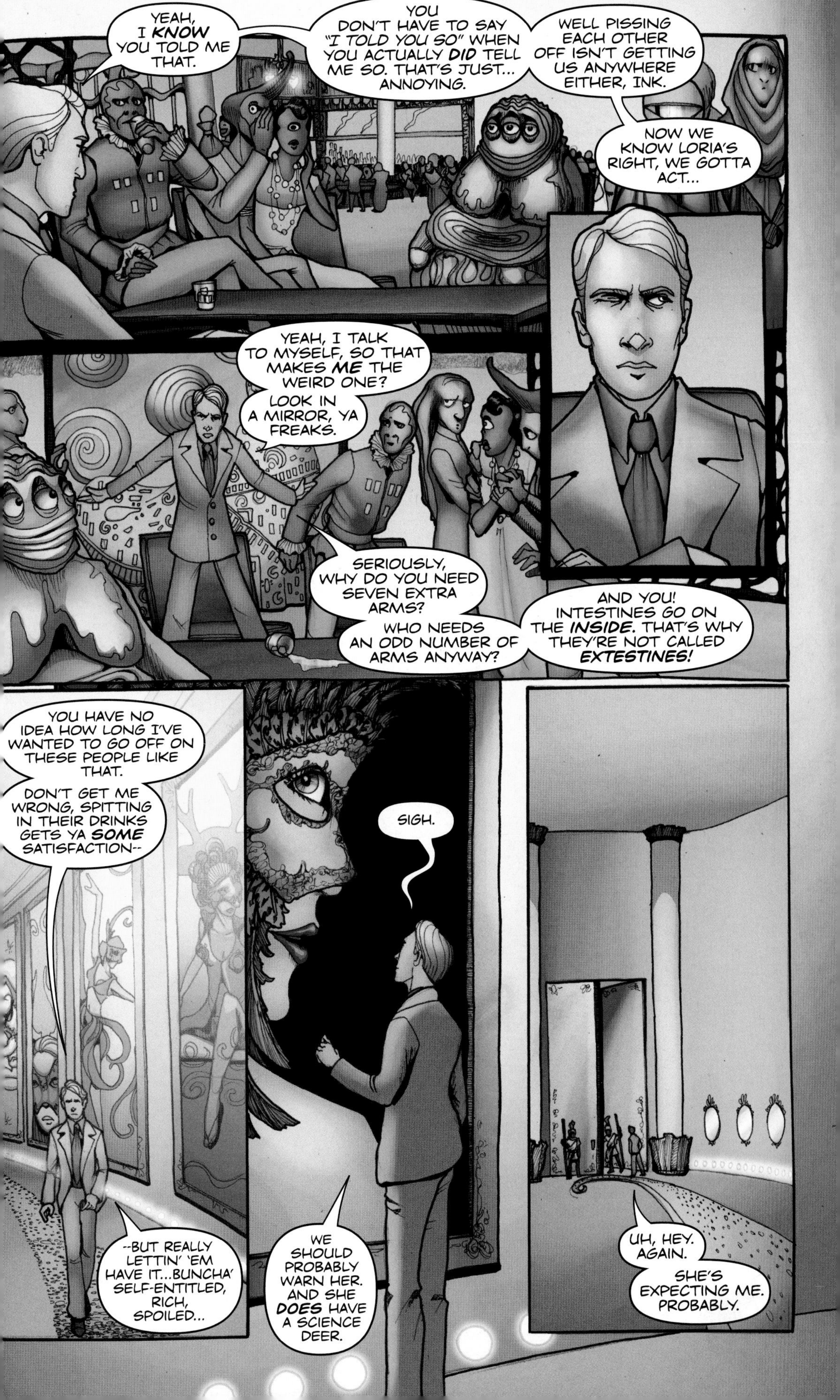
YEAH, I **KNOW** YOU TOLD ME THAT.
YOU DON'T HAVE TO SAY "I TOLD YOU SO" WHEN YOU ACTUALLY **DID** TELL ME SO. THAT'S JUST... ANNOYING.
WELL PISSING EACH OTHER OFF ISN'T GETTING US ANYWHERE EITHER, INK.
NOW WE KNOW LORIA'S RIGHT, WE GOTTA ACT...
YEAH, I TALK TO MYSELF, SO THAT MAKES **ME** THE WEIRD ONE?
LOOK IN A MIRROR, YA FREAKS.
SERIOUSLY, WHY DO YOU NEED SEVEN EXTRA ARMS?
WHO NEEDS AN ODD NUMBER OF ARMS ANYWAY?
AND YOU! INTESTINES GO ON THE **INSIDE**. THAT'S WHY THEY'RE NOT CALLED **EXTESTINES!**
YOU HAVE NO IDEA HOW LONG I'VE WANTED TO GO OFF ON THESE PEOPLE LIKE THAT.
DON'T GET ME WRONG, SPITTING IN THEIR DRINKS GETS YA **SOME** SATISFACTION--
--BUT REALLY LETTIN' 'EM HAVE IT...BUNCHA' SELF-ENTITLED, RICH, SPOILED...
SIGH.
WE SHOULD PROBABLY WARN HER. AND SHE **DOES** HAVE A SCIENCE DEER.
UH, HEY. AGAIN.
SHE'S EXPECTING ME. PROBABLY.

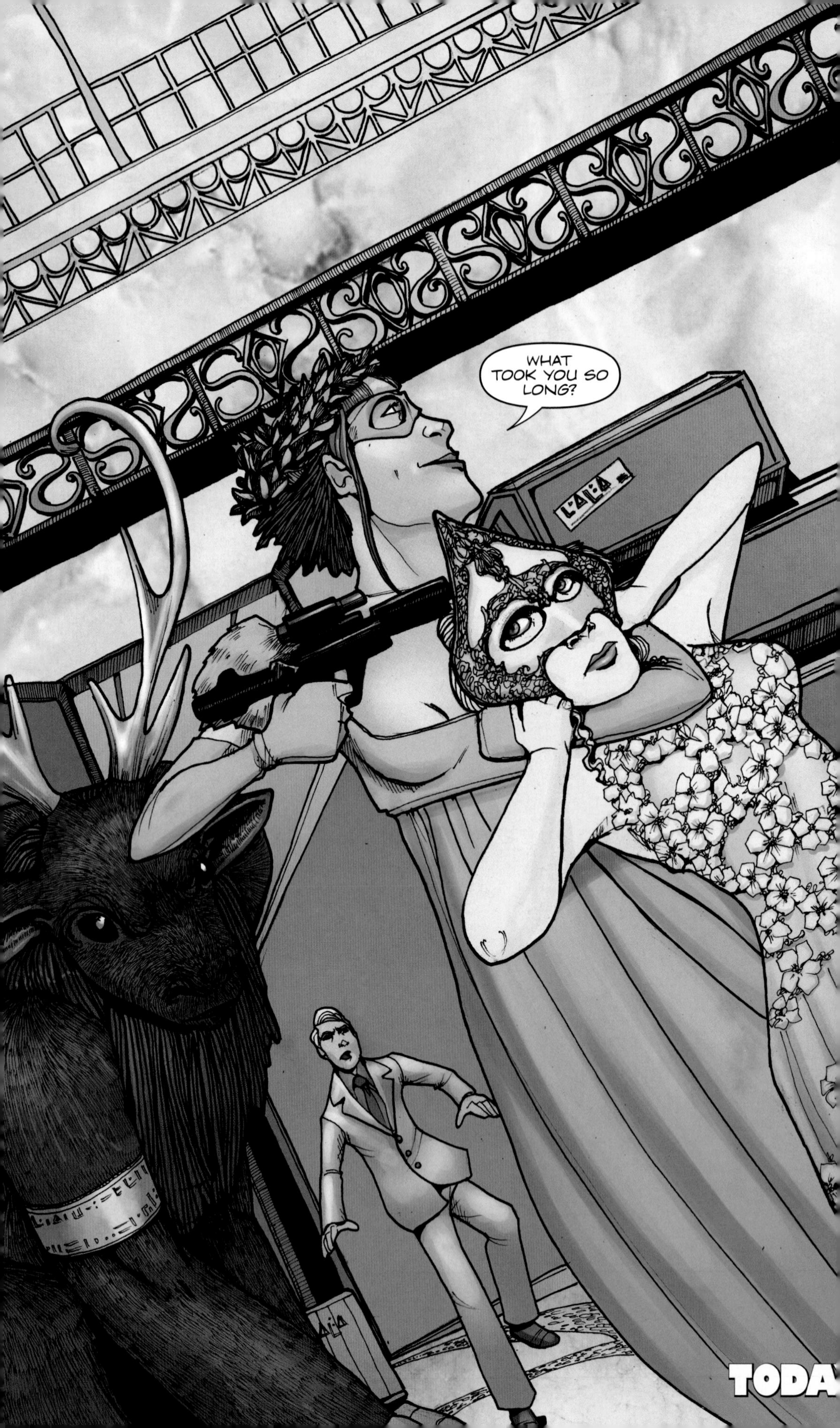
WHAT TOOK YOU SO LONG?
TODA

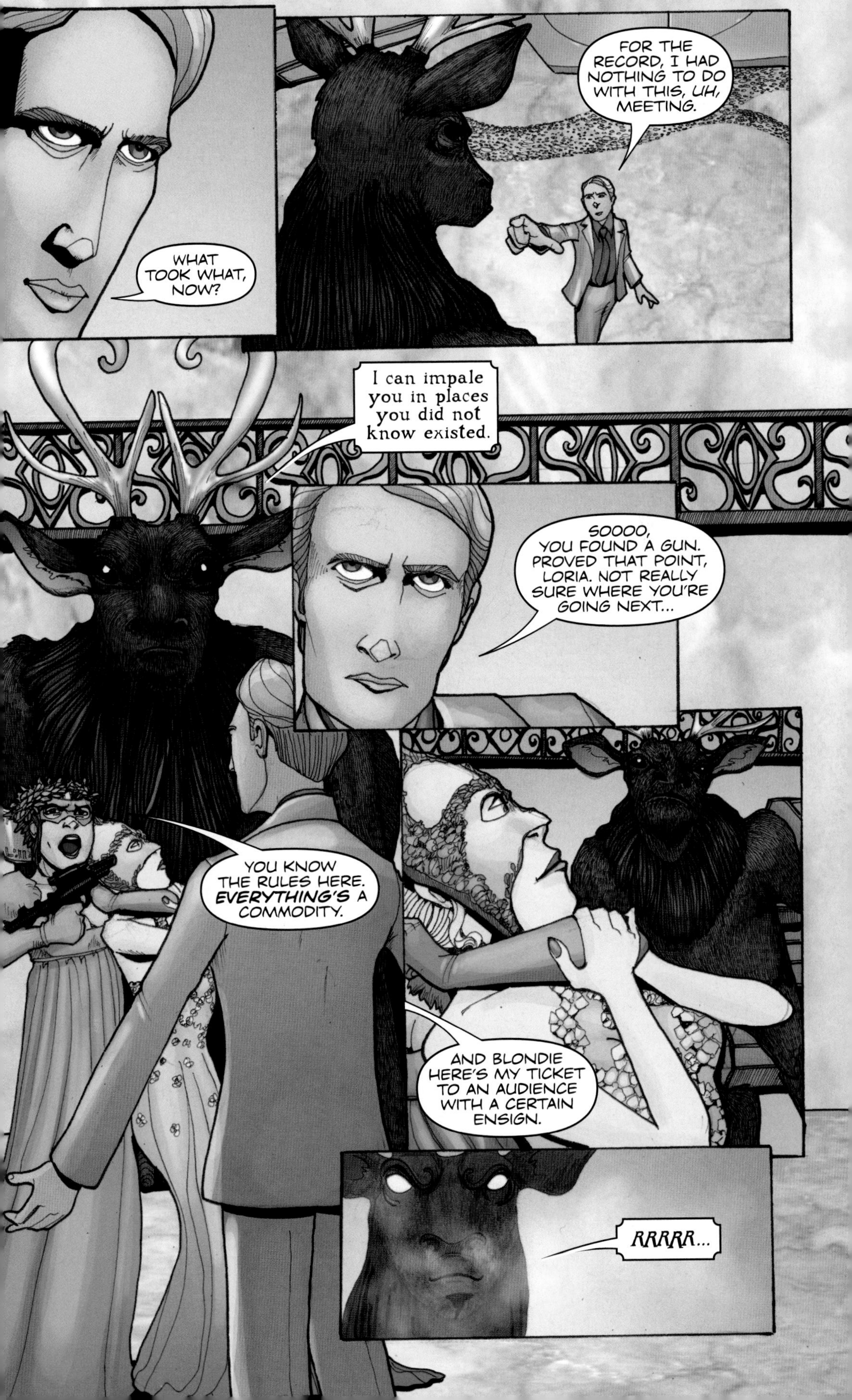
WHAT TOOK WHAT, NOW?
FOR THE RECORD, I HAD NOTHING TO DO WITH THIS, UH, MEETING.
I can impale you in places you did not know existed.
SOOOO, YOU FOUND A GUN. PROVED THAT POINT, LORIA. NOT REALLY SURE WHERE YOU'RE GOING NEXT...
YOU KNOW THE RULES HERE. EVERYTHING'S A COMMODITY.
AND BLONDIE HERE'S MY TICKET TO AN AUDIENCE WITH A CERTAIN ENSIGN.
RRRRR...

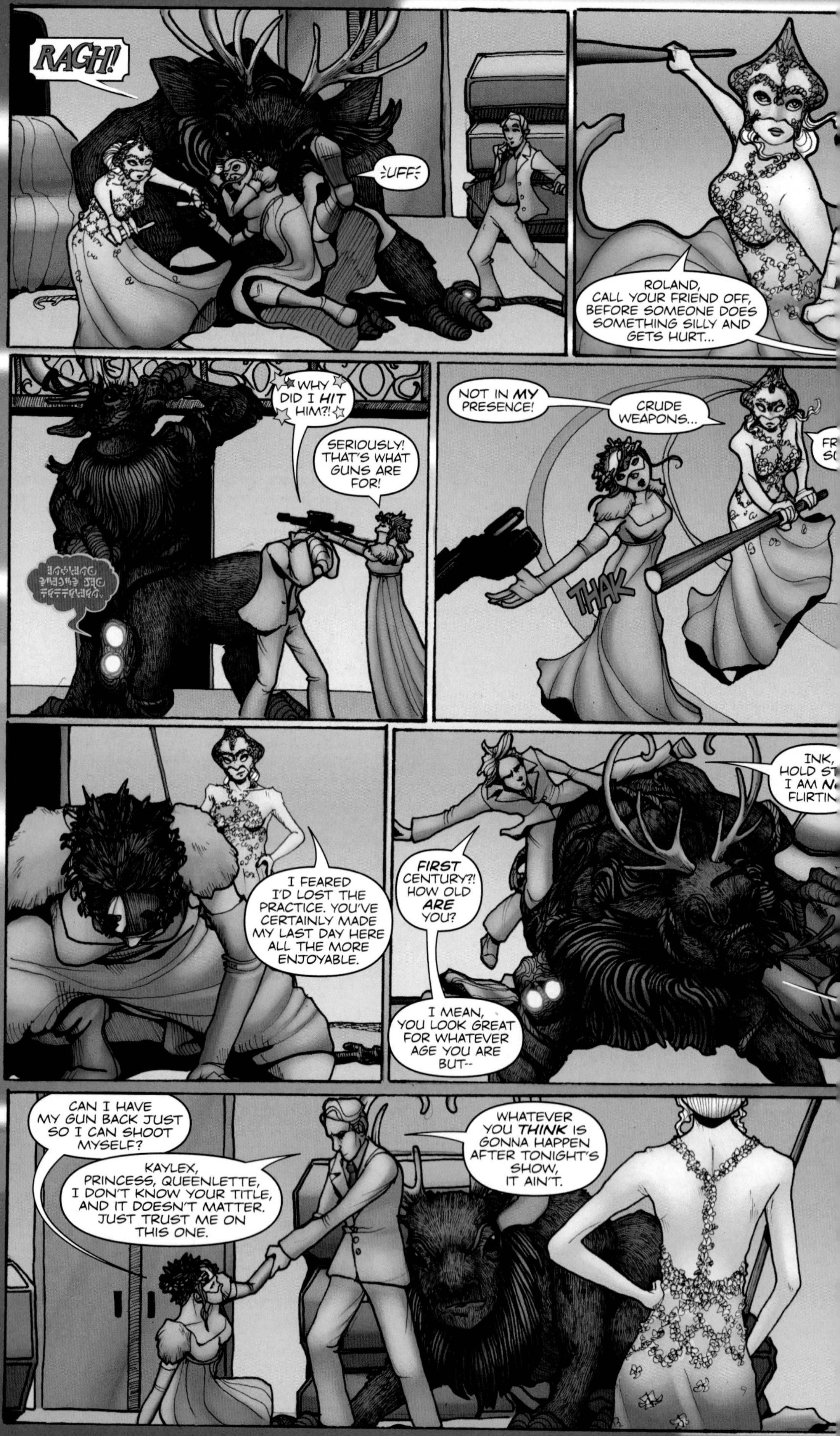
RAGH!
UFF
ROLAND, CALL YOUR FRIEND OFF, BEFORE SOMEONE DOES SOMETHING SILLY AND GETS HURT...
WHY DID I HIT HIM?!
SERIOUSLY! THAT'S WHAT GUNS ARE FOR!
NOT IN MY PRESENCE!
CRUDE WEAPONS...
THAK
I FEARED I'D LOST THE PRACTICE. YOU'VE CERTAINLY MADE MY LAST DAY HERE ALL THE MORE ENJOYABLE.
INK, HOLD ST I AM N FLIRTIN
FIRST CENTURY?! HOW OLD ARE YOU?
I MEAN, YOU LOOK GREAT FOR WHATEVER AGE YOU ARE BUT--
CAN I HAVE MY GUN BACK JUST SO I CAN SHOOT MYSELF?
KAYLEX, PRINCESS, QUEENLETTE, I DON'T KNOW YOUR TITLE, AND IT DOESN'T MATTER. JUST TRUST ME ON THIS ONE.
WHATEVER YOU THINK IS GONNA HAPPEN AFTER TONIGHT'S SHOW, IT AIN'T.

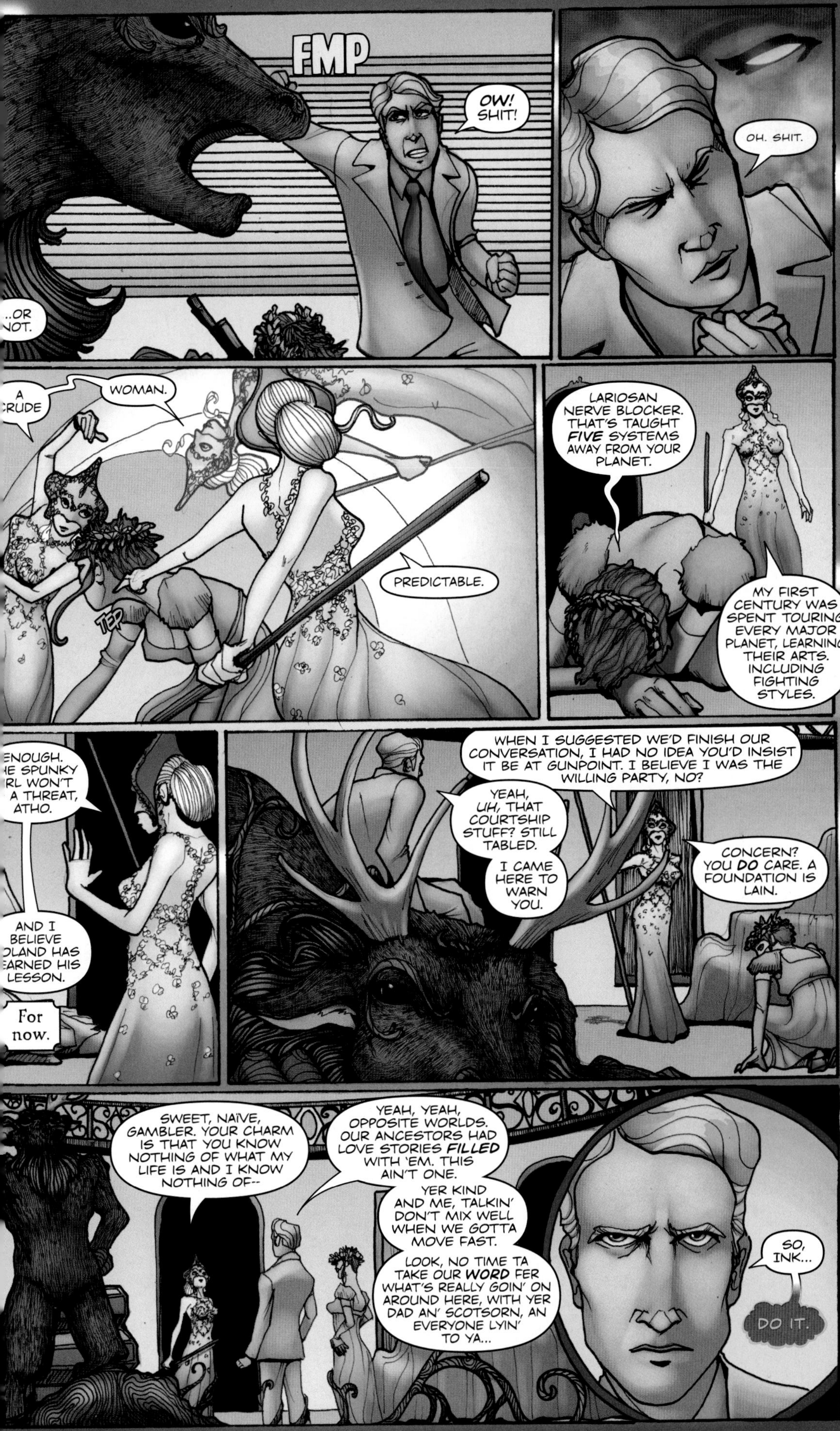
FMP
OW! SHIT!
OH. SHIT.
...OR NOT.
A CRUDE
WOMAN.
PREDICTABLE.
TEP
LARIOSAN NERVE BLOCKER. THAT'S TAUGHT FIVE SYSTEMS AWAY FROM YOUR PLANET.
MY FIRST CENTURY WAS SPENT TOURING EVERY MAJOR PLANET, LEARNING THEIR ARTS. INCLUDING FIGHTING STYLES.
ENOUGH. THE SPUNKY IRL WON'T A THREAT, ATHO.
AND I BELIEVE OLAND HAS EARNED HIS LESSON.
For now.
WHEN I SUGGESTED WE'D FINISH OUR CONVERSATION, I HAD NO IDEA YOU'D INSIST IT BE AT GUNPOINT. I BELIEVE I WAS THE WILLING PARTY, NO?
YEAH, UH, THAT COURTSHIP STUFF? STILL TABLED.
I CAME HERE TO WARN YOU.
CONCERN? YOU DO CARE. A FOUNDATION IS LAIN.
SWEET, NAÏVE, GAMBLER. YOUR CHARM IS THAT YOU KNOW NOTHING OF WHAT MY LIFE IS AND I KNOW NOTHING OF--
YEAH, YEAH, OPPOSITE WORLDS. OUR ANCESTORS HAD LOVE STORIES FILLED WITH 'EM. THIS AIN'T ONE.
YER KIND AND ME, TALKIN' DON'T MIX WELL WHEN WE GOTTA MOVE FAST.
LOOK, NO TIME TA TAKE OUR WORD FER WHAT'S REALLY GOIN' ON AROUND HERE, WITH YER DAD AN' SCOTSORN, AN EVERYONE LYIN' TO YA...
SO, INK...
DO IT.

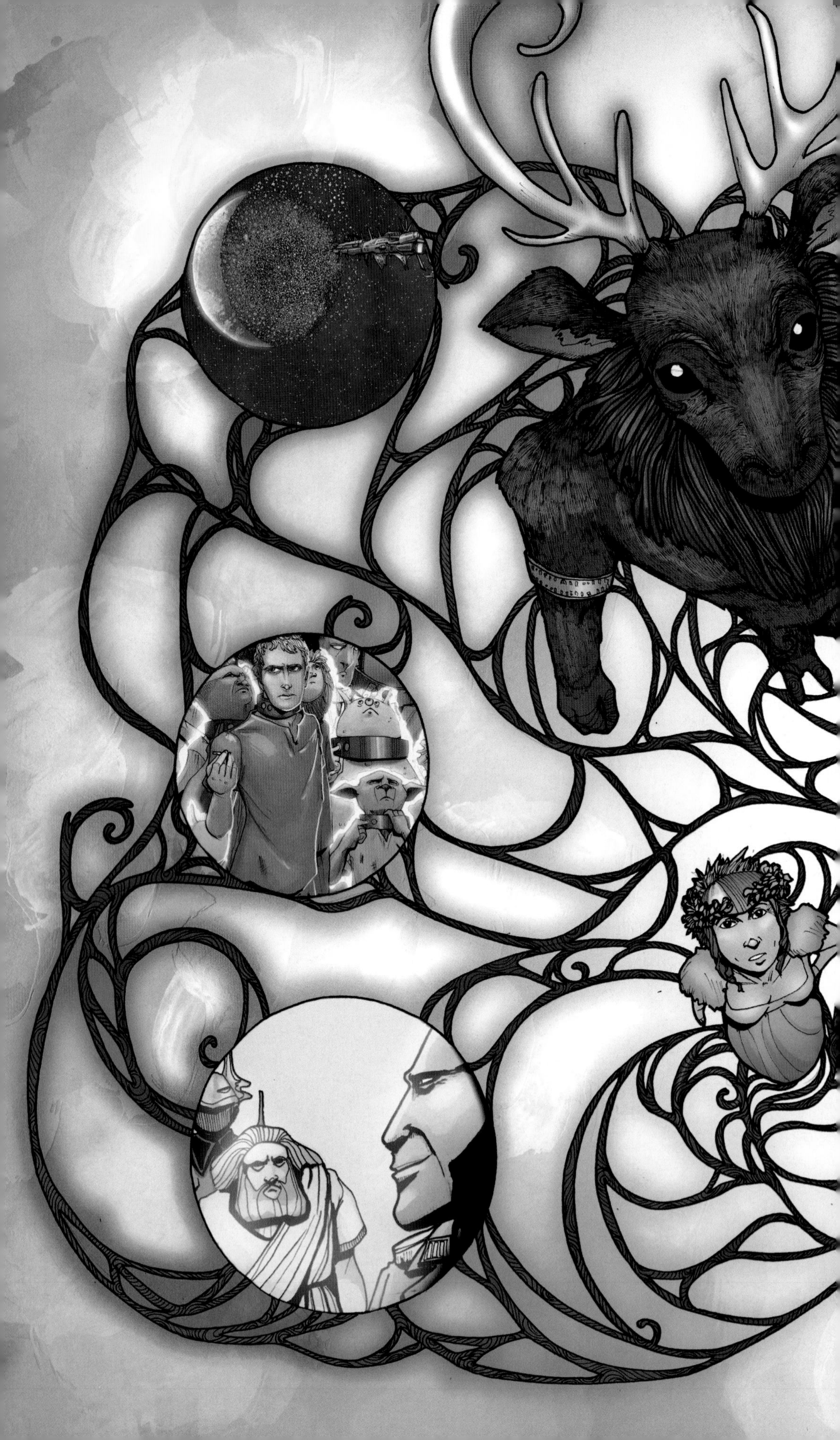

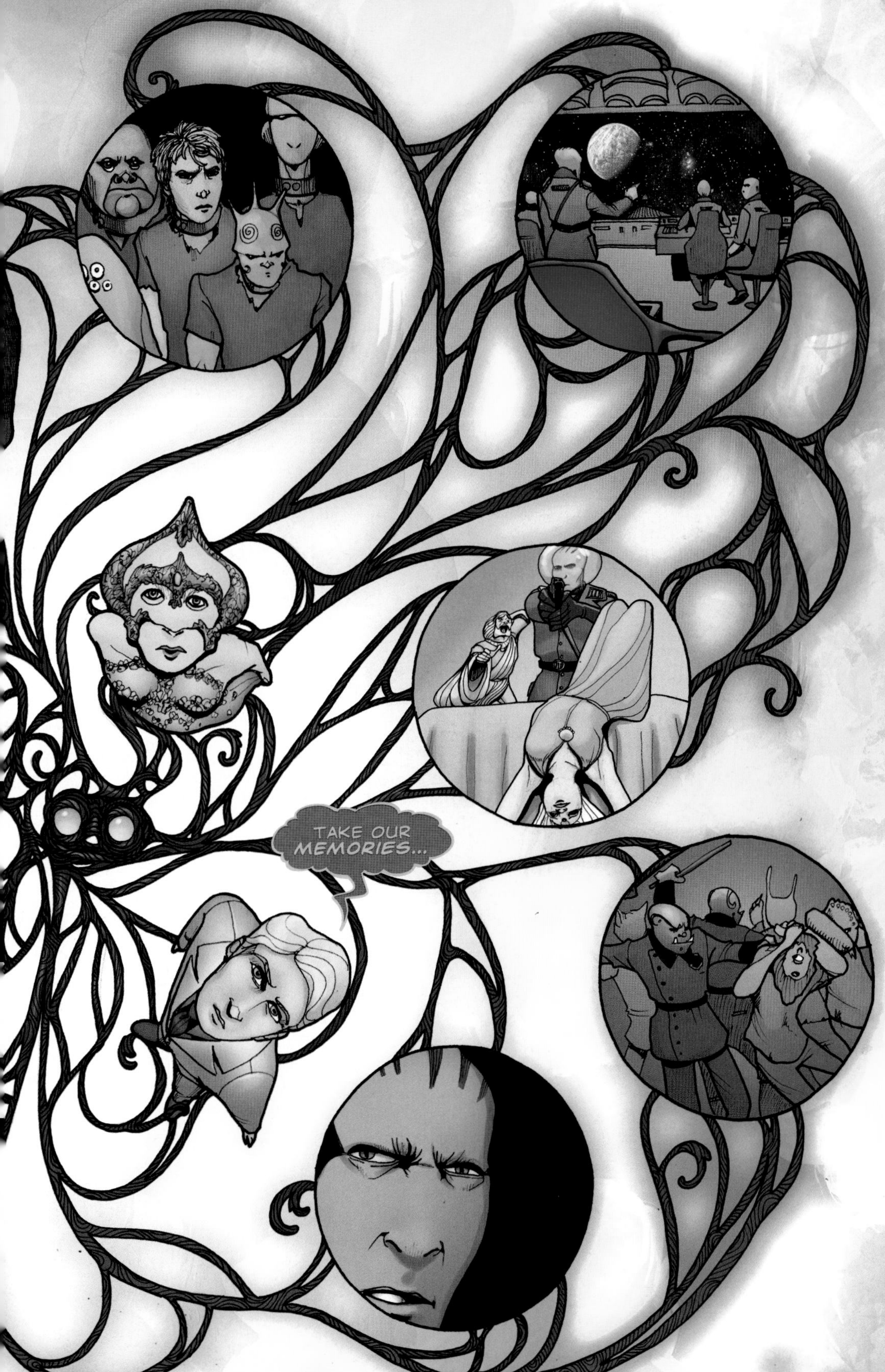
TAKE OUR MEMORIES...

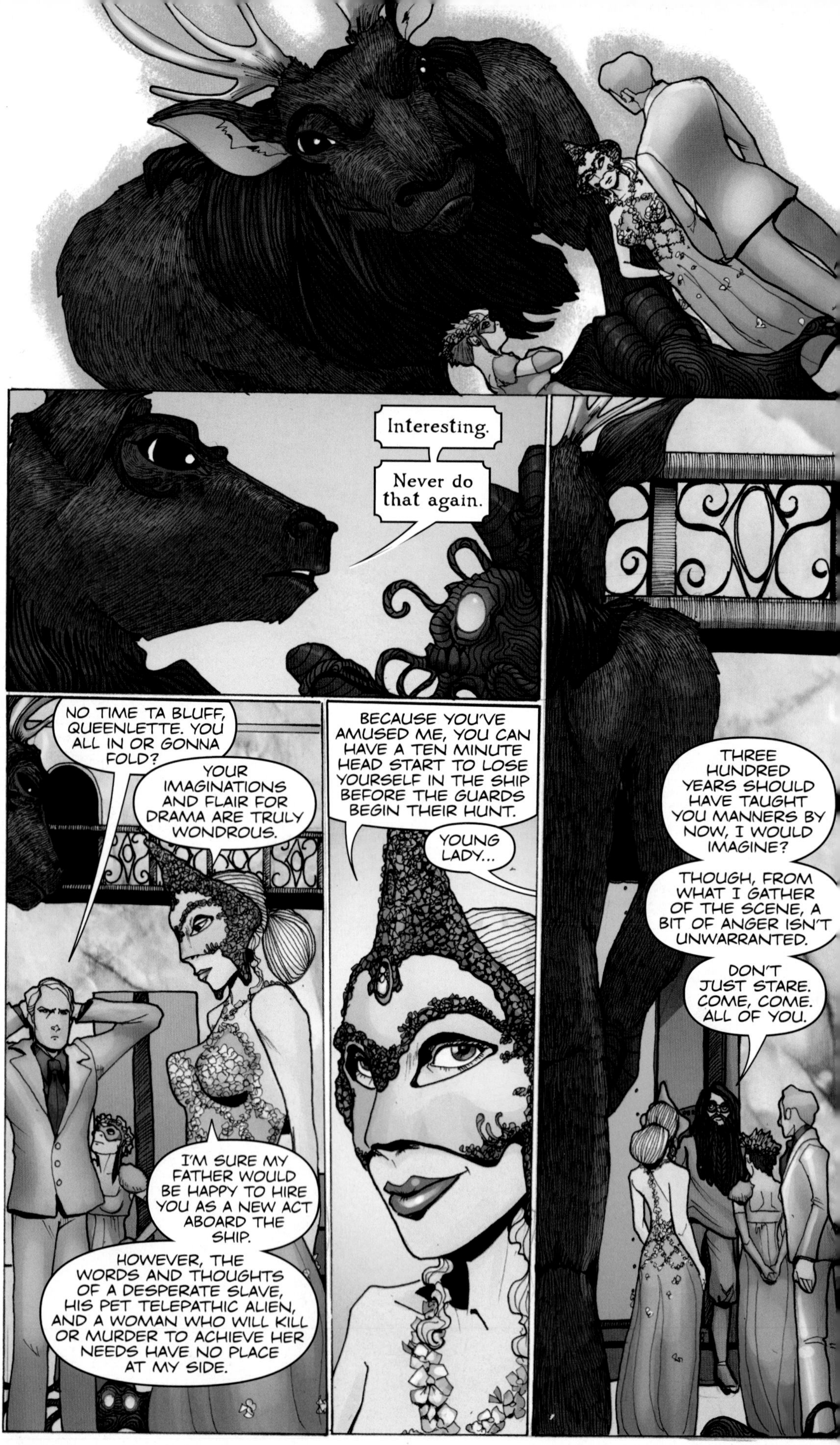

Interesting.
Never do that again.
NO TIME TA BLUFF, QUEENLETTE. YOU ALL IN OR GONNA FOLD?
YOUR IMAGINATIONS AND FLAIR FOR DRAMA ARE TRULY WONDROUS.
I'M SURE MY FATHER WOULD BE HAPPY TO HIRE YOU AS A NEW ACT ABOARD THE SHIP.
HOWEVER, THE WORDS AND THOUGHTS OF A DESPERATE SLAVE, HIS PET TELEPATHIC ALIEN, AND A WOMAN WHO WILL KILL OR MURDER TO ACHIEVE HER NEEDS HAVE NO PLACE AT MY SIDE.
BECAUSE YOU'VE AMUSED ME, YOU CAN HAVE A TEN MINUTE HEAD START TO LOSE YOURSELF IN THE SHIP BEFORE THE GUARDS BEGIN THEIR HUNT.
YOUNG LADY...
THREE HUNDRED YEARS SHOULD HAVE TAUGHT YOU MANNERS BY NOW, I WOULD IMAGINE?
THOUGH, FROM WHAT I GATHER OF THE SCENE, A BIT OF ANGER ISN'T UNWARRANTED.
DON'T JUST STARE. COME, COME. ALL OF YOU.

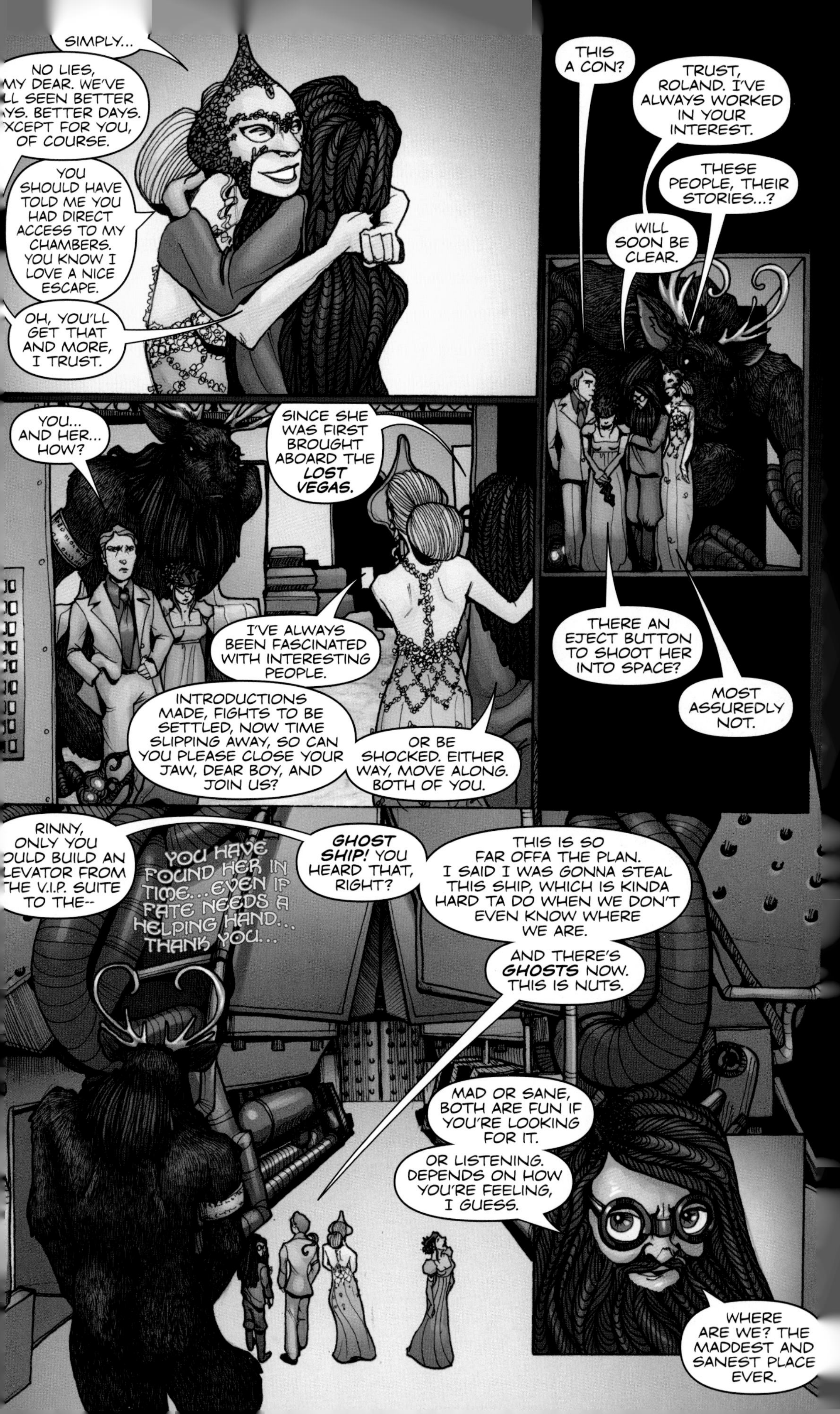
SIMPLY...
NO LIES, MY DEAR. WE'VE LL SEEN BETTER YS. BETTER DAYS. XCEPT FOR YOU, OF COURSE.
YOU SHOULD HAVE TOLD ME YOU HAD DIRECT ACCESS TO MY CHAMBERS. YOU KNOW I LOVE A NICE ESCAPE.
OH, YOU'LL GET THAT AND MORE, I TRUST.
YOU... AND HER... HOW?
SINCE SHE WAS FIRST BROUGHT ABOARD THE **LOST VEGAS.**
I'VE ALWAYS BEEN FASCINATED WITH INTERESTING PEOPLE.
INTRODUCTIONS MADE, FIGHTS TO BE SETTLED, NOW TIME SLIPPING AWAY, SO CAN YOU PLEASE CLOSE YOUR JAW, DEAR BOY, AND JOIN US?
OR BE SHOCKED. EITHER WAY, MOVE ALONG. BOTH OF YOU.
THIS A CON?
TRUST, ROLAND. I'VE ALWAYS WORKED IN YOUR INTEREST.
THESE PEOPLE, THEIR STORIES...?
WILL SOON BE CLEAR.
THERE AN EJECT BUTTON TO SHOOT HER INTO SPACE?
MOST ASSUREDLY NOT.
RINNY, ONLY YOU OULD BUILD AN LEVATOR FROM THE V.I.P. SUITE TO THE--
YOU HAVE FOUND HER IN TIME... EVEN IF FATE NEEDS A HELPING HAND... THANK YOU...
GHOST SHIP! YOU HEARD THAT, RIGHT?
THIS IS SO FAR OFFA THE PLAN. I SAID I WAS GONNA STEAL THIS SHIP, WHICH IS KINDA HARD TA DO WHEN WE DON'T EVEN KNOW WHERE WE ARE.
AND THERE'S **GHOSTS** NOW. THIS IS NUTS.
MAD OR SANE, BOTH ARE FUN IF YOU'RE LOOKING FOR IT.
OR LISTENING. DEPENDS ON HOW YOU'RE FEELING, I GUESS.
WHERE ARE WE? THE MADDEST AND SANEST PLACE EVER.

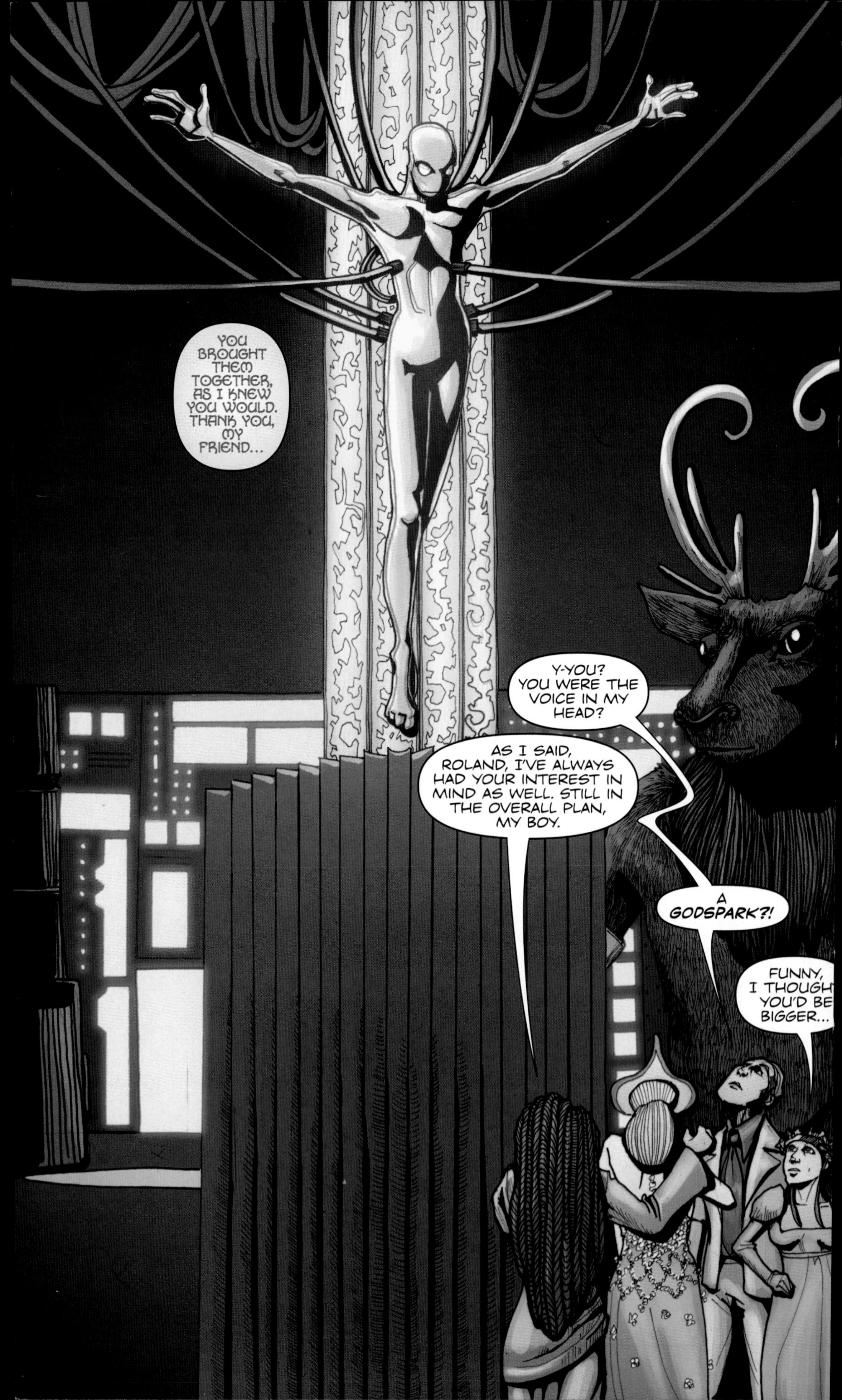

YOU BROUGHT THEM TOGETHER, AS I KNEW YOU WOULD. THANK YOU, MY FRIEND...
Y-YOU? YOU WERE THE VOICE IN MY HEAD?
AS I SAID, ROLAND, I'VE ALWAYS HAD YOUR INTEREST IN MIND AS WELL. STILL IN THE OVERALL PLAN, MY BOY.
A GODSPARK?!
FUNNY, I THOUGHT YOU'D BE BIGGER...

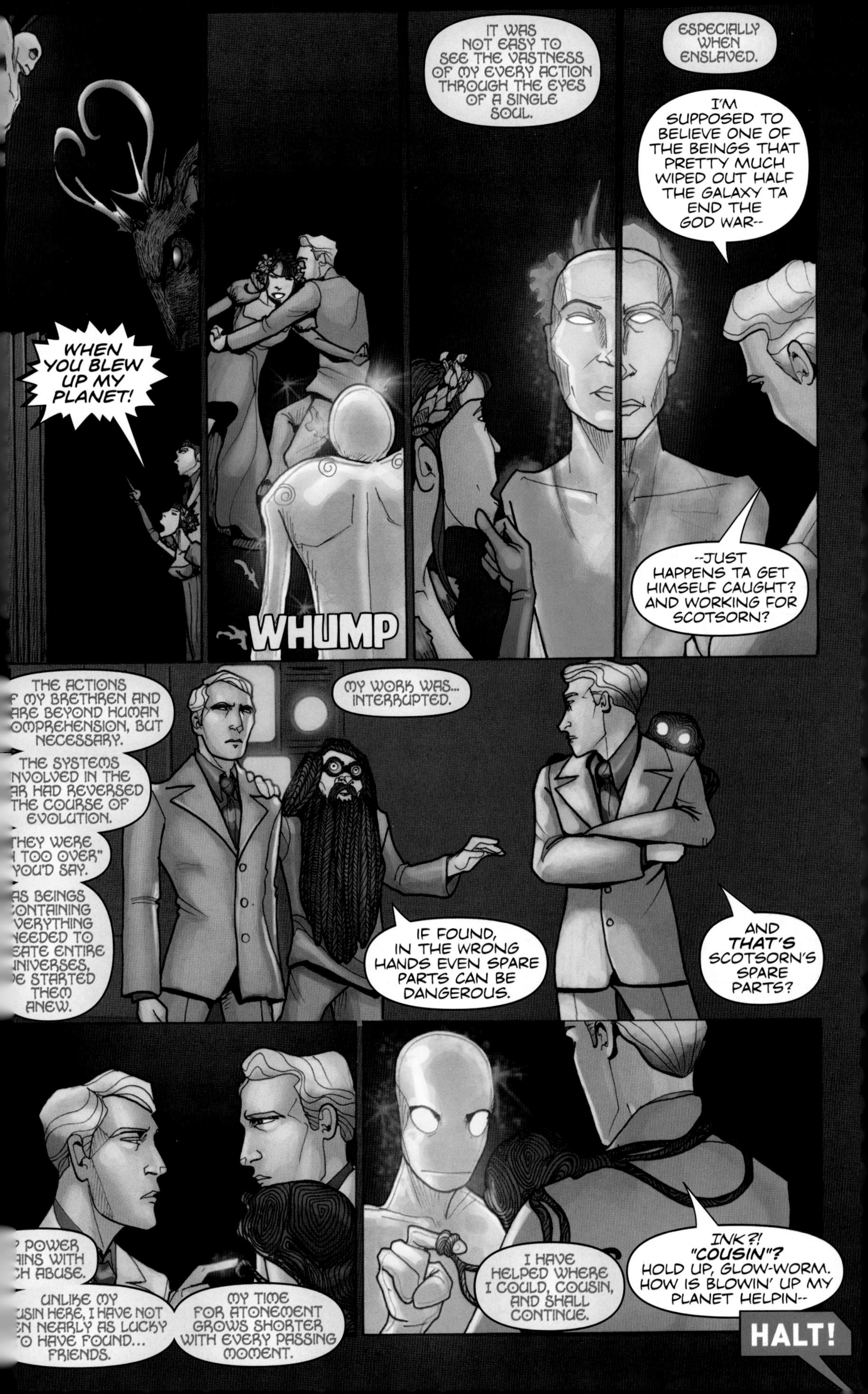
WHEN YOU BLEW UP MY PLANET!
WHUMP
IT WAS NOT EASY TO SEE THE VASTNESS OF MY EVERY ACTION THROUGH THE EYES OF A SINGLE SOUL.
ESPECIALLY WHEN ENSLAVED.
I'M SUPPOSED TO BELIEVE ONE OF THE BEINGS THAT PRETTY MUCH WIPED OUT HALF THE GALAXY TA END THE GOD WAR--
--JUST HAPPENS TA GET HIMSELF CAUGHT? AND WORKING FOR SCOTSORN?
THE ACTIONS F MY BRETHREN AND ARE BEYOND HUMAN OMPREHENSION, BUT NECESSARY.
THE SYSTEMS NVOLVED IN THE AR HAD REVERSED THE COURSE OF EVOLUTION.
THEY WERE N TOO OVER" YOU'D SAY.
AS BEINGS CONTAINING VERYTHING NEEDED TO EATE ENTIRE NIVERSES, E STARTED THEM ANEW.
MY WORK WAS... INTERRUPTED.
IF FOUND, IN THE WRONG HANDS EVEN SPARE PARTS CAN BE DANGEROUS.
AND THAT'S SCOTSORN'S SPARE PARTS?
POWER AINS WITH CH ABUSE.
UNLIKE MY OUSIN HERE, I HAVE NOT EN NEARLY AS LUCKY TO HAVE FOUND... FRIENDS.
MY TIME FOR ATONEMENT GROWS SHORTER WITH EVERY PASSING MOMENT.
I HAVE HELPED WHERE I COULD, COUSIN, AND SHALL CONTINUE.
INK?! "COUSIN"? HOLD UP, GLOW-WORM. HOW IS BLOWIN' UP MY PLANET HELPIN--
HALT!

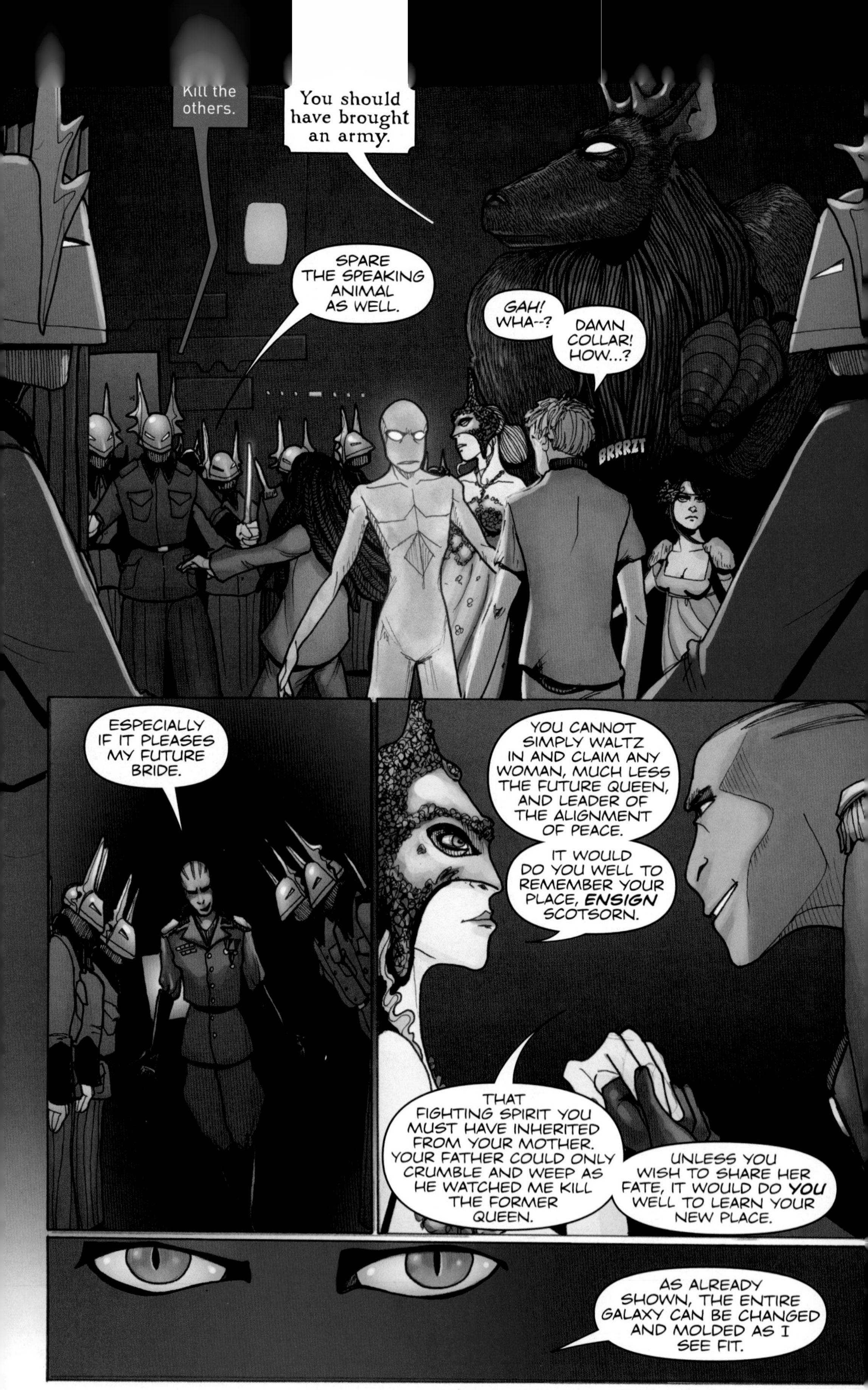

Kill the others.
You should have brought an army.
SPARE THE SPEAKING ANIMAL AS WELL.
GAH! WHA--?
DAMN COLLAR! HOW...?
BRRRZT
ESPECIALLY IF IT PLEASES MY FUTURE BRIDE.
YOU CANNOT SIMPLY WALTZ IN AND CLAIM ANY WOMAN, MUCH LESS THE FUTURE QUEEN, AND LEADER OF THE ALIGNMENT OF PEACE.
IT WOULD DO YOU WELL TO REMEMBER YOUR PLACE, ENSIGN SCOTSORN.
THAT FIGHTING SPIRIT YOU MUST HAVE INHERITED FROM YOUR MOTHER. YOUR FATHER COULD ONLY CRUMBLE AND WEEP AS HE WATCHED ME KILL THE FORMER QUEEN.
UNLESS YOU WISH TO SHARE HER FATE, IT WOULD DO YOU WELL TO LEARN YOUR NEW PLACE.
AS ALREADY SHOWN, THE ENTIRE GALAXY CAN BE CHANGED AND MOLDED AS I SEE FIT.

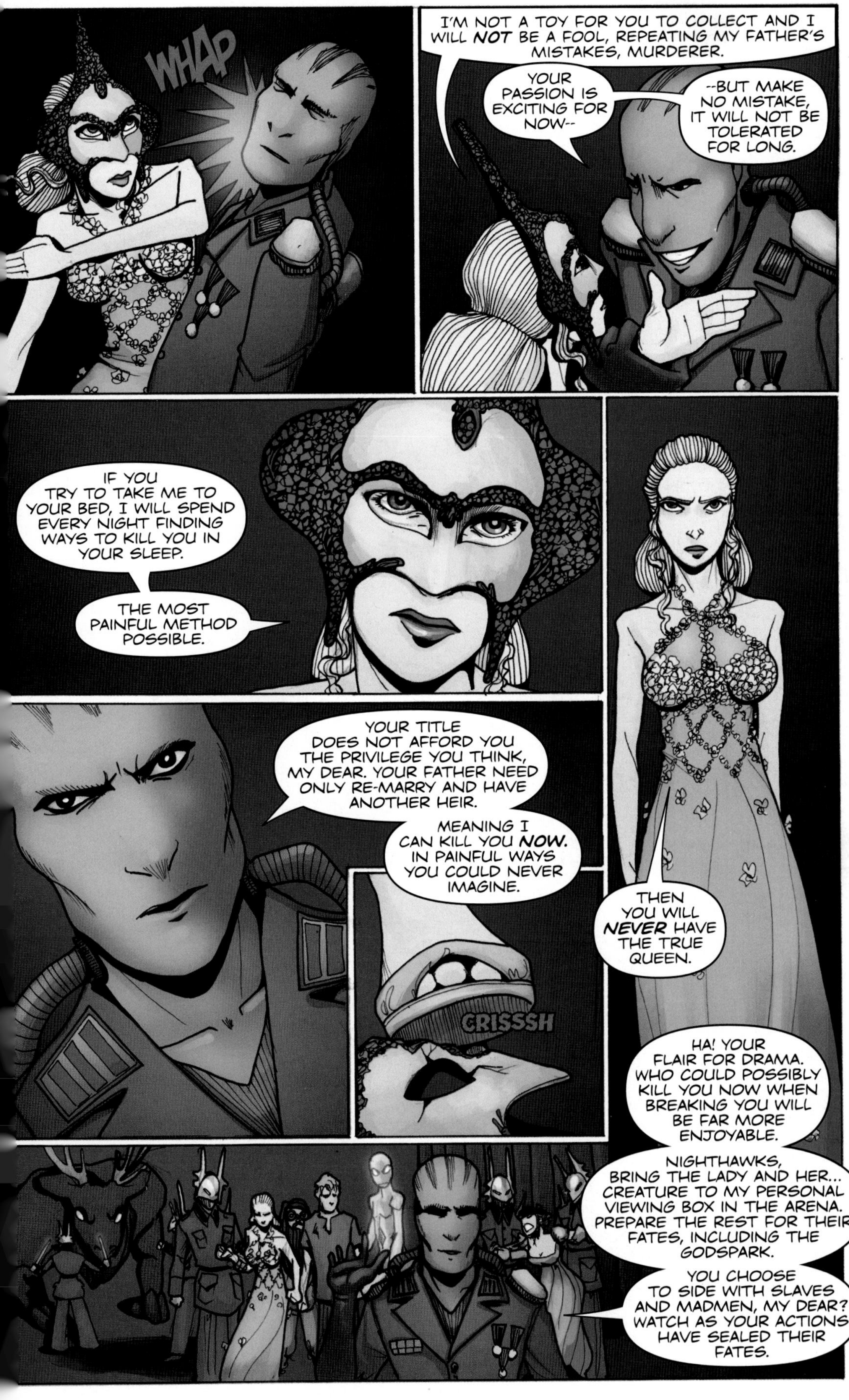
WHAP
I'M NOT A TOY FOR YOU TO COLLECT AND I WILL NOT BE A FOOL, REPEATING MY FATHER'S MISTAKES, MURDERER.
YOUR PASSION IS EXCITING FOR NOW--
--BUT MAKE NO MISTAKE, IT WILL NOT BE TOLERATED FOR LONG.
IF YOU TRY TO TAKE ME TO YOUR BED, I WILL SPEND EVERY NIGHT FINDING WAYS TO KILL YOU IN YOUR SLEEP.
THE MOST PAINFUL METHOD POSSIBLE.
YOUR TITLE DOES NOT AFFORD YOU THE PRIVILEGE YOU THINK, MY DEAR. YOUR FATHER NEED ONLY RE-MARRY AND HAVE ANOTHER HEIR.
MEANING I CAN KILL YOU NOW. IN PAINFUL WAYS YOU COULD NEVER IMAGINE.
CRISSSH
THEN YOU WILL NEVER HAVE THE TRUE QUEEN.
HA! YOUR FLAIR FOR DRAMA. WHO COULD POSSIBLY KILL YOU NOW WHEN BREAKING YOU WILL BE FAR MORE ENJOYABLE.
NIGHTHAWKS, BRING THE LADY AND HER... CREATURE TO MY PERSONAL VIEWING BOX IN THE ARENA. PREPARE THE REST FOR THEIR FATES, INCLUDING THE GODSPARK.
YOU CHOOSE TO SIDE WITH SLAVES AND MADMEN, MY DEAR? WATCH AS YOUR ACTIONS HAVE SEALED THEIR FATES.

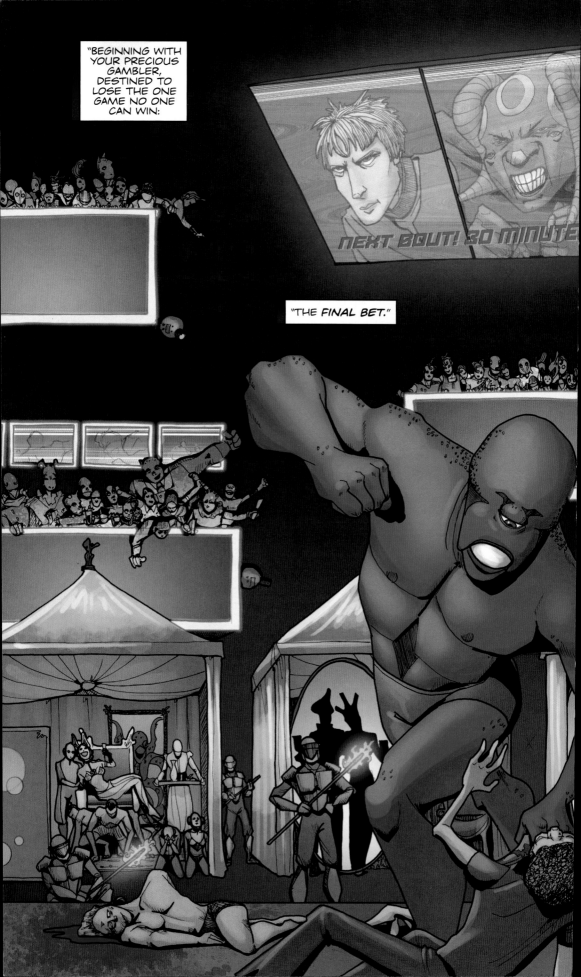

"BEGINNING WITH YOUR PRECIOUS GAMBLER, DESTINED TO LOSE THE ONE GAME NO ONE CAN WIN:

NEXT BOUT! 30 MINUTE

"THE *FINAL BET.*"

END THIRD HAND

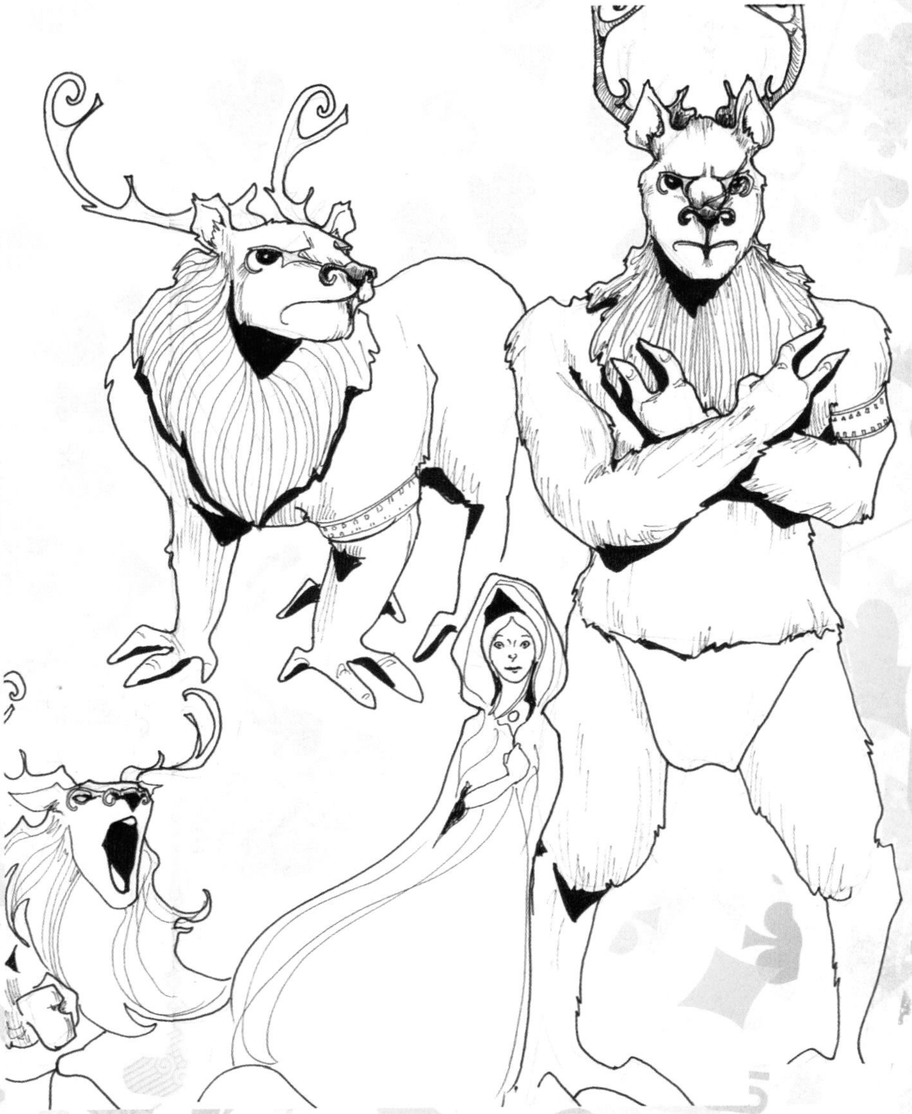

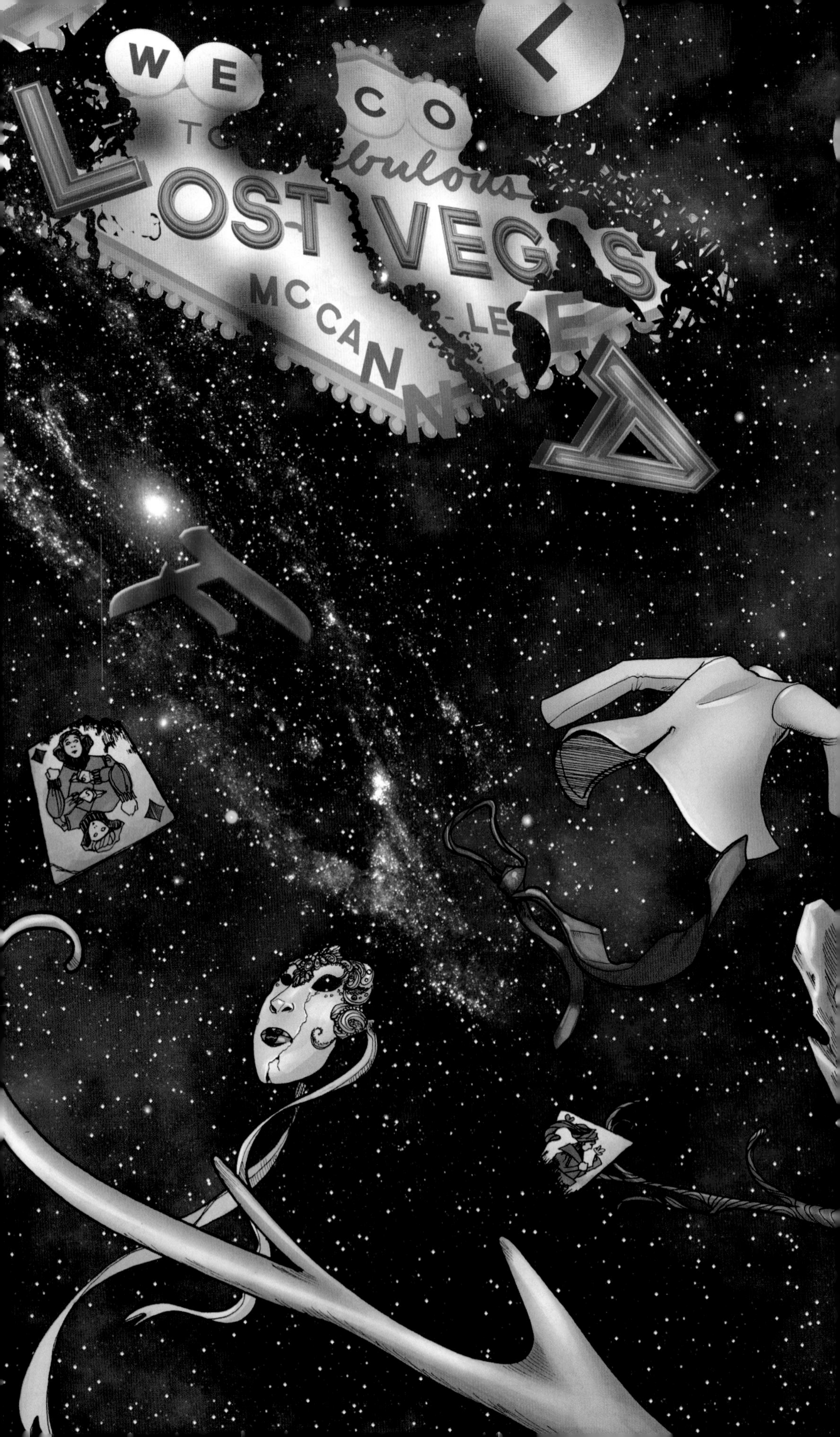
WE
CO
L
TO
bulous
LOST VEG S
MCCAN
-LE
N

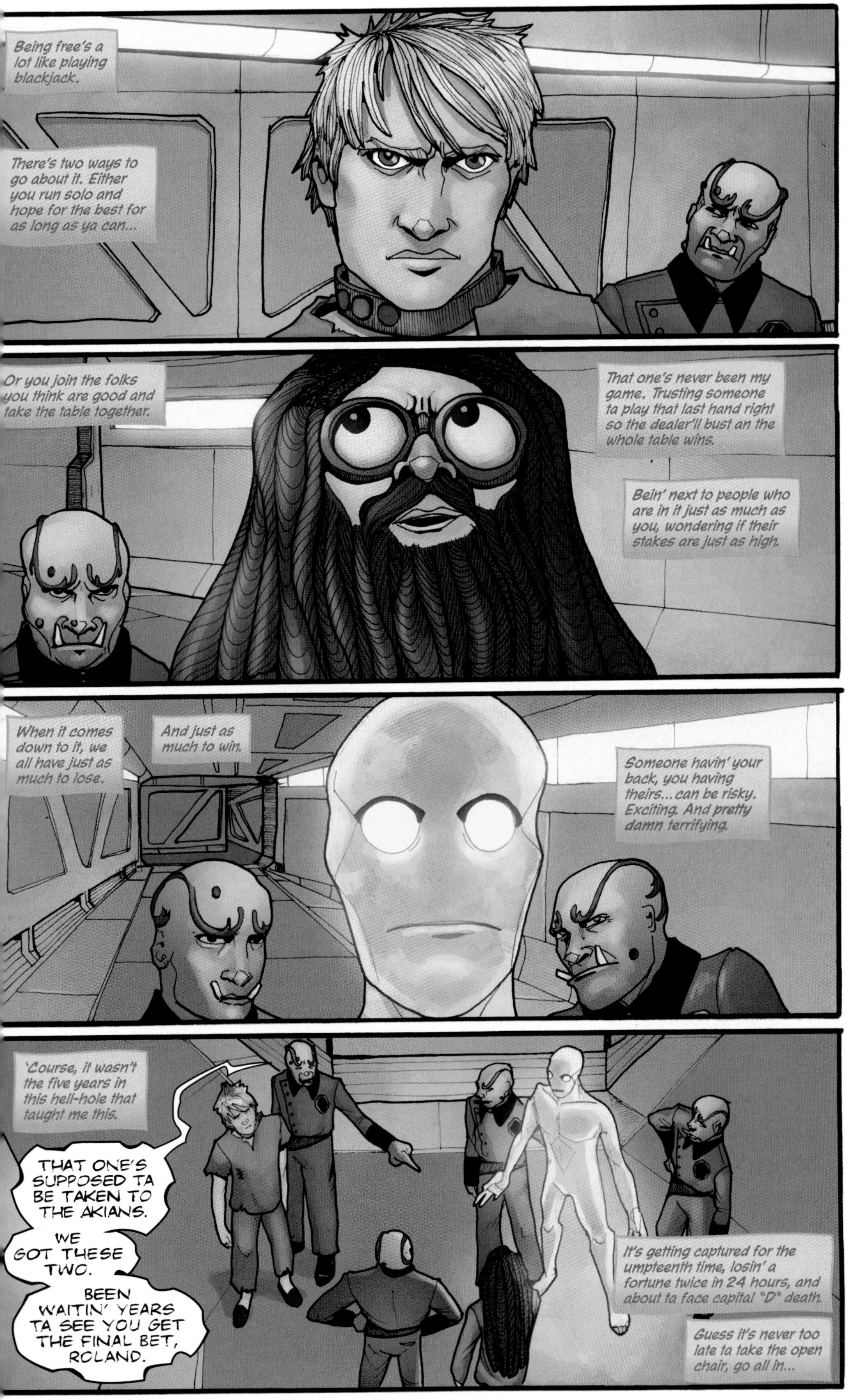

Being free's a lot like playing blackjack.
There's two ways to go about it. Either you run solo and hope for the best for as long as ya can...
Or you join the folks you think are good and take the table together.
That one's never been my game. Trusting someone ta play that last hand right so the dealer'll bust an the whole table wins.
Bein' next to people who are in it just as much as you, wondering if their stakes are just as high.
When it comes down to it, we all have just as much to lose.
And just as much to win.
Someone havin' your back, you having theirs... can be risky. Exciting. And pretty damn terrifying.
'Course, it wasn't the five years in this hell-hole that taught me this.
THAT ONE'S SUPPOSED TA BE TAKEN TO THE AKIANS.
WE GOT THESE TWO.
BEEN WAITIN' YEARS TA SEE YOU GET THE FINAL BET, ROLAND.
It's getting captured for the umpteenth time, losin' a fortune twice in 24 hours, and about ta face capital "D" death.
Guess it's never too late ta take the open chair, go all in...

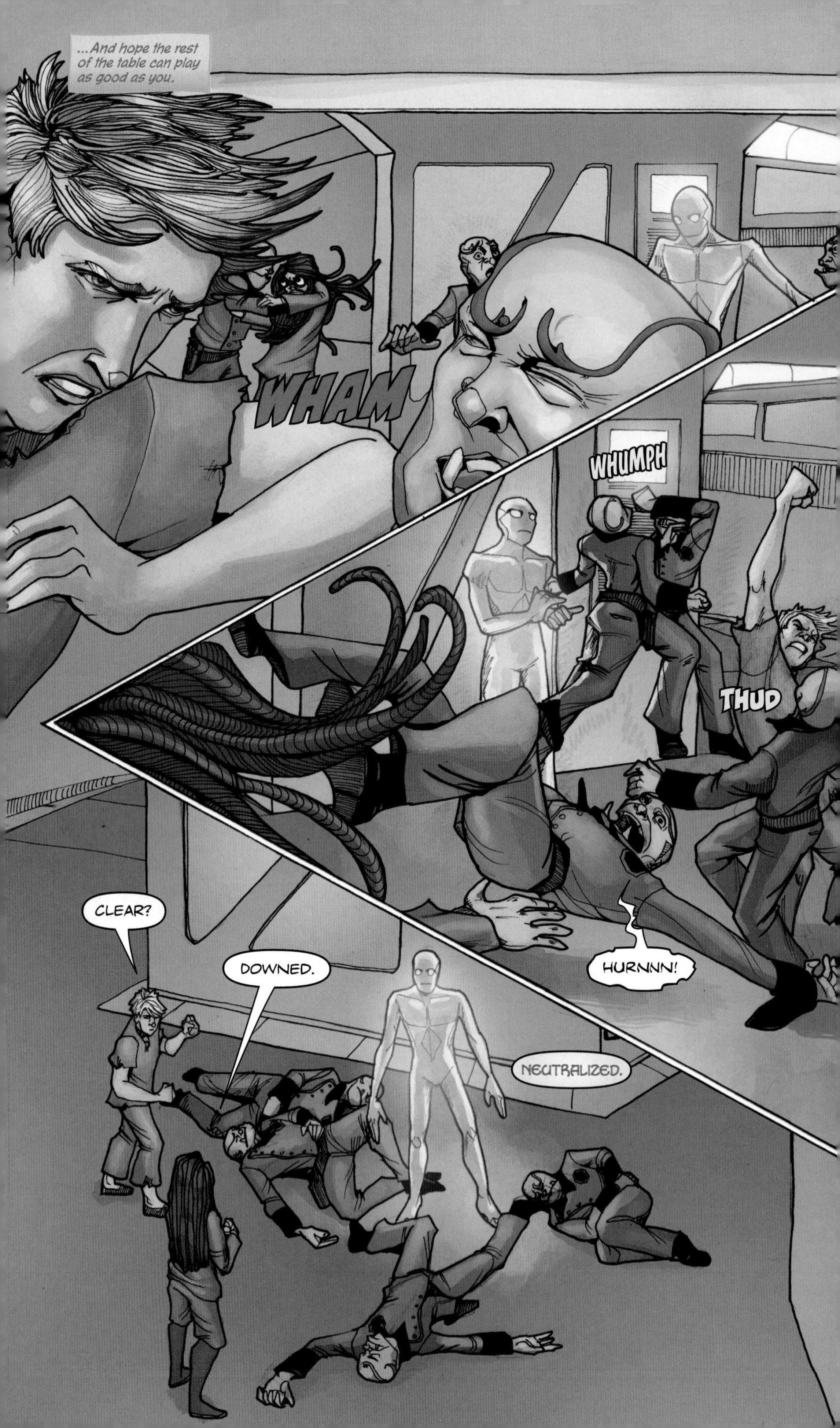
...And hope the rest of the table can play as good as you.
WHAM
WHUMPH
THUD
HURNNN!
CLEAR?
DOWNED.
NEUTRALIZED.

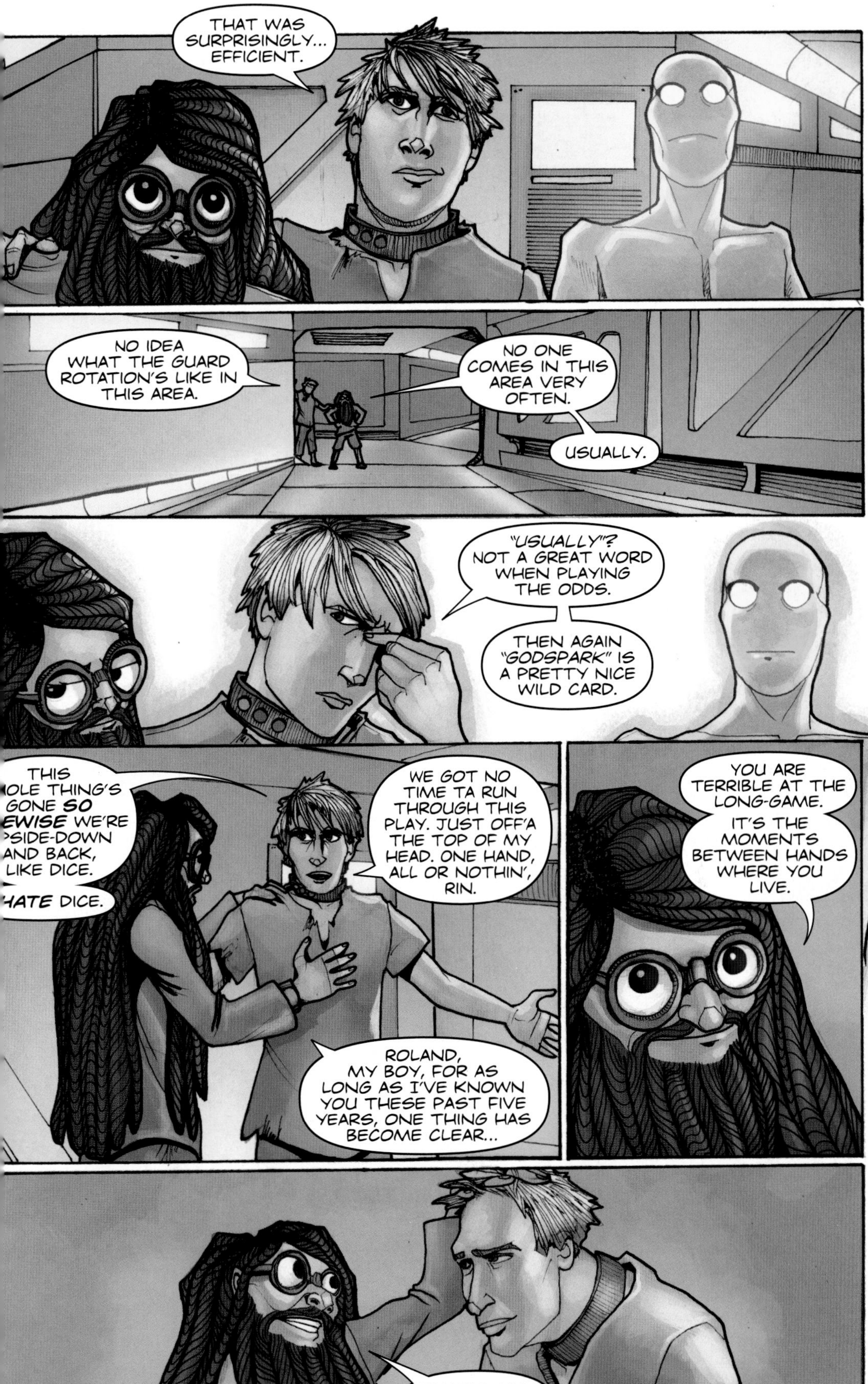
THAT WAS SURPRISINGLY... EFFICIENT.
NO IDEA WHAT THE GUARD ROTATION'S LIKE IN THIS AREA.
NO ONE COMES IN THIS AREA VERY OFTEN.
USUALLY.
"USUALLY"? NOT A GREAT WORD WHEN PLAYING THE ODDS.
THEN AGAIN "GODSPARK" IS A PRETTY NICE WILD CARD.
THIS
OLE THING'S
GONE **SO**
EWISE WE'RE
PSIDE-DOWN
AND BACK,
LIKE DICE.
HATE DICE.
WE GOT NO TIME TA RUN THROUGH THIS PLAY. JUST OFF'A THE TOP OF MY HEAD. ONE HAND, ALL OR NOTHIN', RIN.
ROLAND, MY BOY, FOR AS LONG AS I'VE KNOWN YOU THESE PAST FIVE YEARS, ONE THING HAS BECOME CLEAR...
YOU ARE TERRIBLE AT THE LONG-GAME.
IT'S THE MOMENTS BETWEEN HANDS WHERE YOU LIVE.
THAT'S WHY THIS IS GOING TO WORK.

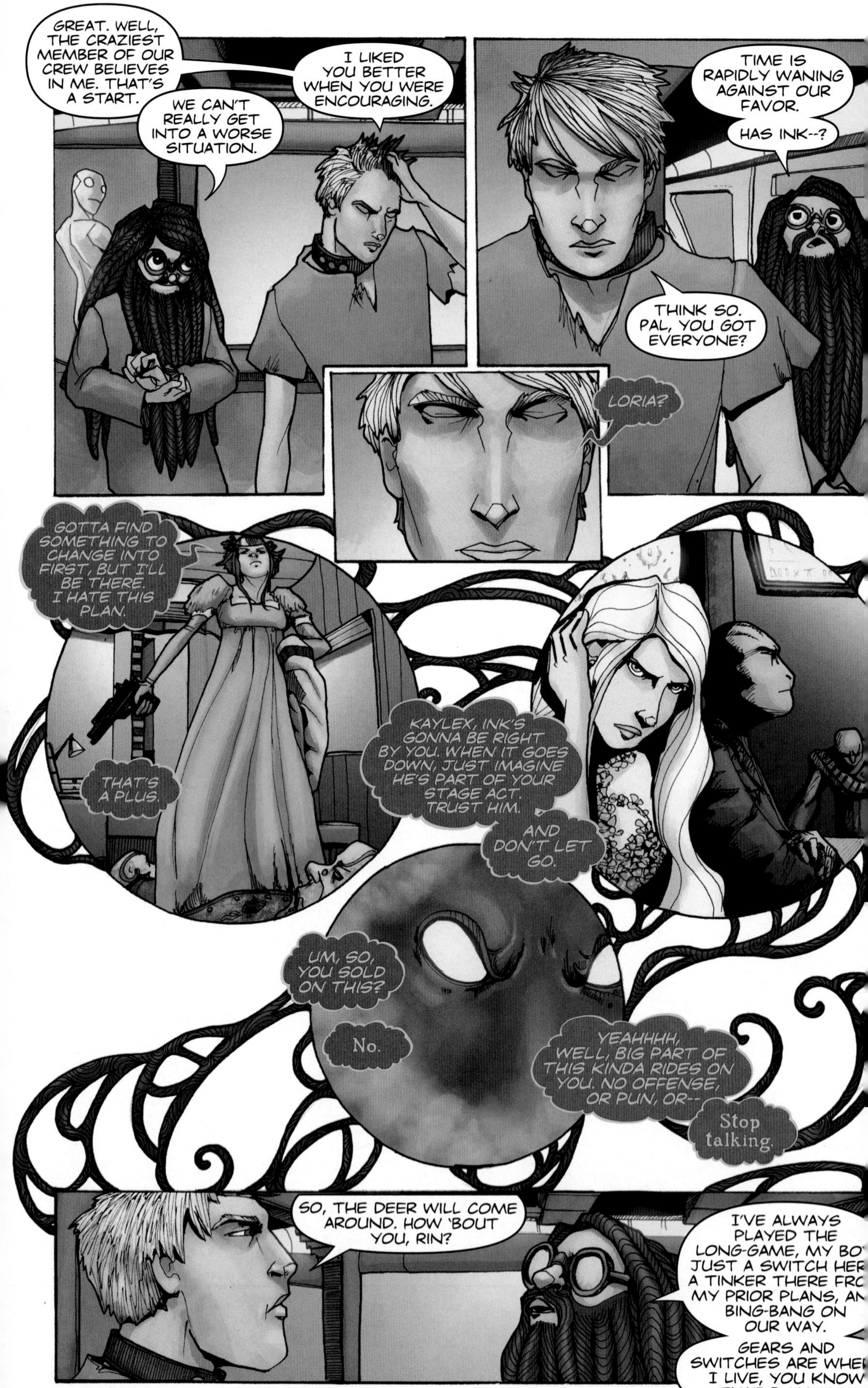

GREAT. WELL, THE CRAZIEST MEMBER OF OUR CREW BELIEVES IN ME. THAT'S A START.
I LIKED YOU BETTER WHEN YOU WERE ENCOURAGING.
WE CAN'T REALLY GET INTO A WORSE SITUATION.
TIME IS RAPIDLY WANING AGAINST OUR FAVOR.
HAS INK--?
THINK SO. PAL, YOU GOT EVERYONE?
LORIA?
GOTTA FIND SOMETHING TO CHANGE INTO FIRST, BUT I'LL BE THERE. I HATE THIS PLAN.
THAT'S A PLUS.
KAYLEX, INK'S GONNA BE RIGHT BY YOU. WHEN IT GOES DOWN, JUST IMAGINE HE'S PART OF YOUR STAGE ACT. TRUST HIM.
AND DON'T LET GO.
UM, SO, YOU SOLD ON THIS?
No.
YEAHHHH, WELL, BIG PART OF THIS KINDA RIDES ON YOU. NO OFFENSE, OR PUN, OR--
Stop talking.
SO, THE DEER WILL COME AROUND. HOW 'BOUT YOU, RIN?
I'VE ALWAYS PLAYED THE LONG-GAME, MY BO JUST A SWITCH HER A TINKER THERE FRO MY PRIOR PLANS, AN BING-BANG ON OUR WAY.
GEARS AND SWITCHES ARE WHE I LIVE, YOU KNOW THAT BY KNOW.

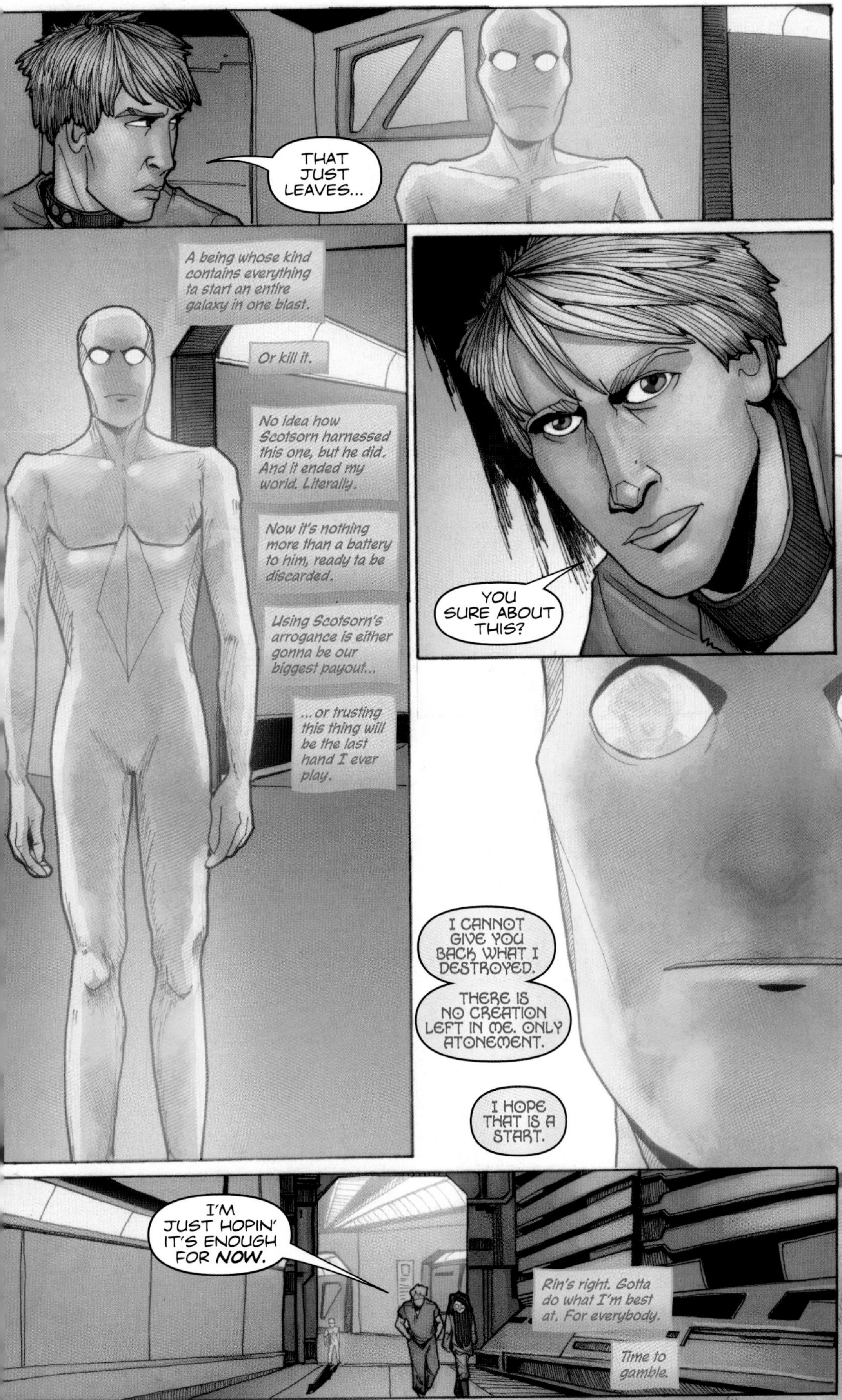
THAT JUST LEAVES...
A being whose kind contains everything ta start an entire galaxy in one blast.
Or kill it.
No idea how Scotsorn harnessed this one, but he did. And it ended my world. Literally.
Now it's nothing more than a battery to him, ready ta be discarded.
Using Scotsorn's arrogance is either gonna be our biggest payout...
...or trusting this thing will be the last hand I ever play.
YOU SURE ABOUT THIS?
I CANNOT GIVE YOU BACK WHAT I DESTROYED.
THERE IS NO CREATION LEFT IN ME. ONLY ATONEMENT.
I HOPE THAT IS A START.
I'M JUST HOPIN' IT'S ENOUGH FOR NOW.
Rin's right. Gotta do what I'm best at. For everybody.
Time to gamble.

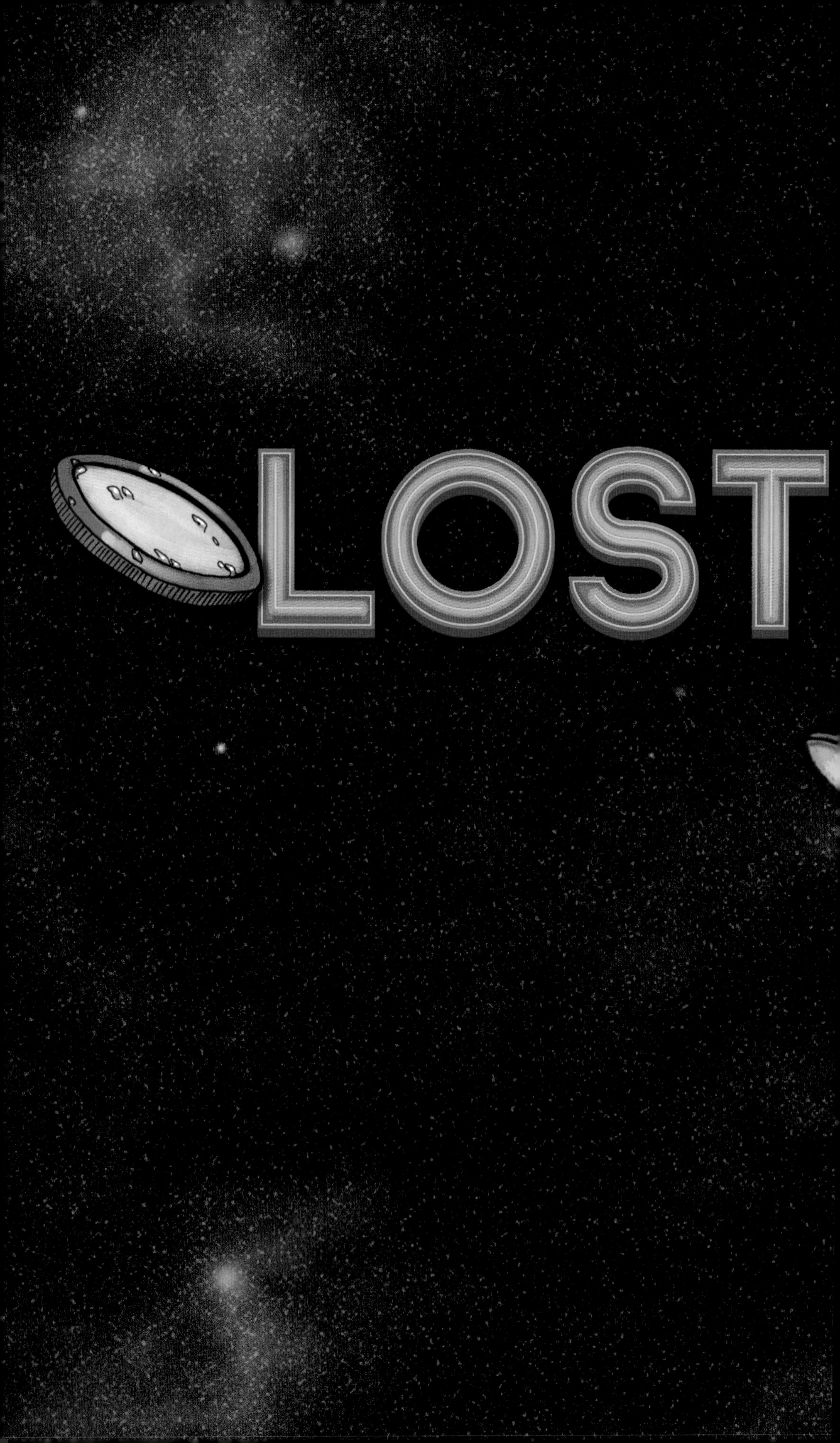
LOST

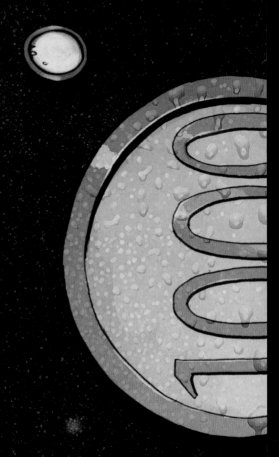

VEGAS

FOURTH HAND | KNOW WHEN TO RUN

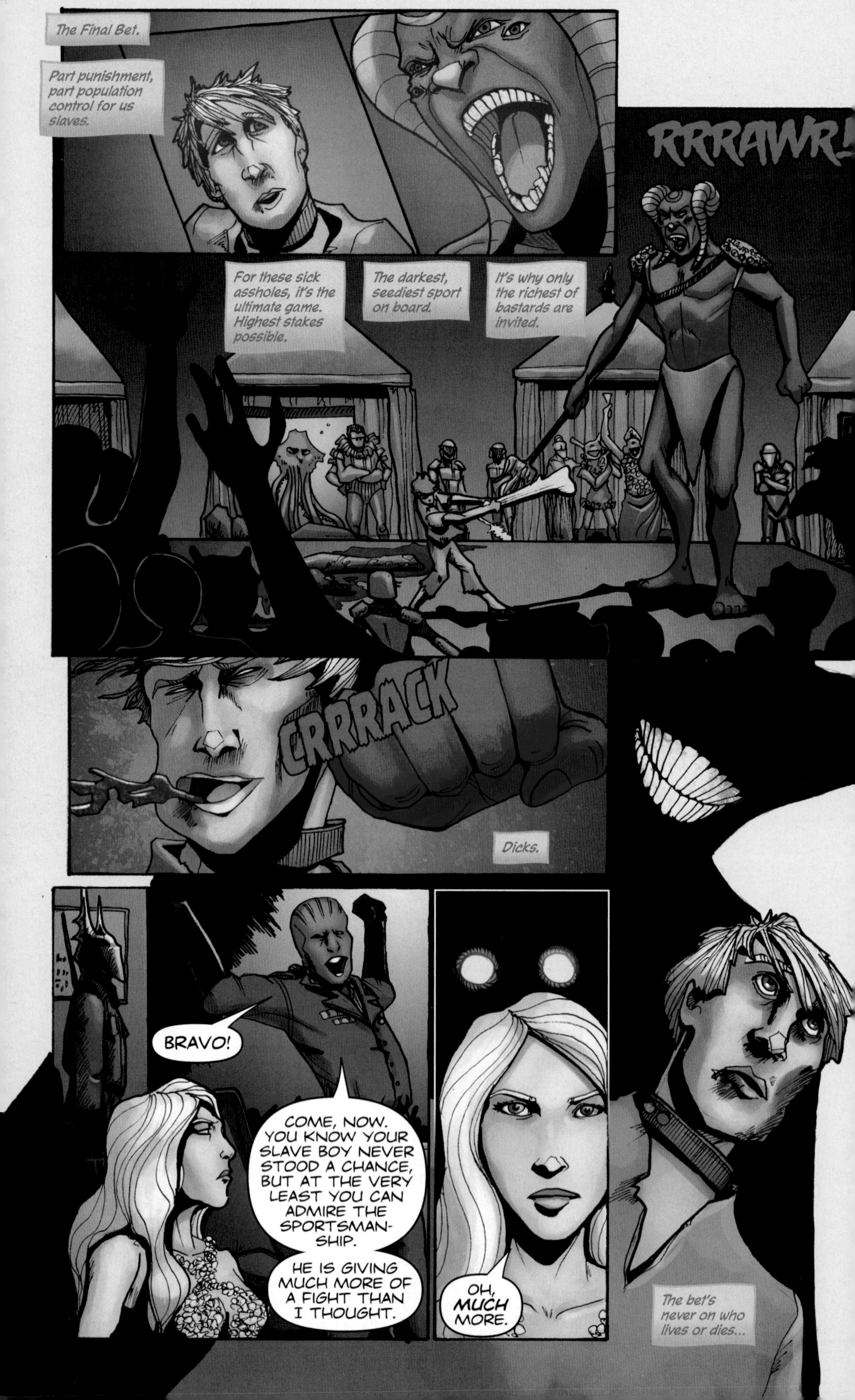
The Final Bet.
Part punishment, part population control for us slaves.
RRRAWR!
For these sick assholes, it's the ultimate game. Highest stakes possible.
The darkest, seediest sport on board.
It's why only the richest of bastards are invited.
CRRRACK
Dicks.
BRAVO!
COME, NOW. YOU KNOW YOUR SLAVE BOY NEVER STOOD A CHANCE, BUT AT THE VERY LEAST YOU CAN ADMIRE THE SPORTSMAN-SHIP.
HE IS GIVING MUCH MORE OF A FIGHT THAN I THOUGHT.
OH, MUCH MORE.
The bet's never on who lives or dies...

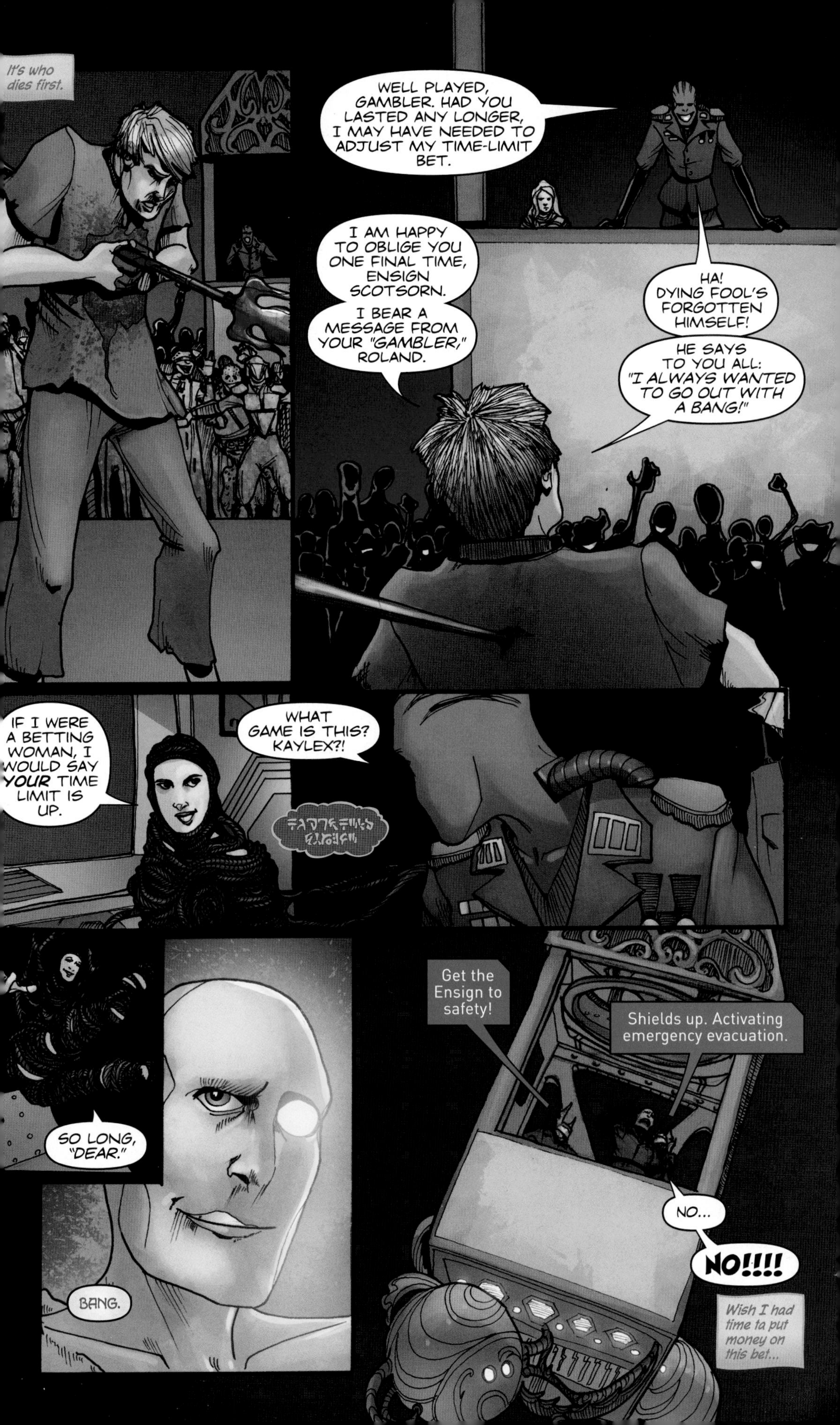
It's who dies first.
WELL PLAYED, GAMBLER. HAD YOU LASTED ANY LONGER, I MAY HAVE NEEDED TO ADJUST MY TIME-LIMIT BET.
I AM HAPPY TO OBLIGE YOU ONE FINAL TIME, ENSIGN SCOTSORN.
I BEAR A MESSAGE FROM YOUR "GAMBLER," ROLAND.
HA! DYING FOOL'S FORGOTTEN HIMSELF!
HE SAYS TO YOU ALL: "I ALWAYS WANTED TO GO OUT WITH A BANG!"
IF I WERE A BETTING WOMAN, I WOULD SAY YOUR TIME LIMIT IS UP.
WHAT GAME IS THIS? KAYLEX?!
SO LONG, "DEAR."
BANG.
Get the Ensign to safety!
Shields up. Activating emergency evacuation.
NO...
NO!!!!
Wish I had time ta put money on this bet...

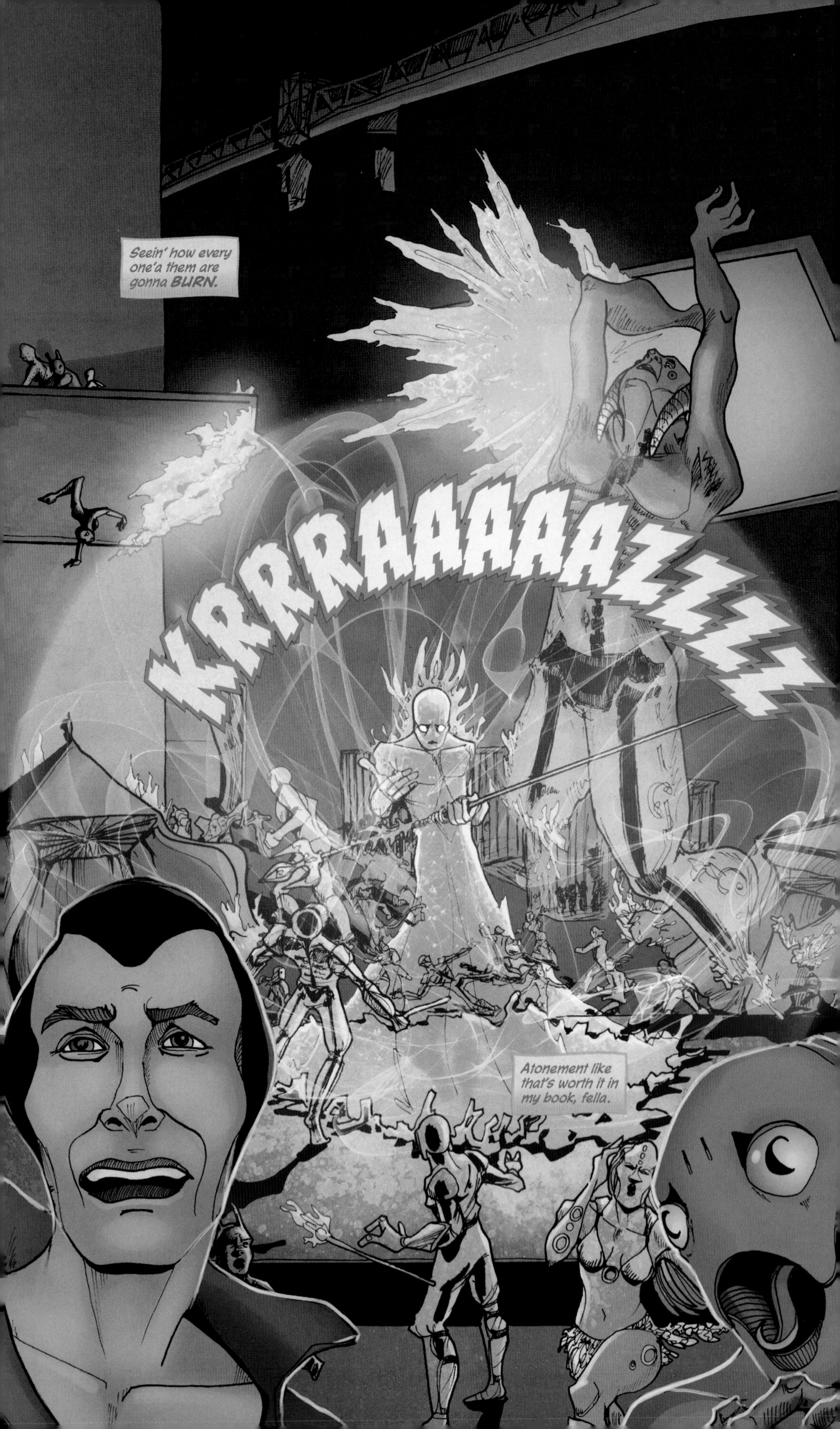
Seein' how every one'a them are gonna BURN.
KRRRAAAAAAZZZZ
Atonement like that's worth it in my book, fella.

WHOA.

IT WOULD APPEAR OUR FRIEND'S SACRIFICE WORKED. WE HAVE LITTLE TIME BEFORE THEY RECOVER, THOUGH!

DON'T WORRY. ATHO'LL BE HERE IN TIME... I HOPE.

Sigh.

SEE?

GODSPARK'S BOOM GAVE US OUR OPENING. IT'S OUR TURN TA MAKE THIS WHOLE SHIP GO BANG.

THE ATMO-SHIELD'S STILL UP. WE BREAK THAT BUBBLE BEFORE THE HULL BELOW CAN BE SEALED--

--THIS HOUSE OF CARDS GOES DOWN. YOU CALCULATED OUR JUMP, BIG GUY?

$$\frac{DE}{Dt}\left[-\frac{1}{r^2}\frac{\partial}{\partial r}(r^2 F)\right]^{-1}$$
$$=\Delta\left[-1+\frac{\beta_d}{\beta}\frac{v\Phi P}{\varnothing}-\frac{4\beta_d}{t_{sc}\beta}\left(1+\frac{\beta}{t_{sc}}\right)^{-2}\right.$$

RIGHT. XACTLY LIKE... WHATEVER. INK, YOU GOT US?

Kaylex is safe?

WOULDN'T DO THIS IF SH WASN'T.

THAT MAKE YOU FEEL BETTER?

No.

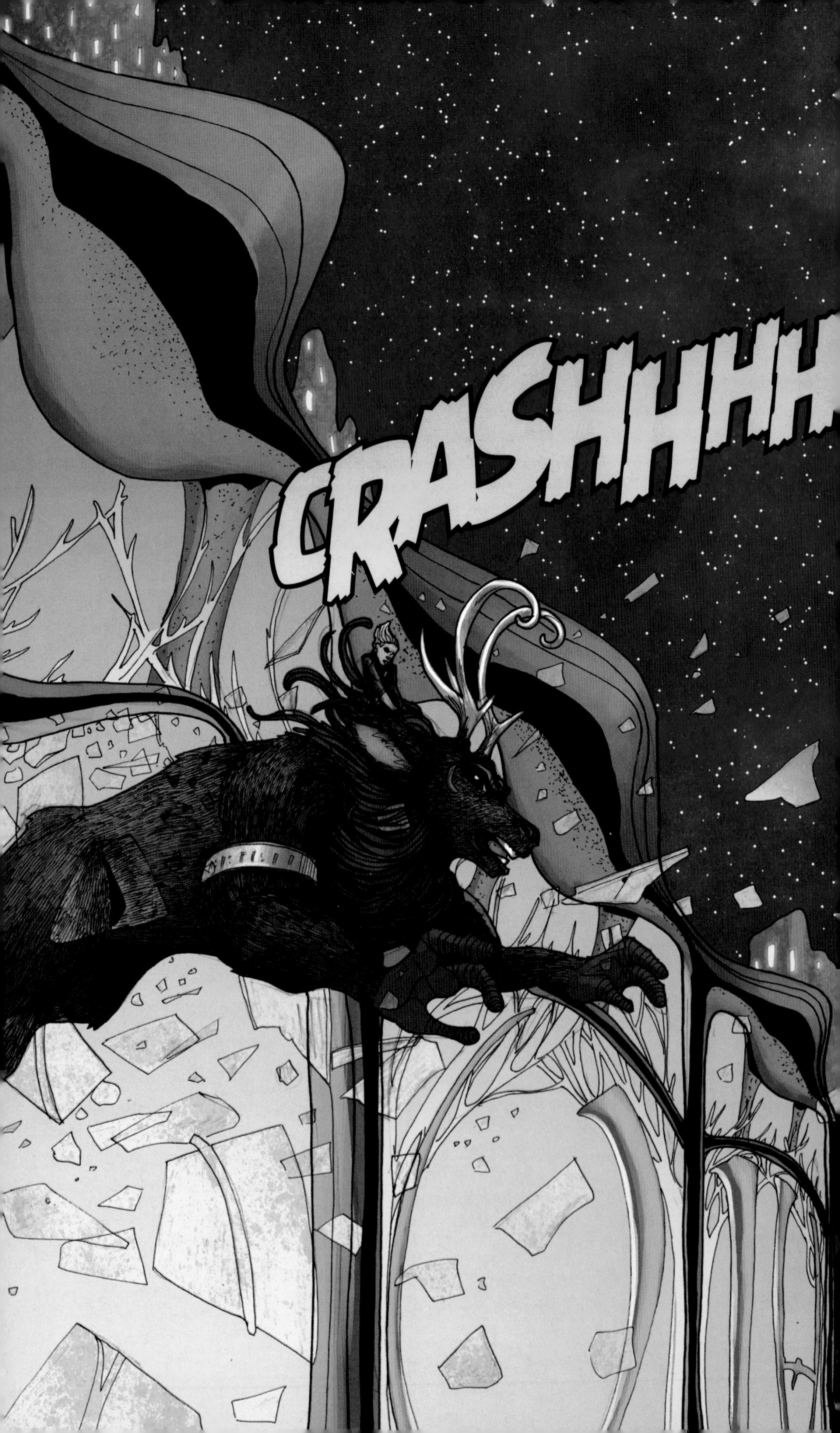
CRASHHHH

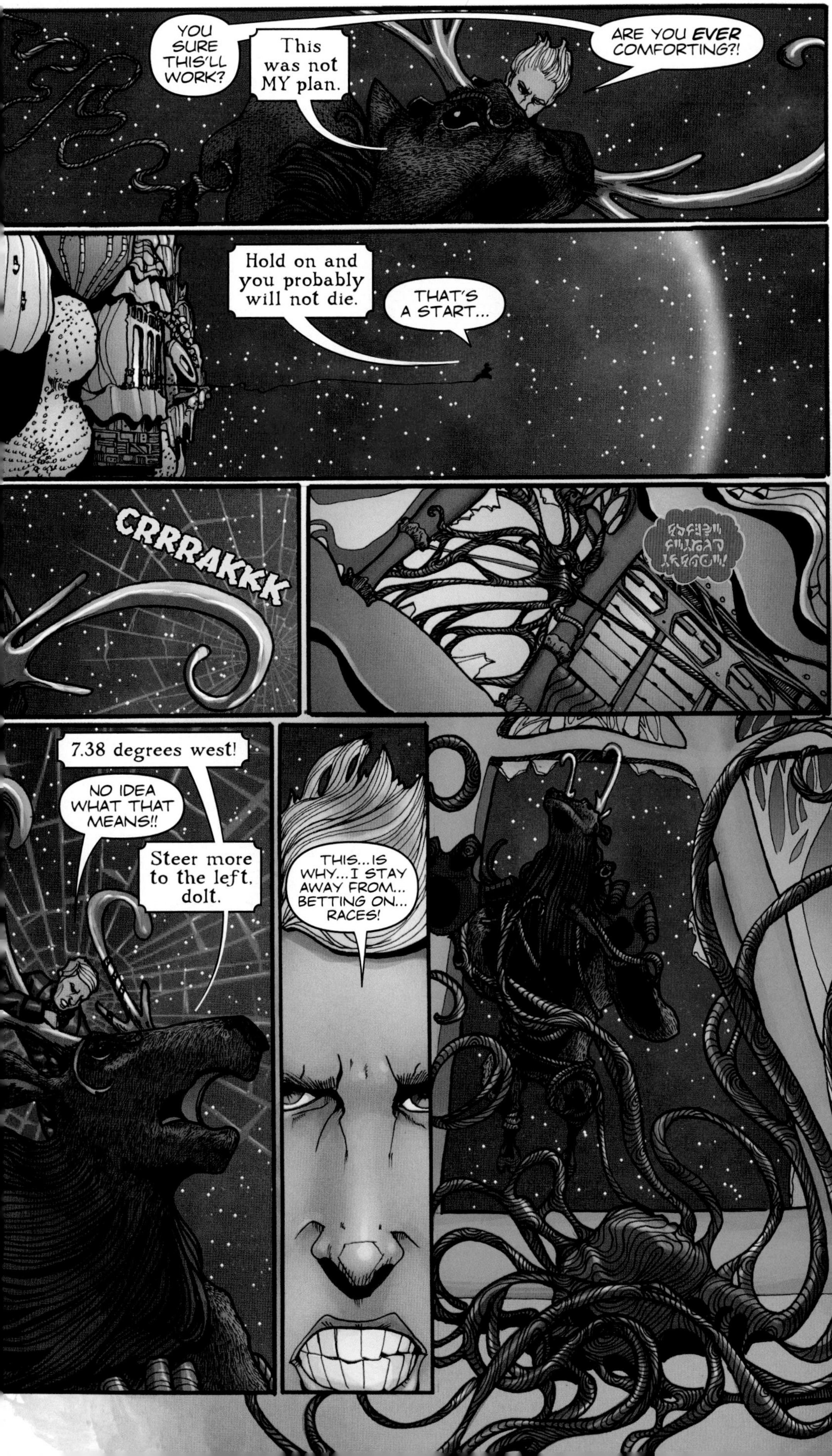
YOU SURE THIS'LL WORK?
This was not MY plan.
ARE YOU EVER COMFORTING?!
Hold on and you probably will not die.
THAT'S A START...
CRRRAKKK
7.38 degrees west!
NO IDEA WHAT THAT MEANS!!
Steer more to the left, dolt.
THIS...IS WHY...I STAY AWAY FROM... BETTING ON... RACES!

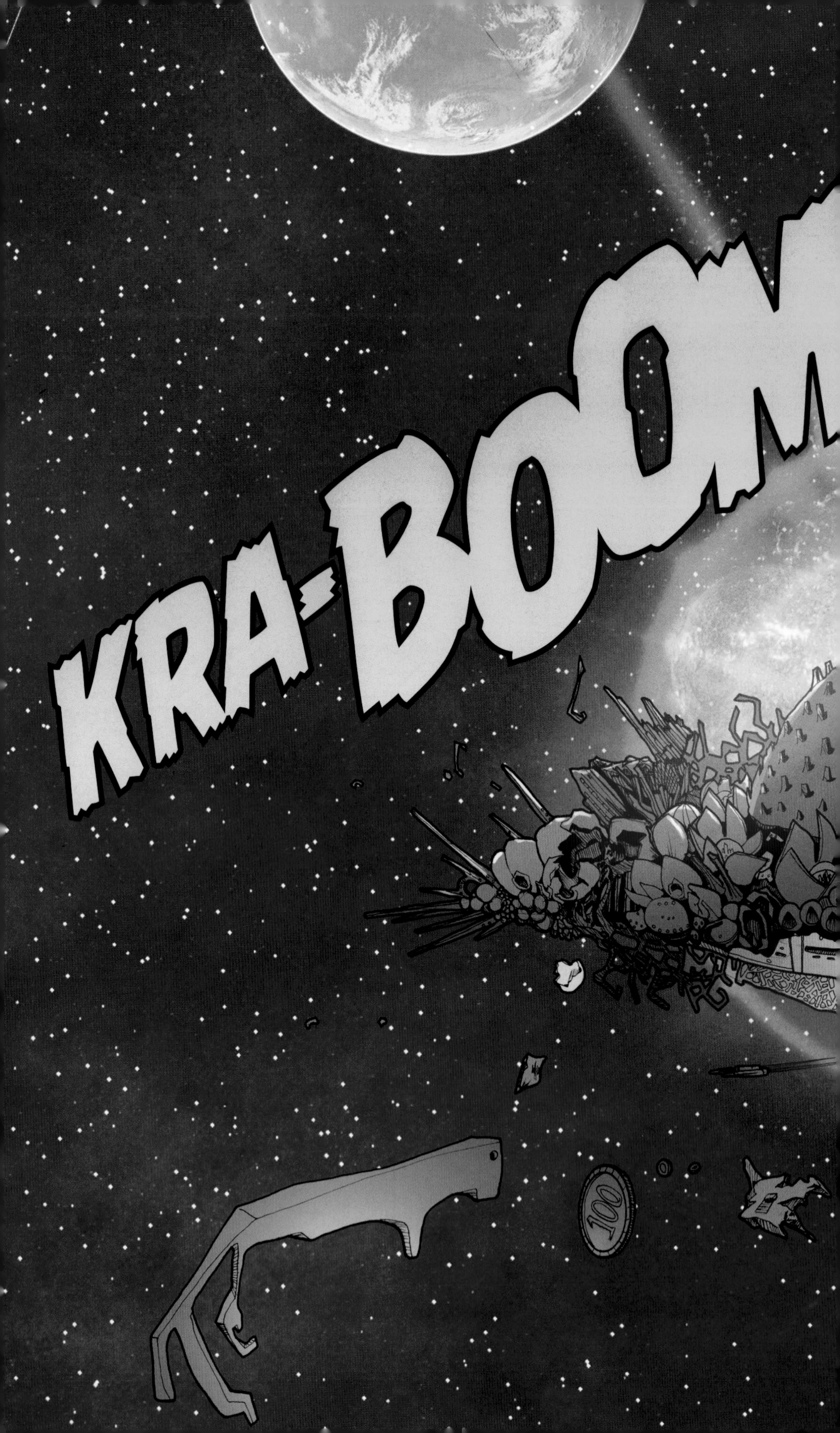
KRA-BOOM

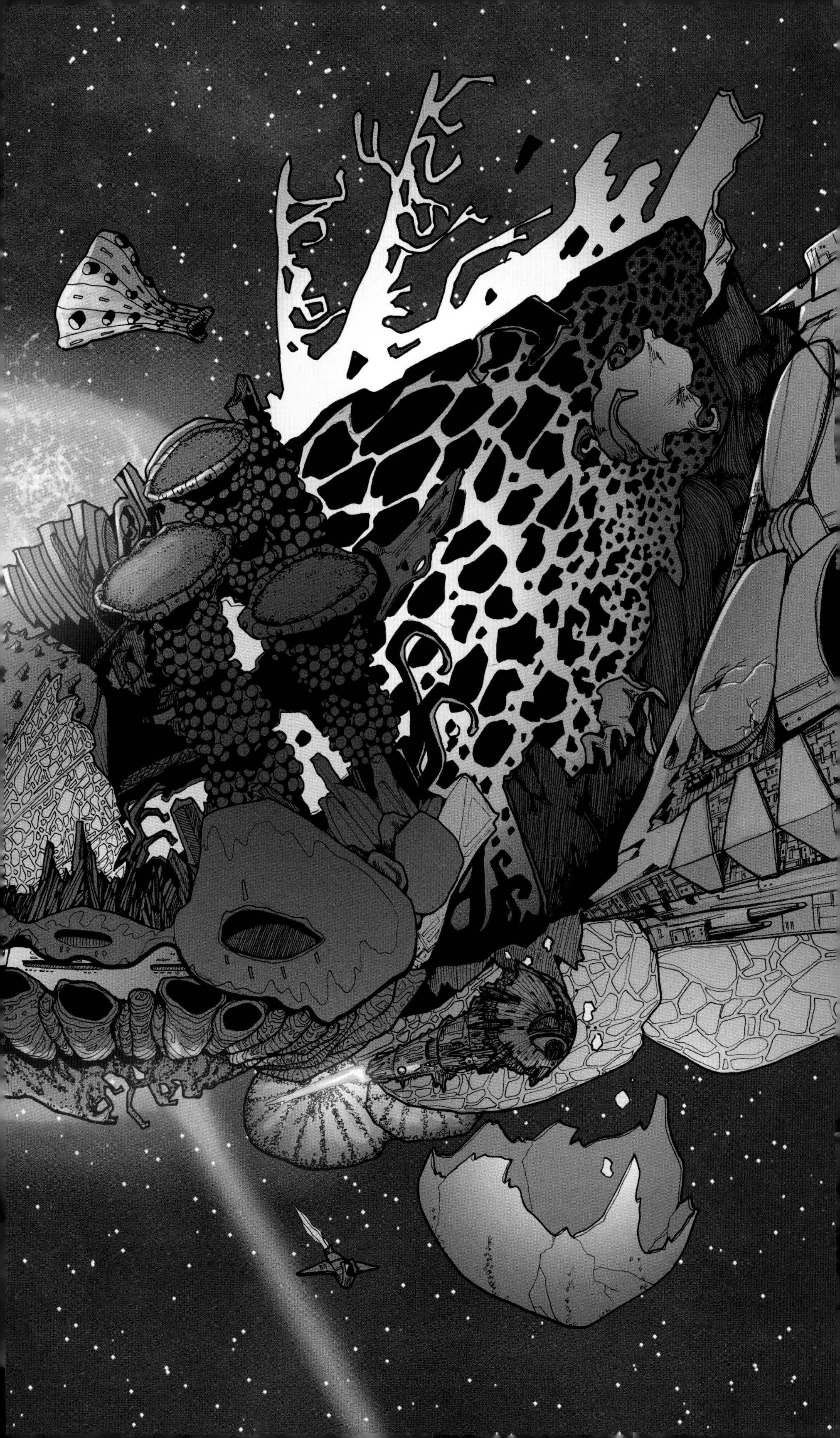

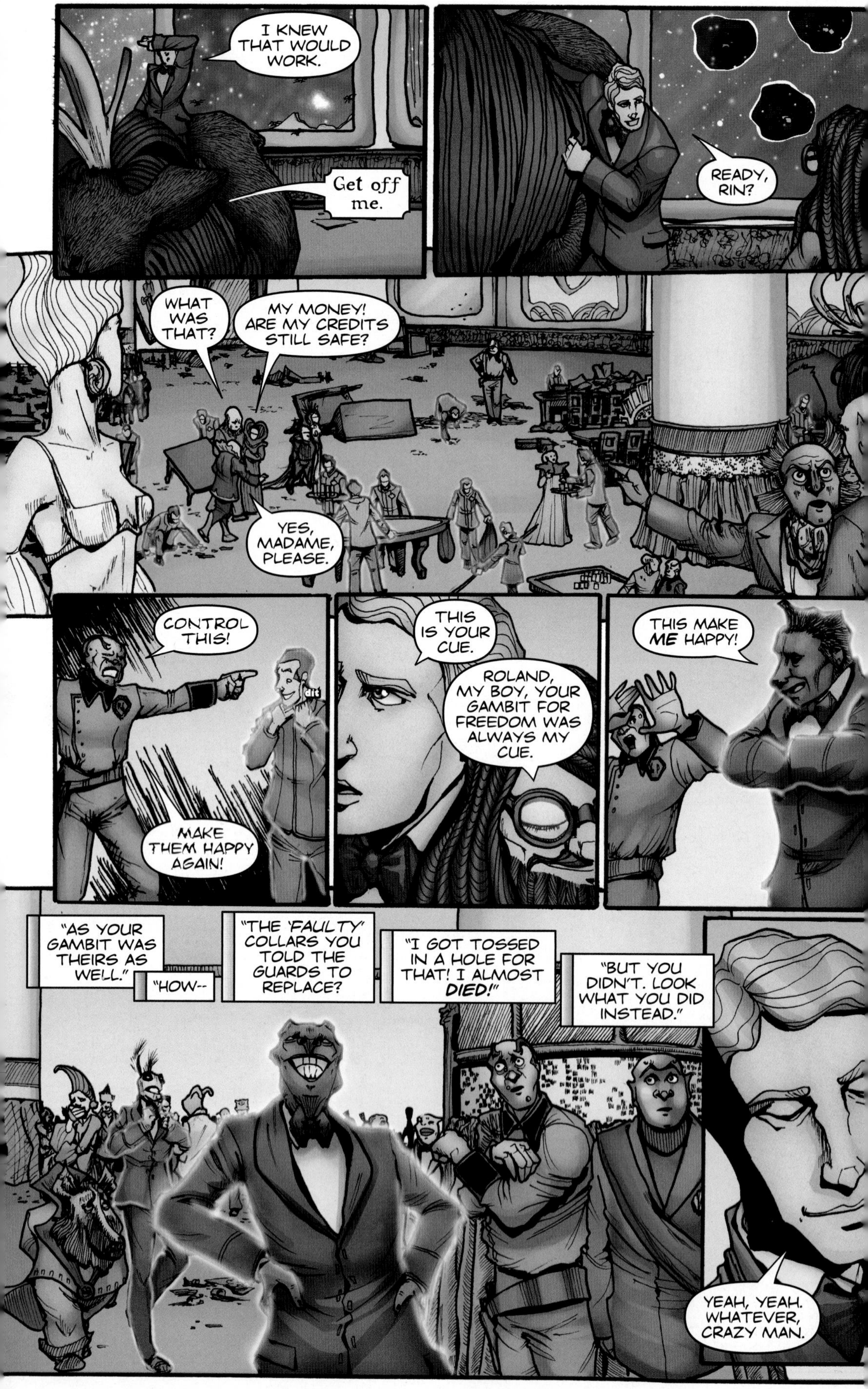
I KNEW THAT WOULD WORK.
Get off me.
READY, RIN?
WHAT WAS THAT?
MY MONEY! ARE MY CREDITS STILL SAFE?
YES, MADAME, PLEASE.
CONTROL THIS!
dit
MAKE THEM HAPPY AGAIN!
THIS IS YOUR CUE.
ROLAND, MY BOY, YOUR GAMBIT FOR FREEDOM WAS ALWAYS MY CUE.
THIS MAKE *ME* HAPPY!
"AS YOUR GAMBIT WAS THEIRS AS WELL."
"HOW--
"THE *'FAULTY'* COLLARS YOU TOLD THE GUARDS TO REPLACE?
"I GOT TOSSED IN A HOLE FOR THAT! I ALMOST *DIED!*"
"BUT YOU DIDN'T. LOOK WHAT YOU DID INSTEAD."
YEAH, YEAH. WHATEVER, CRAZY MAN.

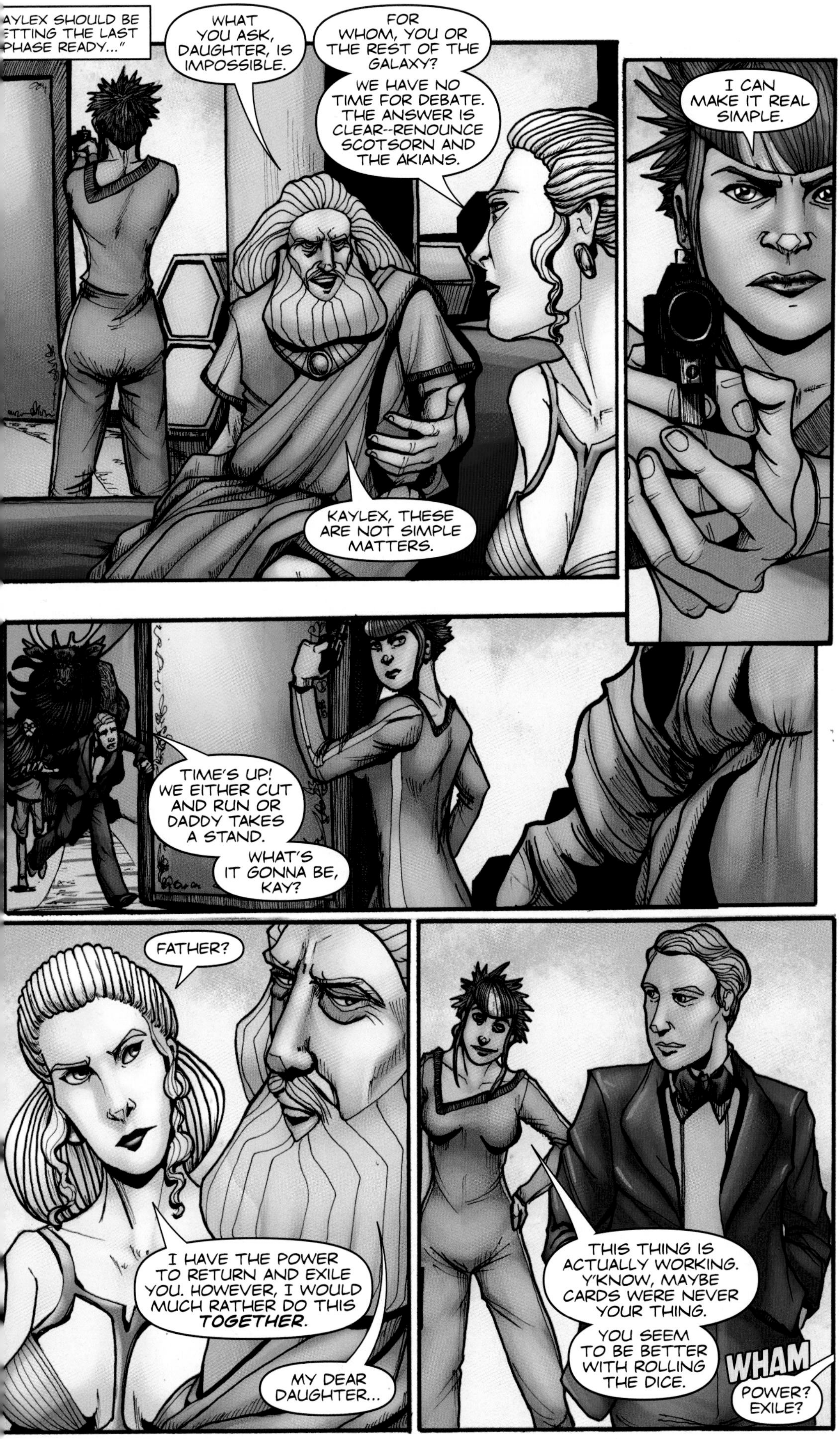

AYLEX SHOULD BE ETTING THE LAST PHASE READY..."
WHAT YOU ASK, DAUGHTER, IS IMPOSSIBLE.
FOR WHOM, YOU OR THE REST OF THE GALAXY?
WE HAVE NO TIME FOR DEBATE. THE ANSWER IS CLEAR--RENOUNCE SCOTSORN AND THE AKIANS.
KAYLEX, THESE ARE NOT SIMPLE MATTERS.
I CAN MAKE IT REAL SIMPLE.
TIME'S UP! WE EITHER CUT AND RUN OR DADDY TAKES A STAND.
WHAT'S IT GONNA BE, KAY?
FATHER?
I HAVE THE POWER TO RETURN AND EXILE YOU. HOWEVER, I WOULD MUCH RATHER DO THIS ***TOGETHER***.
MY DEAR DAUGHTER...
THIS THING IS ACTUALLY WORKING. Y'KNOW, MAYBE CARDS WERE NEVER YOUR THING.
YOU SEEM TO BE BETTER WITH ROLLING THE DICE.
WHAM
POWER? EXILE?

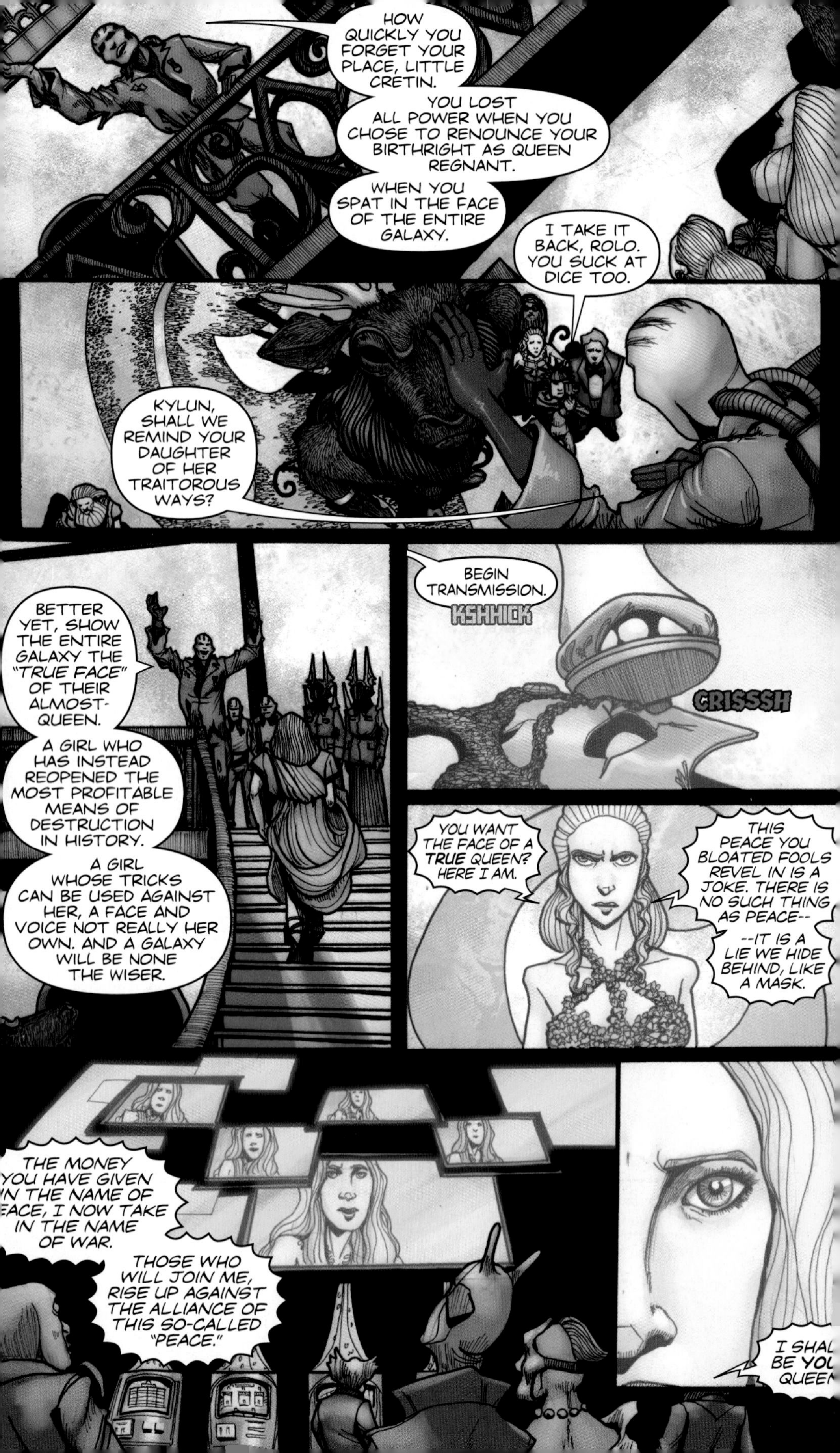
HOW QUICKLY YOU FORGET YOUR PLACE, LITTLE CRETIN.
YOU LOST ALL POWER WHEN YOU CHOSE TO RENOUNCE YOUR BIRTHRIGHT AS QUEEN REGNANT.
WHEN YOU SPAT IN THE FACE OF THE ENTIRE GALAXY.
I TAKE IT BACK, ROLO. YOU SUCK AT DICE TOO.
KYLUN, SHALL WE REMIND YOUR DAUGHTER OF HER TRAITOROUS WAYS?
BETTER YET, SHOW THE ENTIRE GALAXY THE "TRUE FACE" OF THEIR ALMOST-QUEEN.
A GIRL WHO HAS INSTEAD REOPENED THE MOST PROFITABLE MEANS OF DESTRUCTION IN HISTORY.
A GIRL WHOSE TRICKS CAN BE USED AGAINST HER, A FACE AND VOICE NOT REALLY HER OWN. AND A GALAXY WILL BE NONE THE WISER.
BEGIN TRANSMISSION.
KSHHICK
CRISSSH
YOU WANT THE FACE OF A TRUE QUEEN? HERE I AM.
THIS PEACE YOU BLOATED FOOLS REVEL IN IS A JOKE. THERE IS NO SUCH THING AS PEACE--
--IT IS A LIE WE HIDE BEHIND, LIKE A MASK.
THE MONEY YOU HAVE GIVEN IN THE NAME OF PEACE, I NOW TAKE IN THE NAME OF WAR.
THOSE WHO WILL JOIN ME, RISE UP AGAINST THE ALLIANCE OF THIS SO-CALLED "PEACE."
I SHAL BE YOU QUEEN

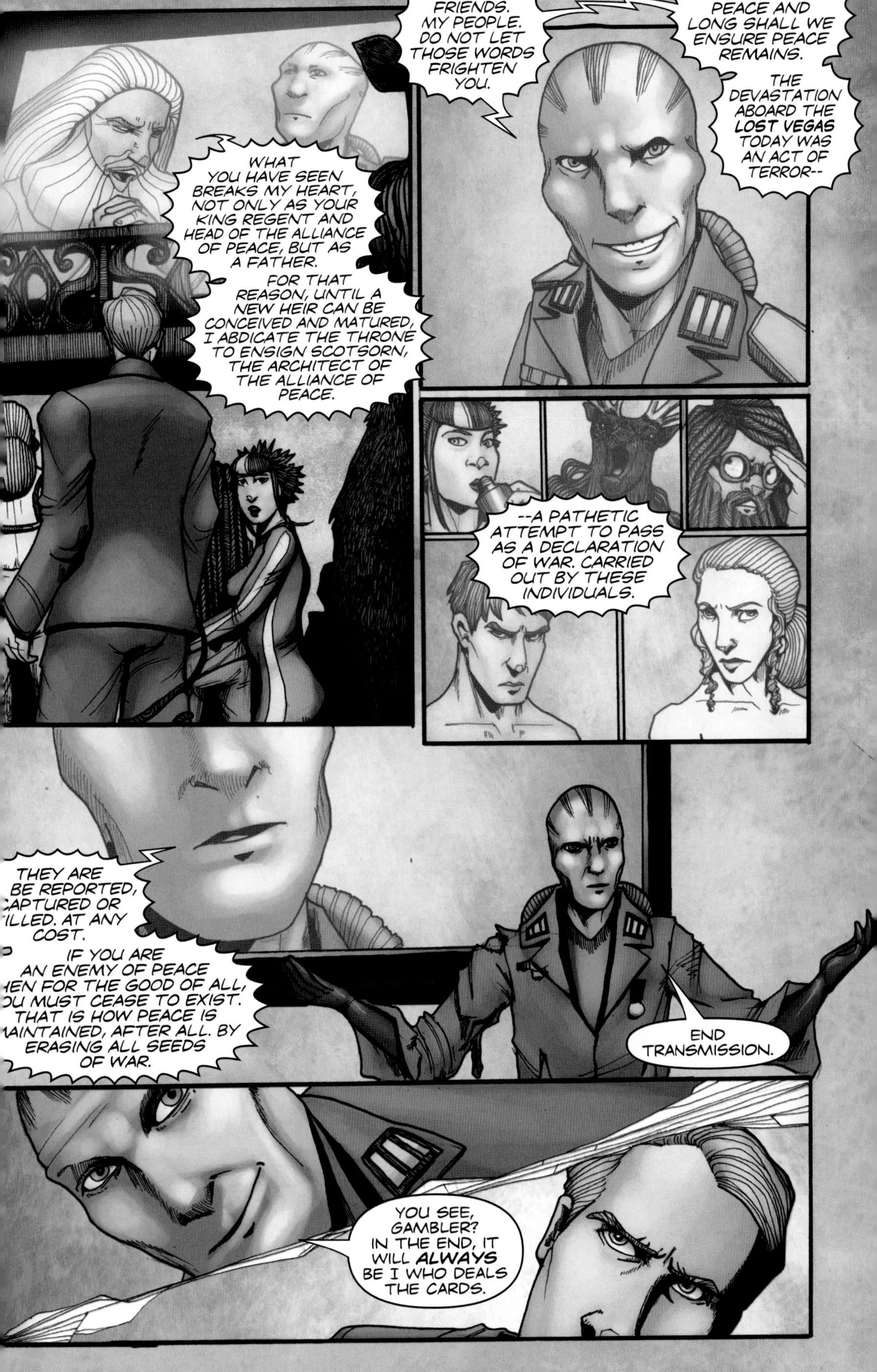
MY FRIENDS. MY PEOPLE. DO NOT LET THOSE WORDS FRIGHTEN YOU.
LONG DID WE FIGHT FOR PEACE AND LONG SHALL WE ENSURE PEACE REMAINS.
THE DEVASTATION ABOARD THE **LOST VEGAS** TODAY WAS AN ACT OF TERROR--
WHAT YOU HAVE SEEN BREAKS MY HEART, NOT ONLY AS YOUR KING REGENT AND HEAD OF THE ALLIANCE OF PEACE, BUT AS A FATHER.
FOR THAT REASON, UNTIL A NEW HEIR CAN BE CONCEIVED AND MATURED, I ABDICATE THE THRONE TO ENSIGN SCOTSORN, THE ARCHITECT OF THE ALLIANCE OF PEACE.
--A PATHETIC ATTEMPT TO PASS AS A DECLARATION OF WAR. CARRIED OUT BY THESE INDIVIDUALS.
THEY ARE BE REPORTED, CAPTURED OR KILLED. AT ANY COST.
IF YOU ARE AN ENEMY OF PEACE THEN FOR THE GOOD OF ALL, YOU MUST CEASE TO EXIST. THAT IS HOW PEACE IS MAINTAINED, AFTER ALL. BY ERASING ALL SEEDS OF WAR.
END TRANSMISSION.
YOU SEE, GAMBLER? IN THE END, IT WILL **ALWAYS** BE I WHO DEALS THE CARDS.

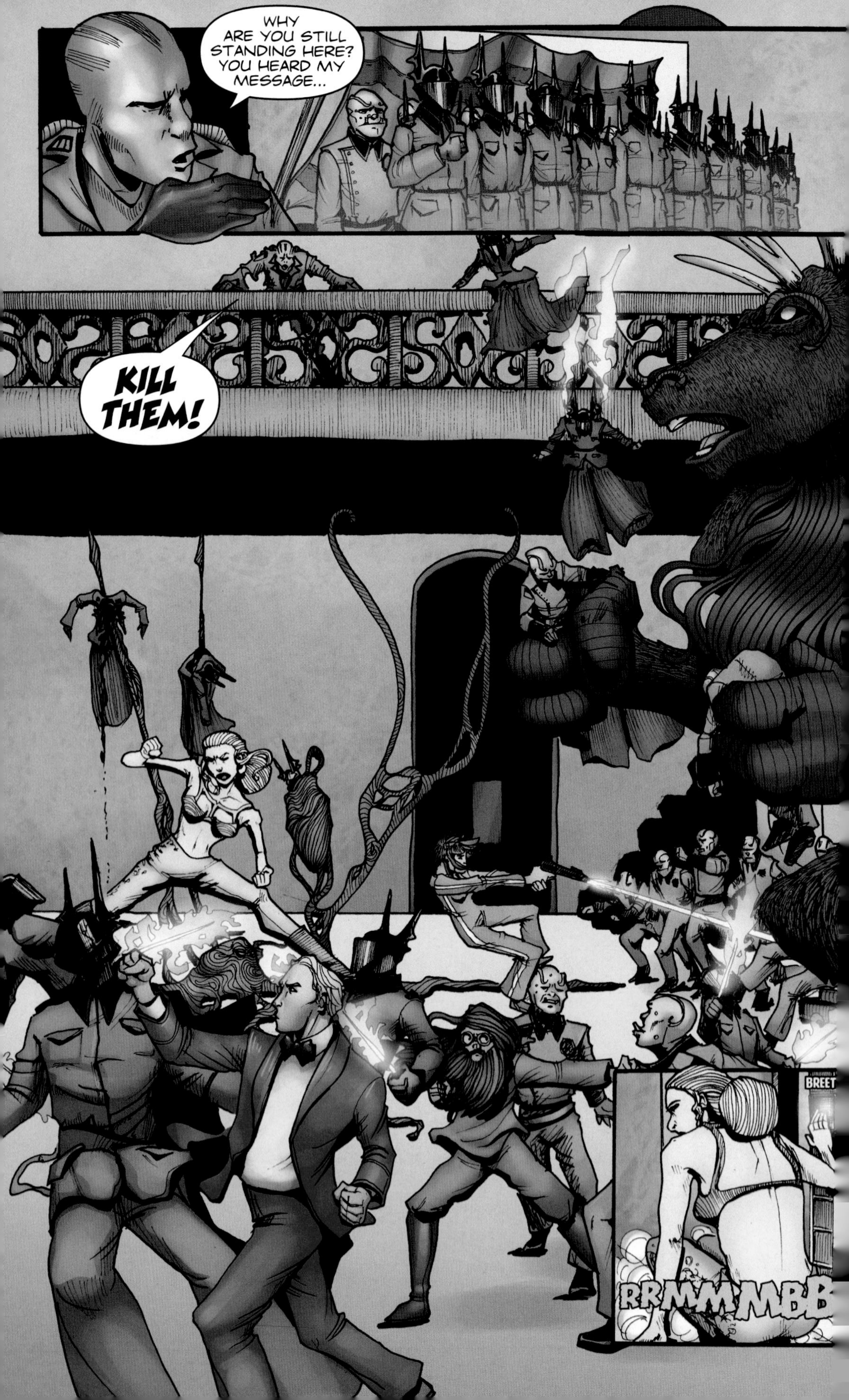
WHY ARE YOU STILL STANDING HERE? YOU HEARD MY MESSAGE...
KILL THEM!
BREET
RRMMMBB

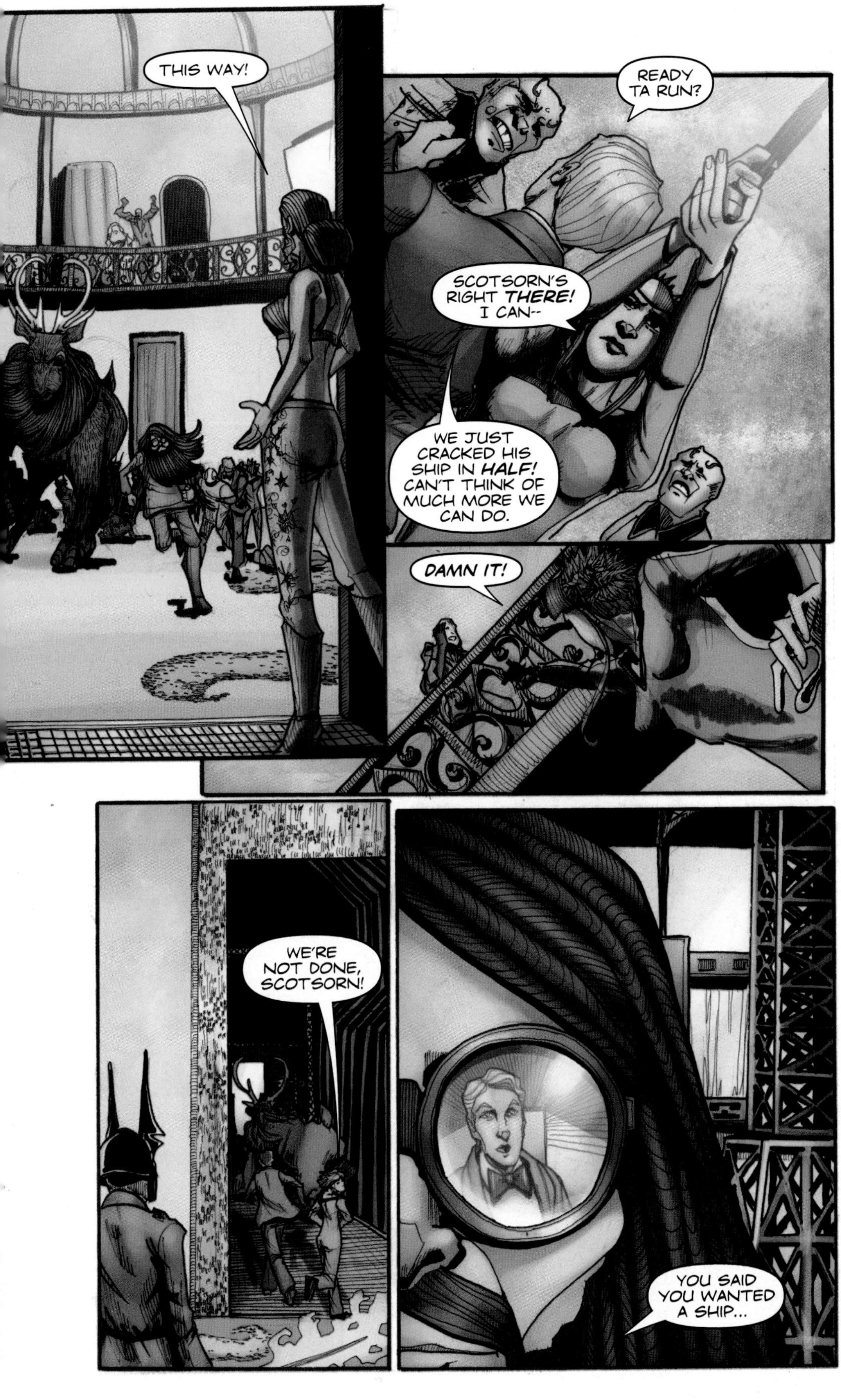
THIS WAY!
READY TA RUN?
SCOTSORN'S RIGHT THERE! I CAN--
WE JUST CRACKED HIS SHIP IN HALF! CAN'T THINK OF MUCH MORE WE CAN DO.
DAMN IT!
WE'RE NOT DONE, SCOTSORN!
YOU SAID YOU WANTED A SHIP...

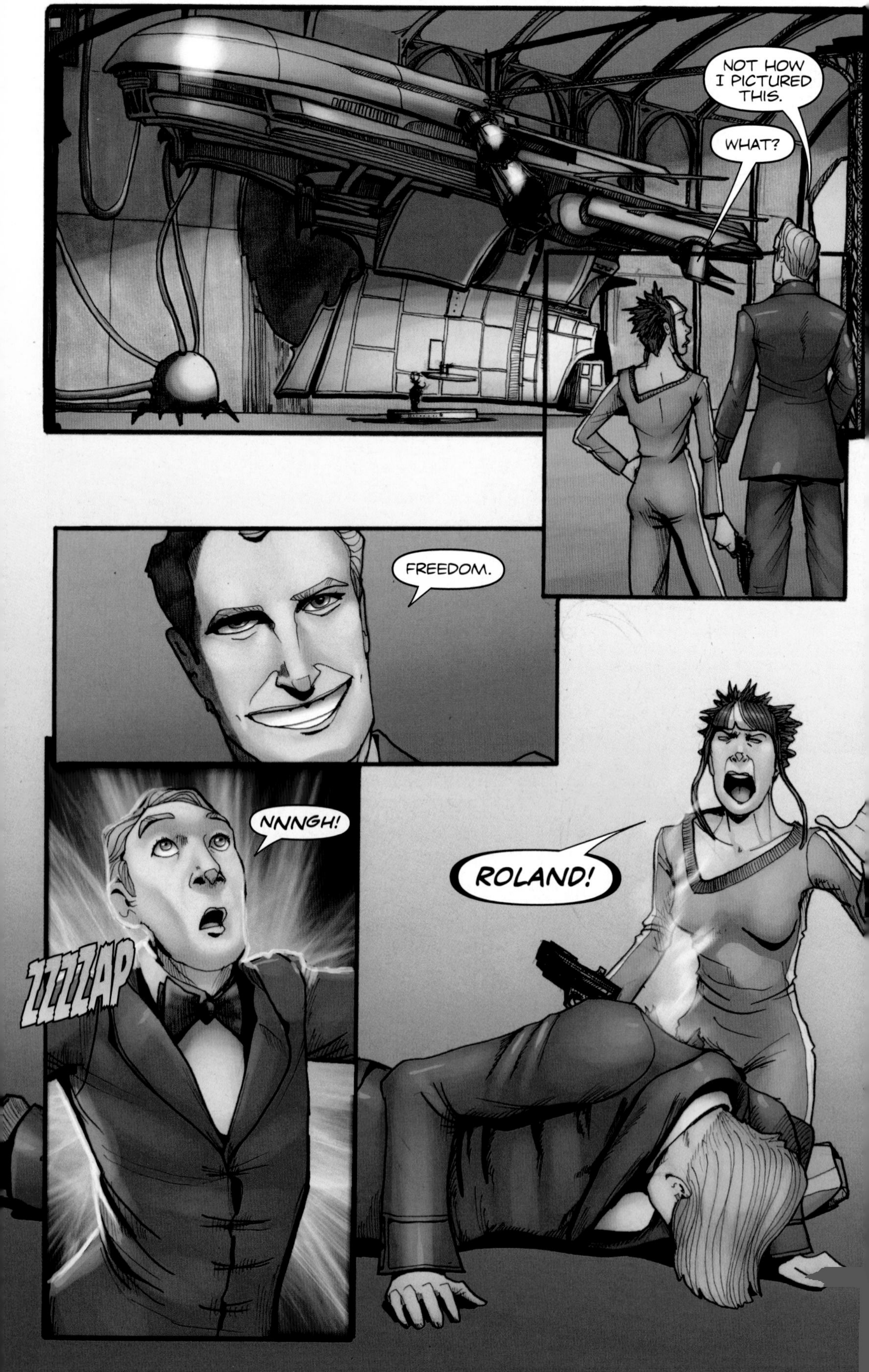
NOT HOW I PICTURED THIS.
WHAT?
FREEDOM.
NNNGH!
ZZZZAP
ROLAND!

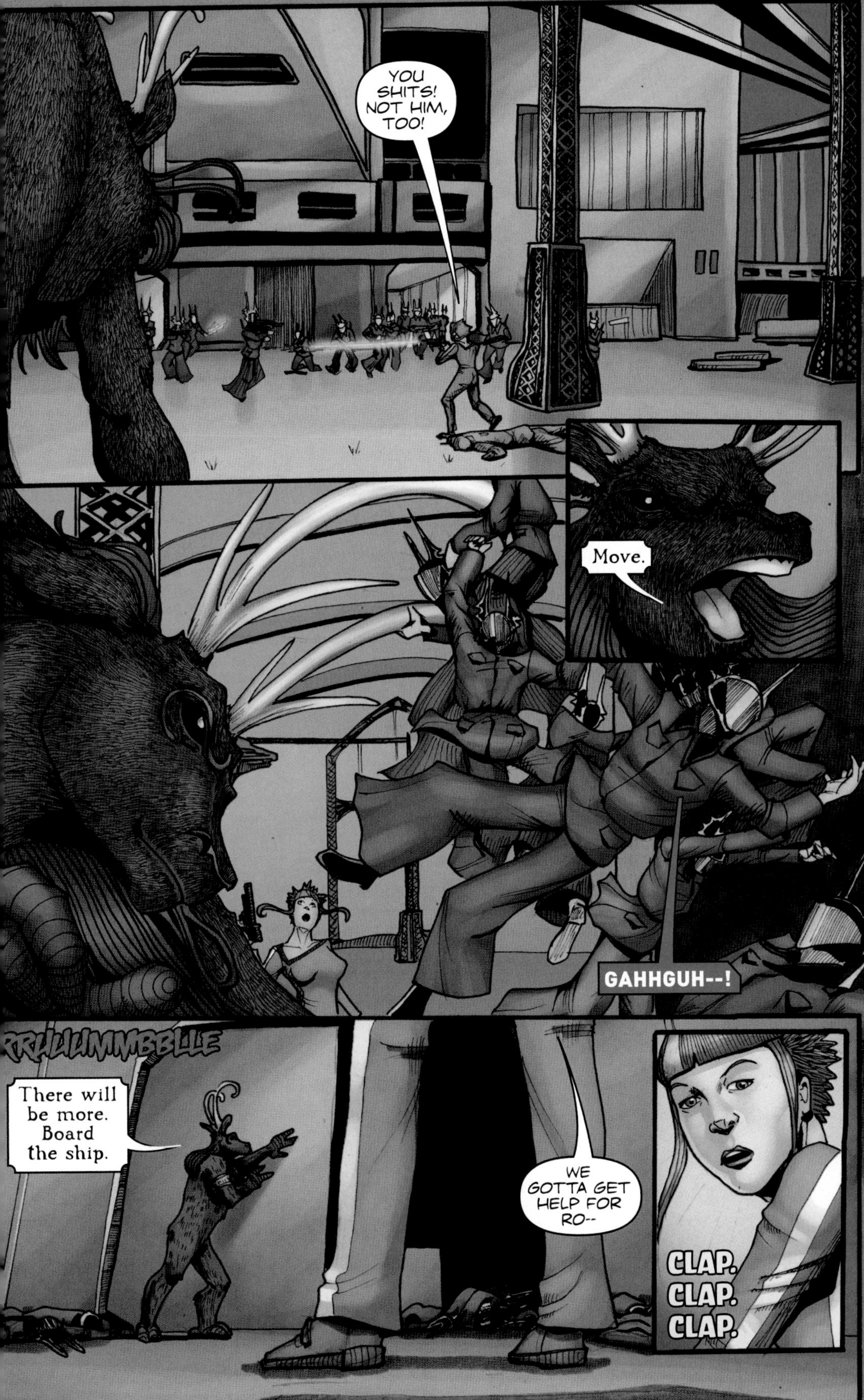
YOU SHITS! NOT HIM, TOO!
Move.
GAHHGUH--!
RRUULLMMBBLLE
There will be more. Board the ship.
WE GOTTA GET HELP FOR RO--
CLAP. CLAP. CLAP.

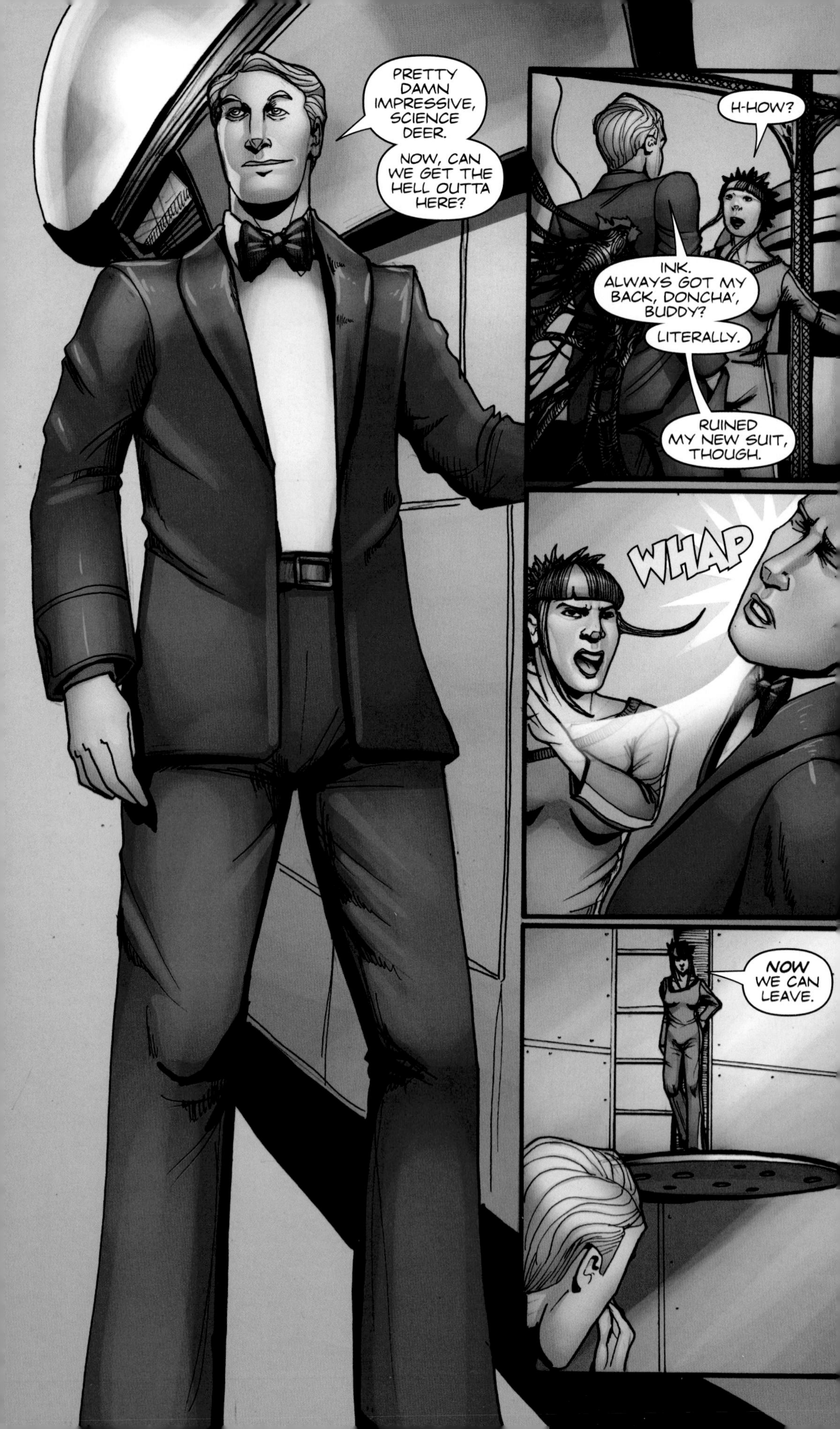
PRETTY DAMN IMPRESSIVE, SCIENCE DEER.
NOW, CAN WE GET THE HELL OUTTA HERE?
H-HOW?
INK. ALWAYS GOT MY BACK, DONCHA', BUDDY?
LITERALLY.
RUINED MY NEW SUIT, THOUGH.
WHAP
NOW WE CAN LEAVE.

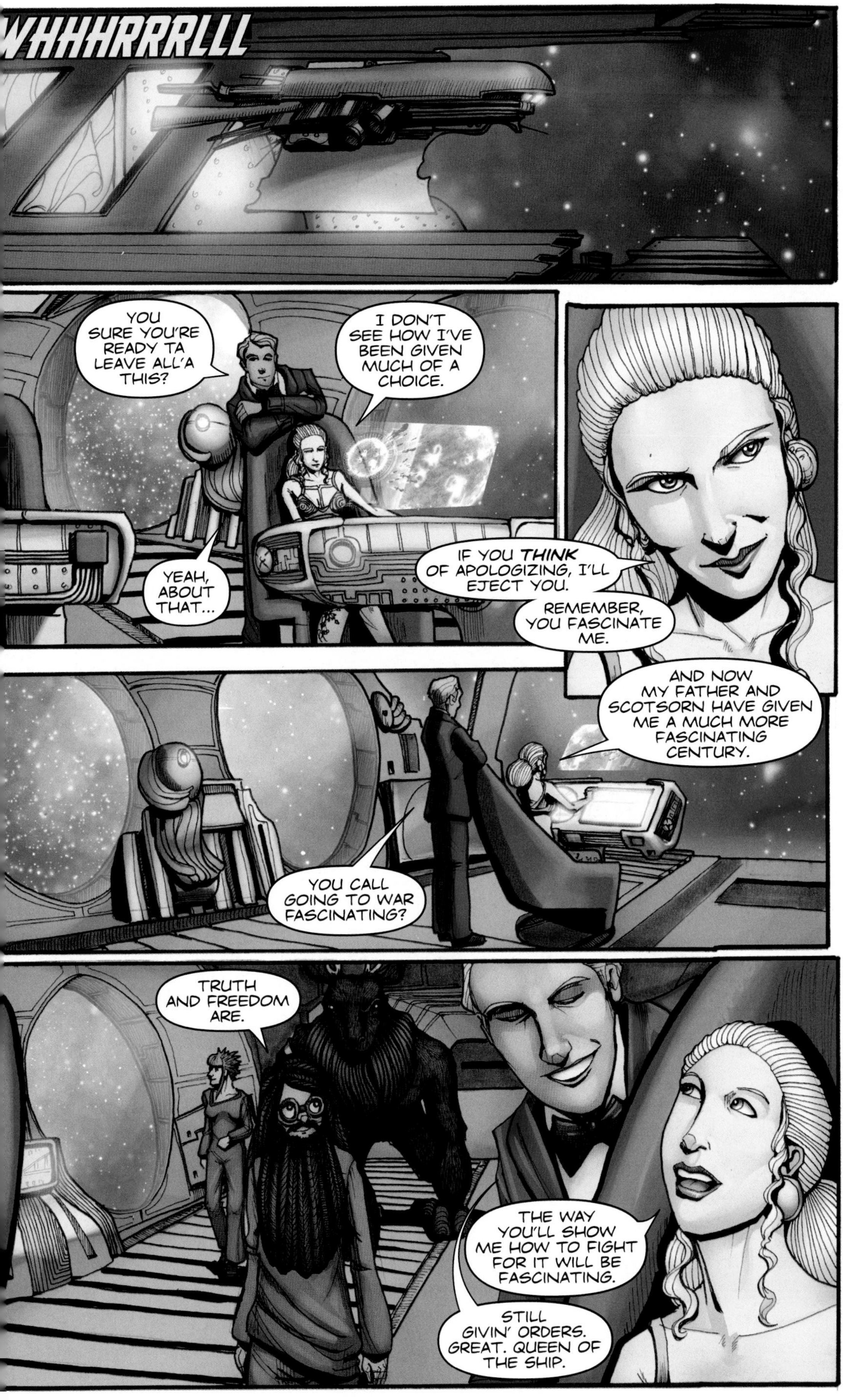
WHHHRRRLLL
YOU SURE YOU'RE READY TA LEAVE ALL'A THIS?
I DON'T SEE HOW I'VE BEEN GIVEN MUCH OF A CHOICE.
YEAH, ABOUT THAT...
IF YOU THINK OF APOLOGIZING, I'LL EJECT YOU.
REMEMBER, YOU FASCINATE ME.
AND NOW MY FATHER AND SCOTSORN HAVE GIVEN ME A MUCH MORE FASCINATING CENTURY.
YOU CALL GOING TO WAR FASCINATING?
TRUTH AND FREEDOM ARE.
THE WAY YOU'LL SHOW ME HOW TO FIGHT FOR IT WILL BE FASCINATING.
STILL GIVIN' ORDERS. GREAT. QUEEN OF THE SHIP.

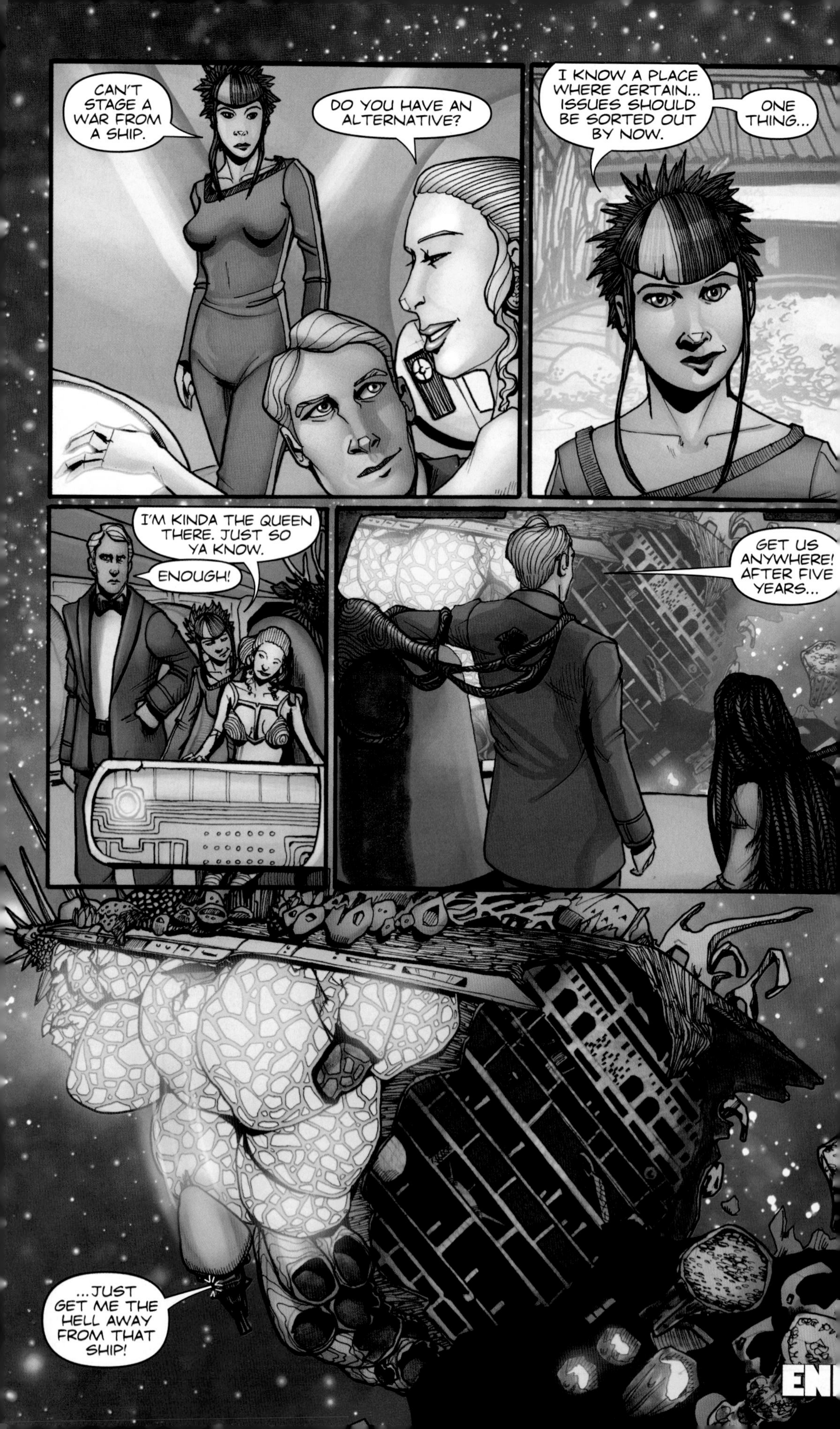
CAN'T STAGE A WAR FROM A SHIP.
DO YOU HAVE AN ALTERNATIVE?
I KNOW A PLACE WHERE CERTAIN... ISSUES SHOULD BE SORTED OUT BY NOW.
ONE THING...
I'M KINDA THE QUEEN THERE. JUST SO YA KNOW.
ENOUGH!
GET US ANYWHERE! AFTER FIVE YEARS...
...JUST GET ME THE HELL AWAY FROM THAT SHIP!

VARIANT COVER GALLERY

◆ JANET K. LEE & CHRIS SOTOMAYOR
114 – PROMO IMAGE ♣

◆ DAN McDAID
115 – ECCC CON EXCLUSIVE
116 – #1 B COVER ♣

◆ DECLAN SHALVEY
117 – #2 B COVER ♣

◆ TONY FLEECS
118 – #3 B COVER ♣

◆ RON SALAS
119 – #4 B COVER ♣

◆ SKOTTIE YOUNG
120 – 123 – PHANTOM VARIANTS ♣

◆ FRANCESCO FRANCAVILLA
124 – 127 – RETAILER INCENTIVE VARIANTS ♣

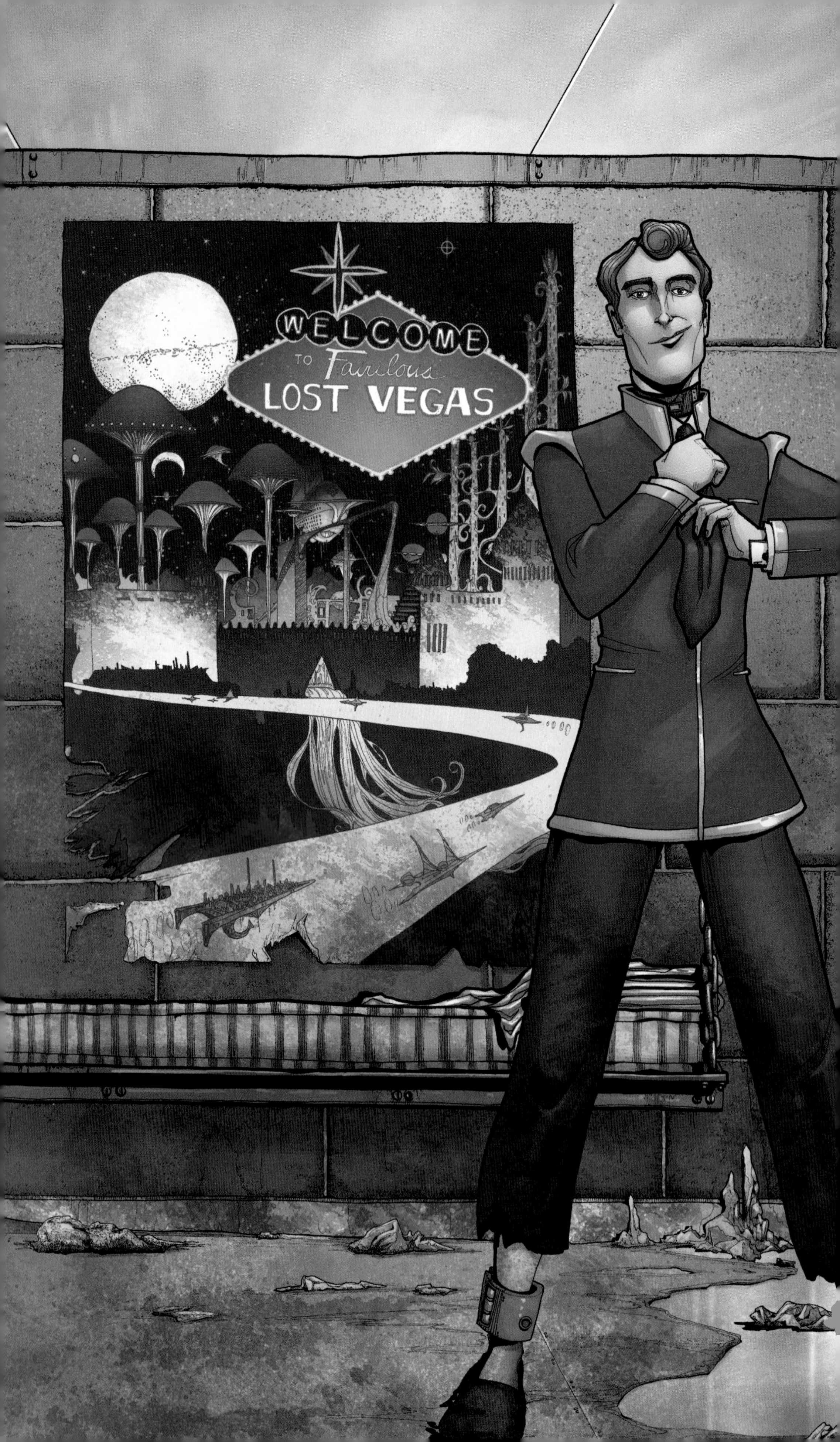
WELCOME
to Fabulous
LOST VEGAS

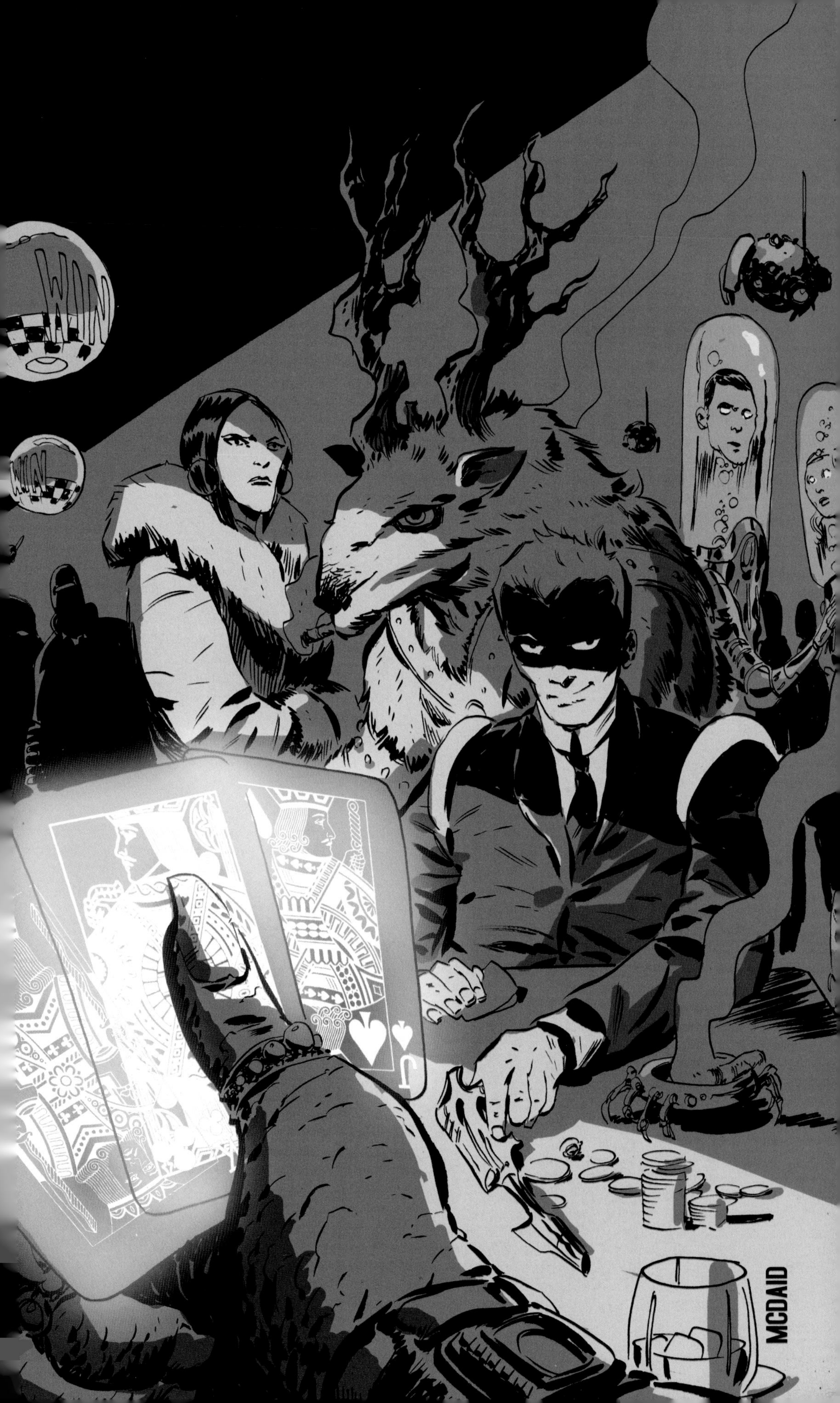
WIN
WIN
MCDAID

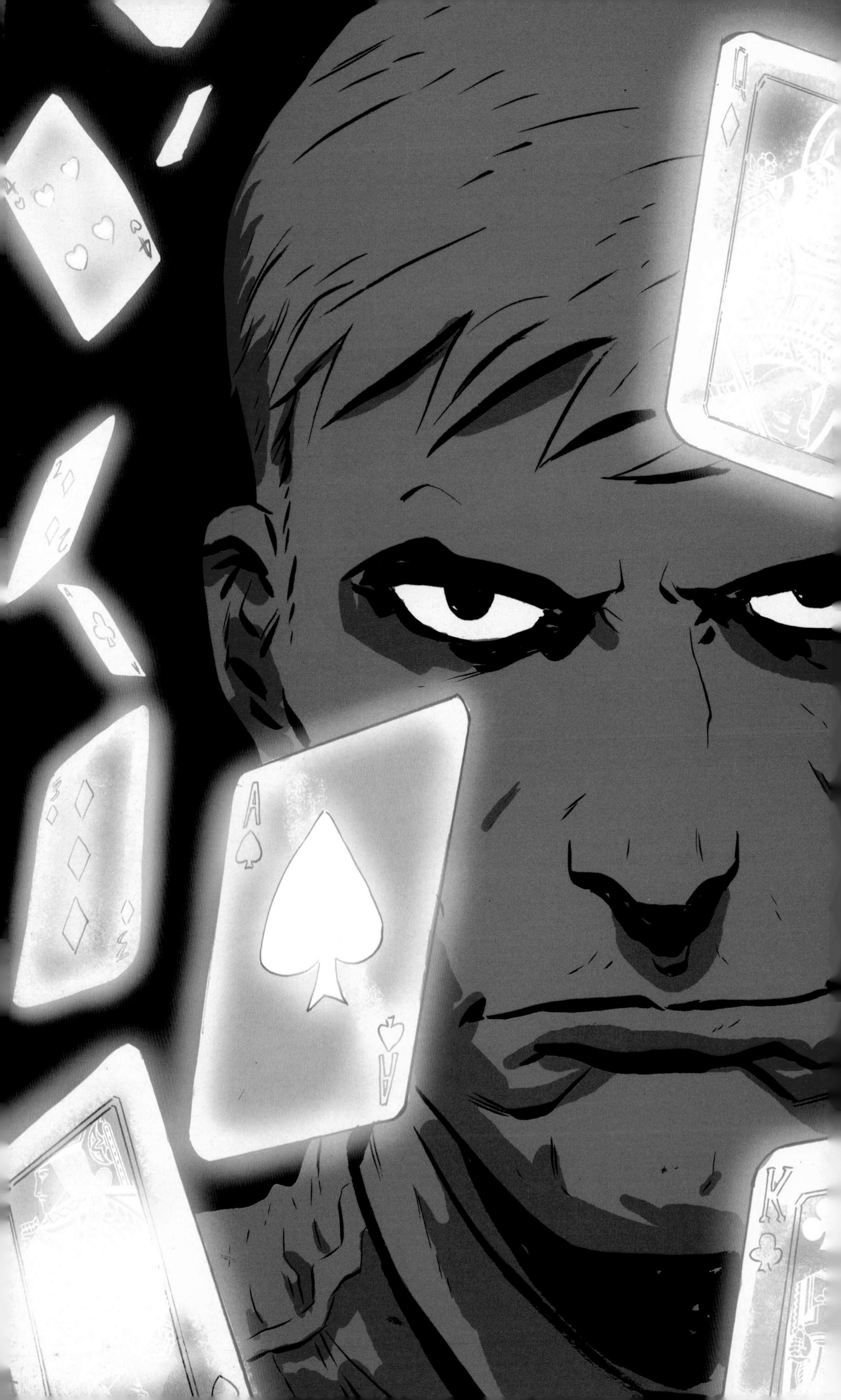

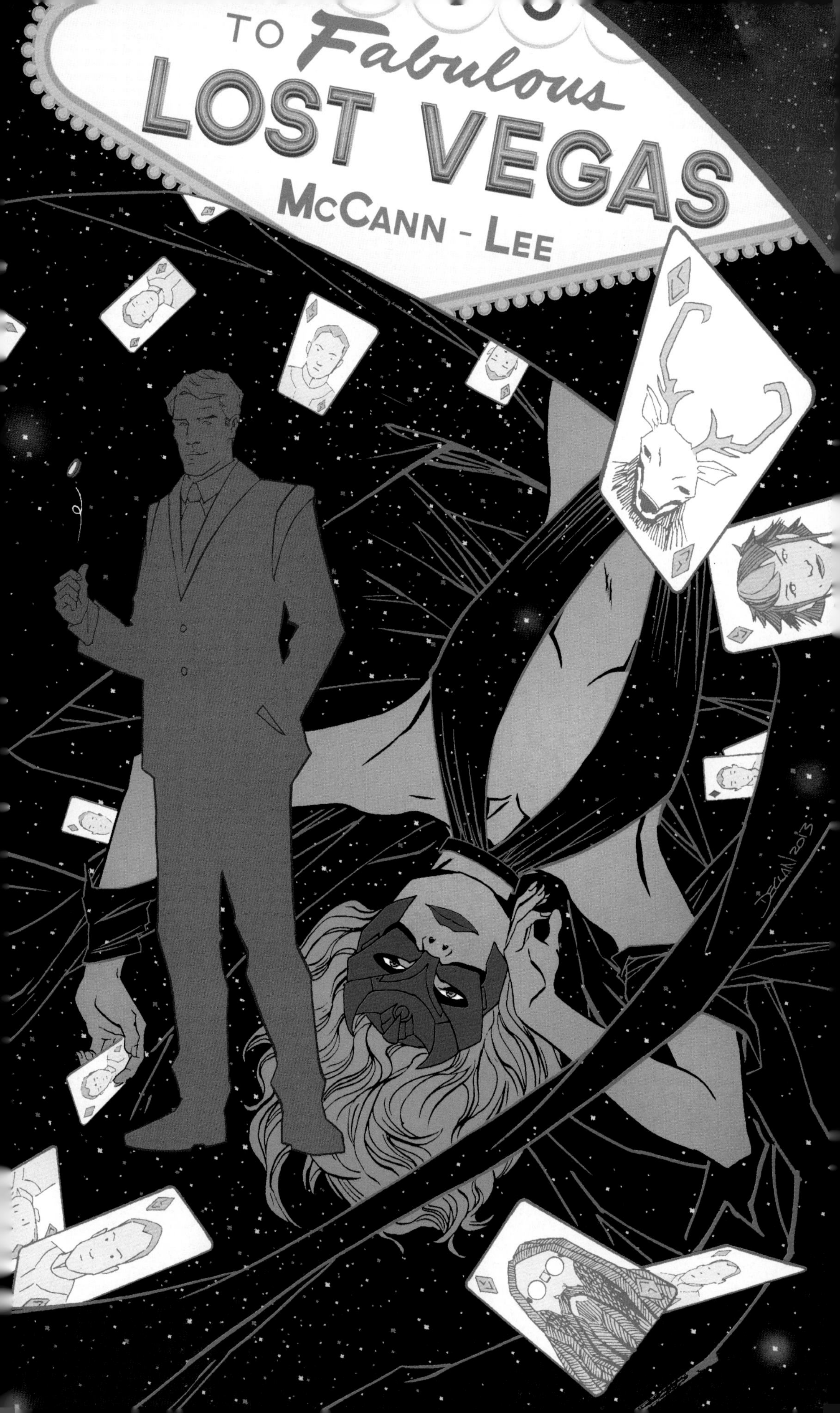
TO Fabulous
LOST VEGAS
McCANN - LEE
DECLAN 2013

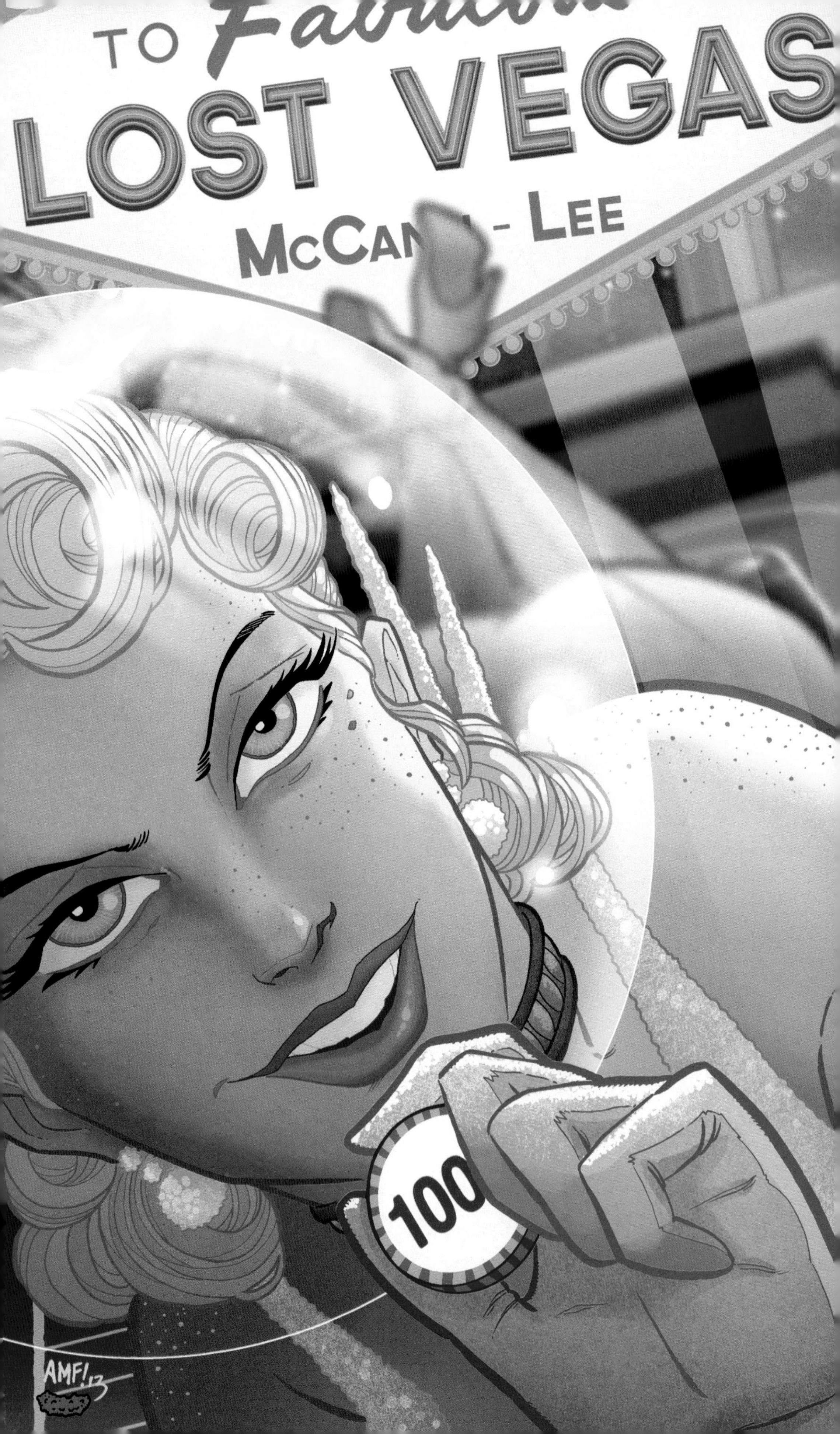

TO
LOST VEGAS
- LEE
100
AMF! 13

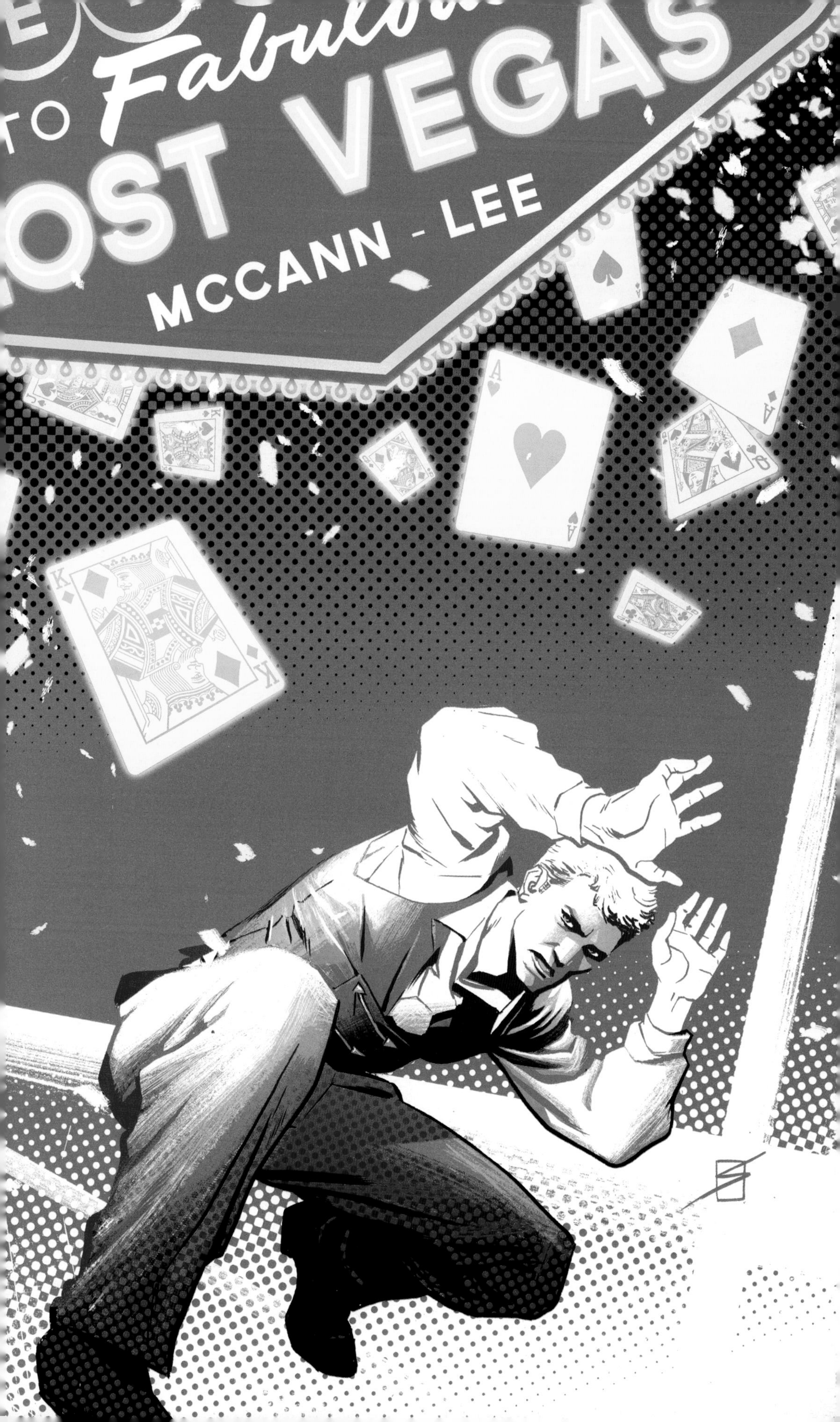

TO Fabulou
OST VEGAS
MCCANN - LEE

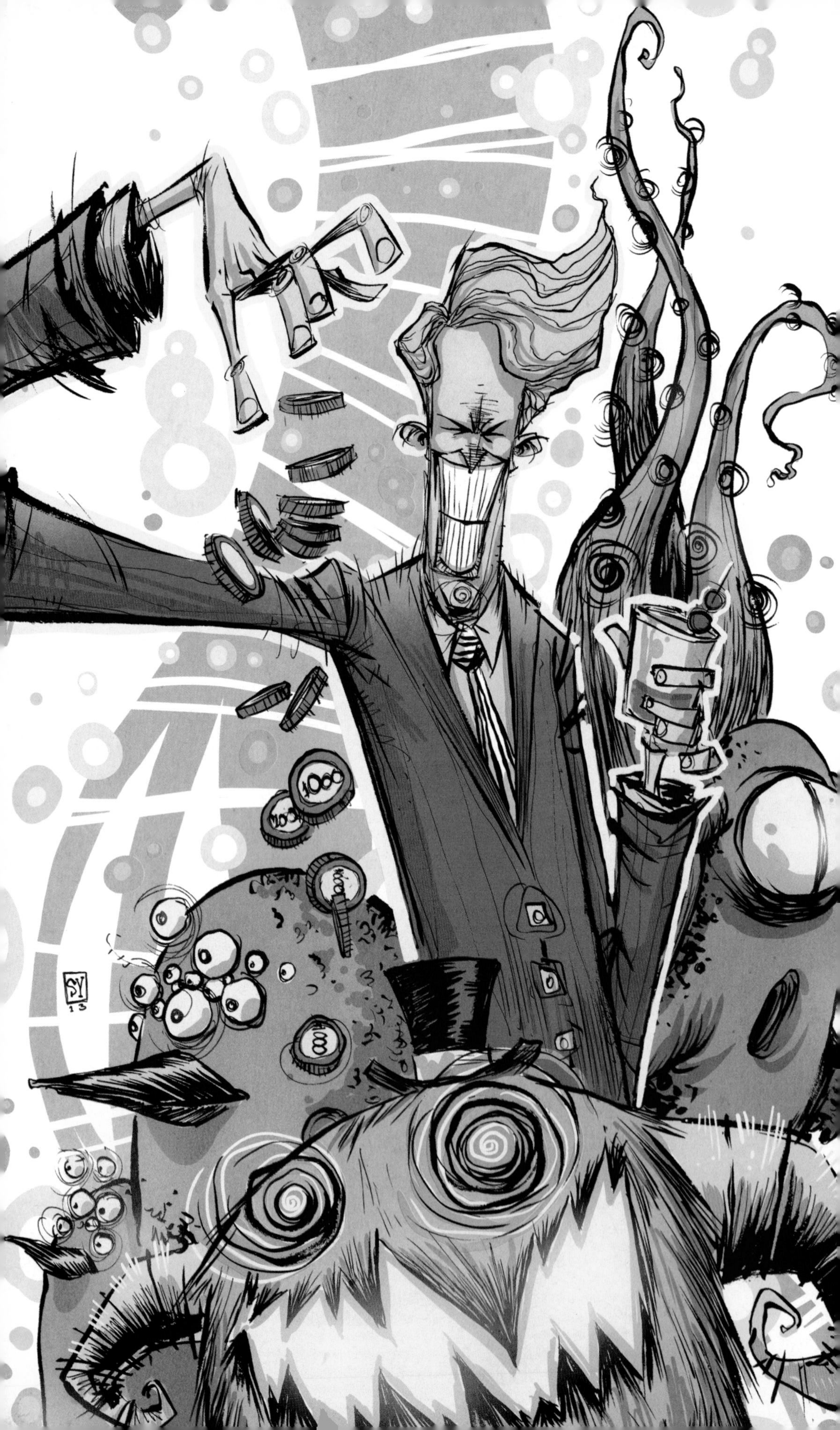

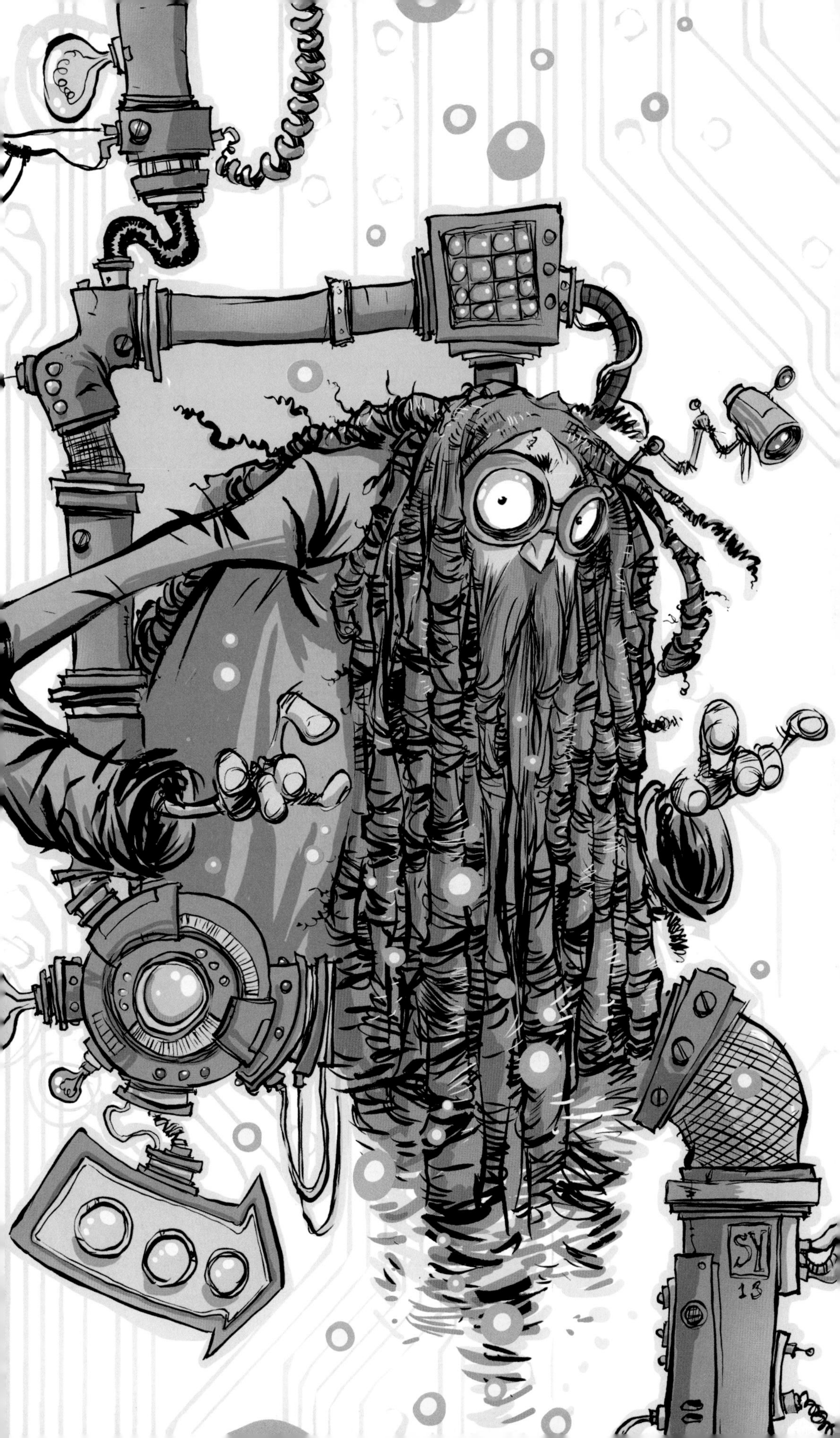
SY
13

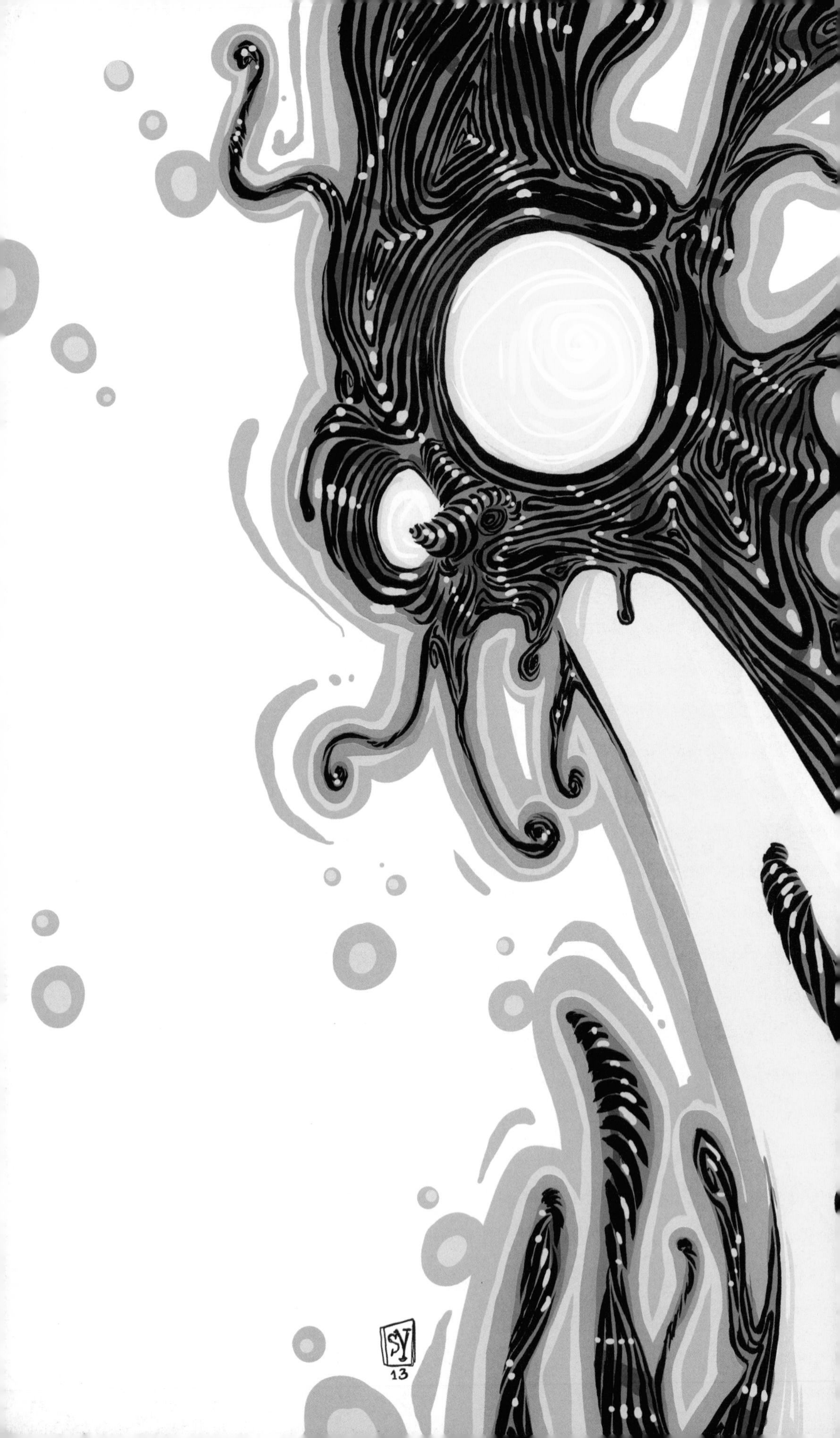
SY
13

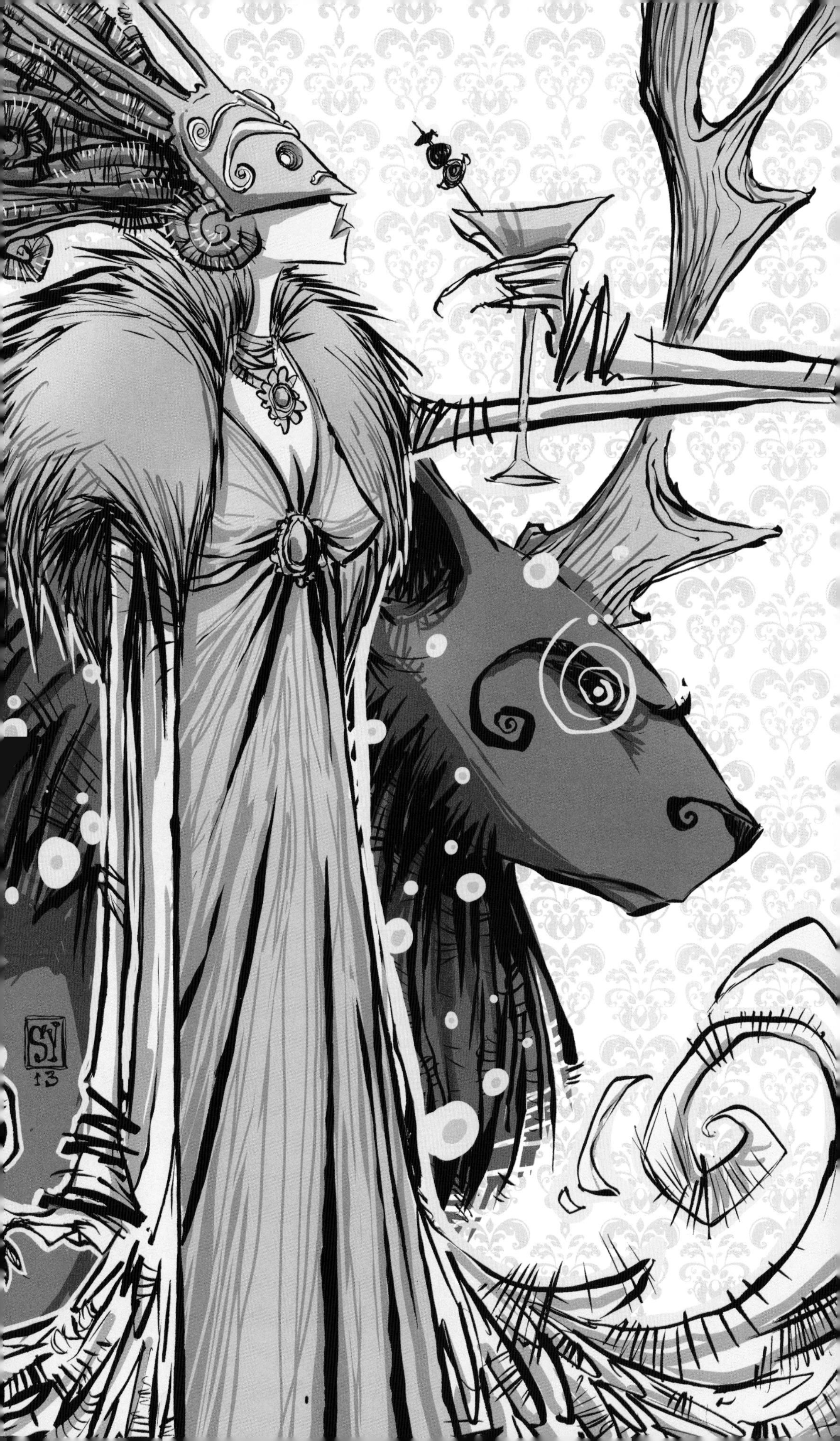
SY
13

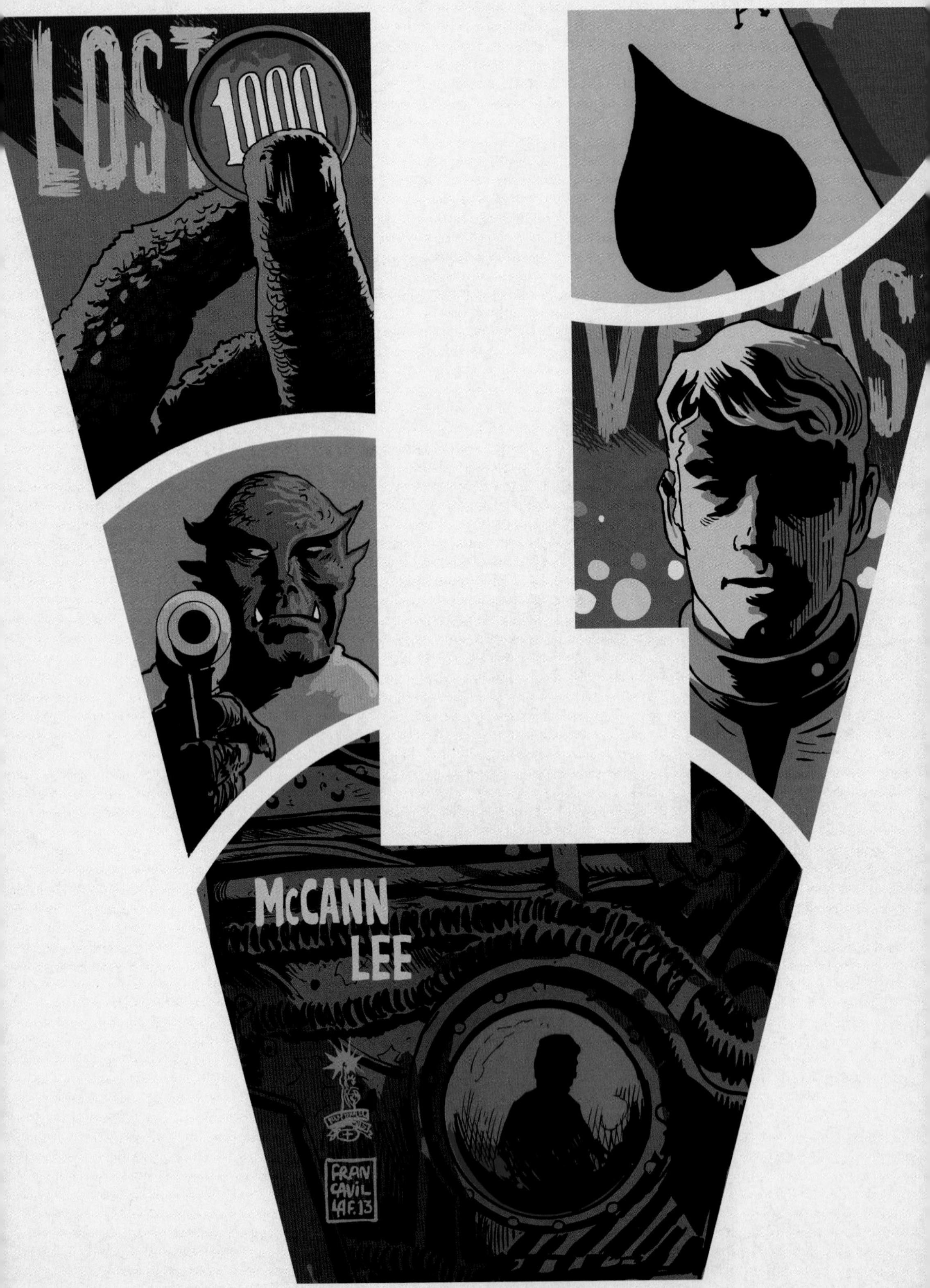
LOST
1000
McCANN
LEE
FRAN
CAVIL
LAF.13

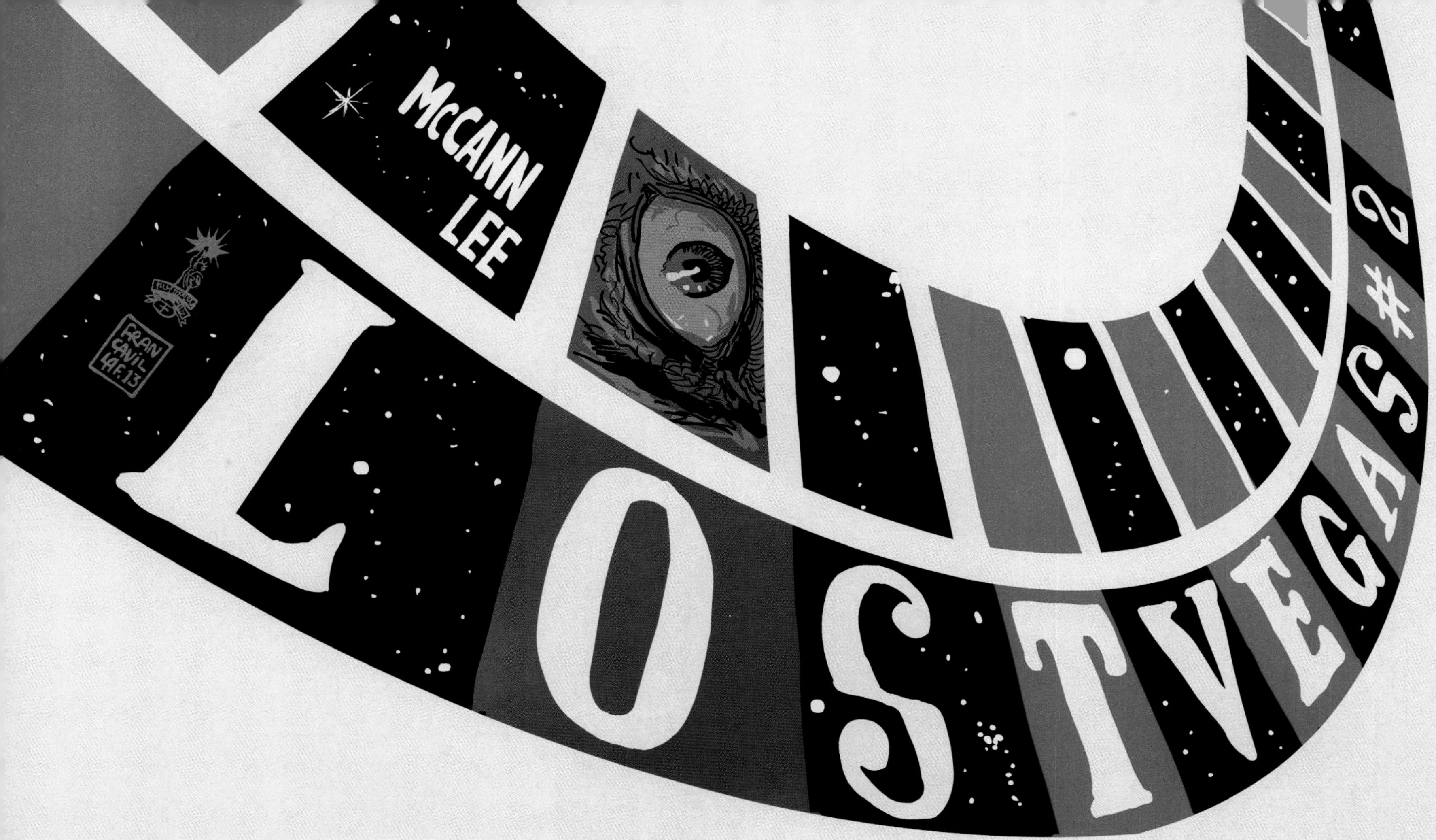
LOST VEGAS #2
McCANN
LEE
FRAN GAVIL LAF.13

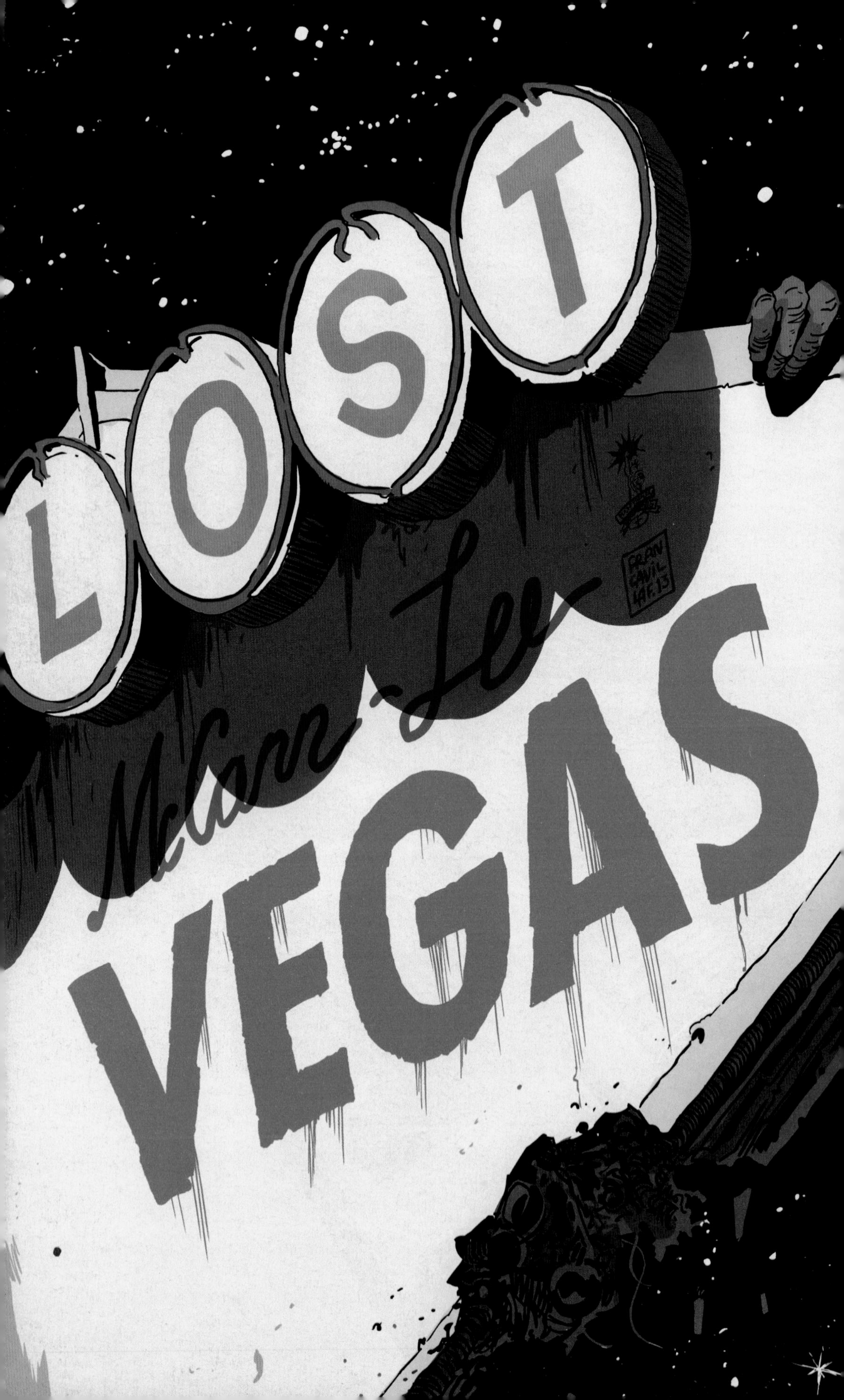
LOST
VEGAS

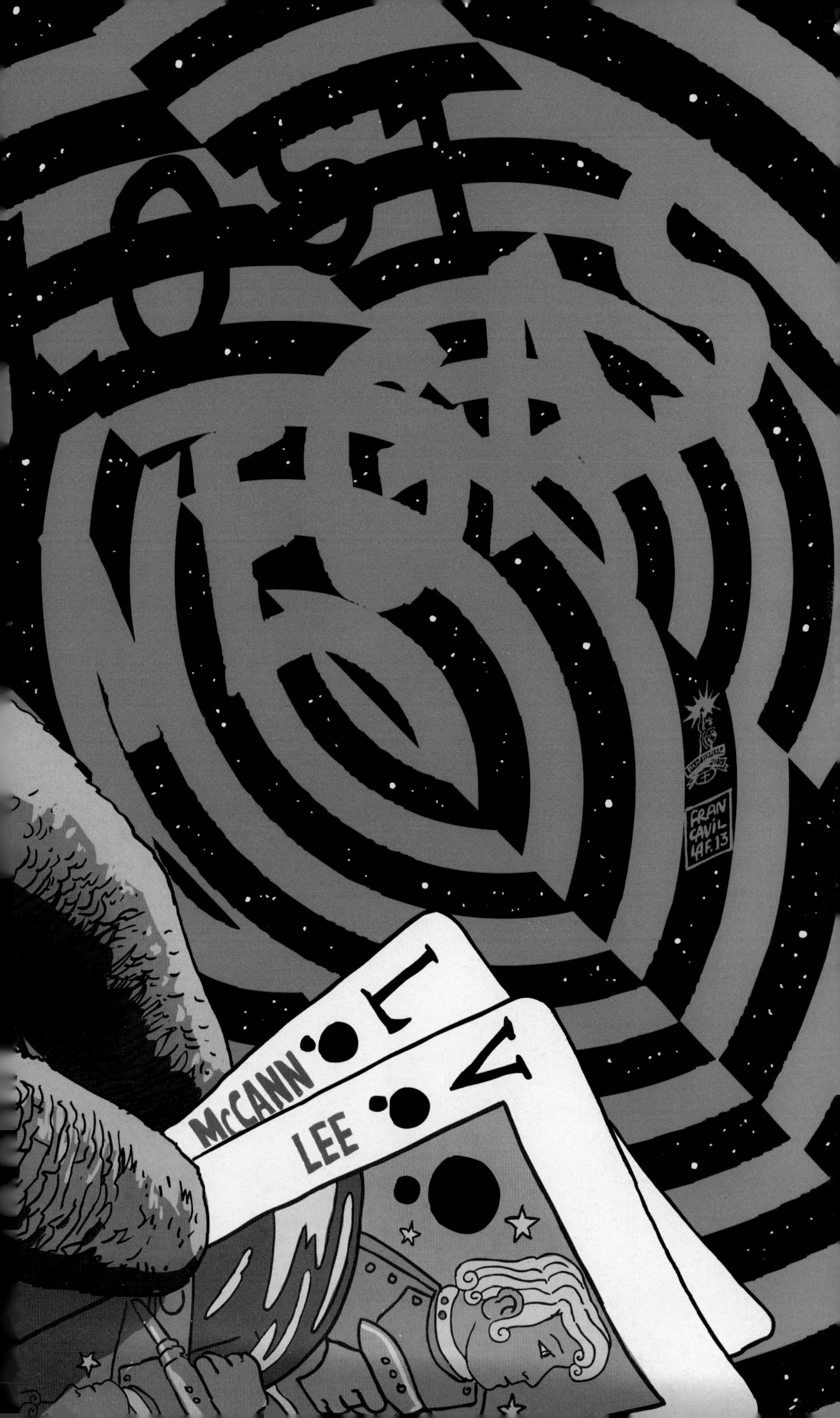
McCANN
LEE

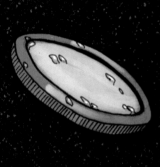